THE SPE
COMMUN

Douglas Ehninger
University of Iowa
Consulting Editor in Speech Communication

SCOTT, FORESMAN'S 〰〰 COLLEGE SPEECH SERIES

THEODORE CLEVENGER, JR.
FLORIDA STATE UNIVERSITY

JACK MATTHEWS
UNIVERSITY OF PITTSBURGH

THE SPEECH
COMMUNICATION PROCESS

SCOTT, FORESMAN AND COMPANY
GLENVIEW, ILLINOIS   LONDON

Library of Congress Catalog Card No. 70–120695

Copyright © 1971 by Scott, Foresman and Company, Glenview, Illinois 60025.
Philippines Copyright 1971 by Scott, Foresman and Company.
All Rights Reserved. Printed in the United States of America.

Regional offices of Scott, Foresman and Company are located in Dallas, Oakland,
N. J., Palo Alto, and Tucker, Ga.

FOREWORD

Variety is the keynote of undergraduate instruction in speech today. In some institutions of higher learning the basic speech course deals with public speaking; in others, with the fundamentals of speech; in still others, with an introduction to speech communication theory. Moreover, within these broad categories, as one moves from school to school and even from instructor to instructor within the same department, one finds that the basic speech course differs greatly in both activity and content. Subject matter that is taught in the introductory course at one institution is reserved for advanced courses at another.

One reason for this state of affairs is that the beginning undergraduate instruction in speech encompasses a wide range of subject matter—far more than can be offered in a single course. From this wealth of topics, instructors and course committees must select material that can be organized into a meaningful pattern of instruction. In addition, since the needs of students in various institutions and curricula differ considerably, textbooks that try to cover an entire semester's work have proved increasingly unable to bear the whole burden of undergraduate instruction. Writing a good survey text is further hindered by the rapid advances in knowledge and research taking place in the field. It is clear that more flexible instructional material is required.

In response to that need, Scott, Foresman's College Speech Series has been designed to provide maximum adaptability to varying instructional goals. Our objective is to make it possible for the instructor to combine just those units of content which best serve the needs of his course: particular subject matter selected for a certain population of students at a given time. The format of the series has developed from that goal. Each title focuses on a single topic, which is developed by an "expert" in much fuller detail than is possible in a survey textbook. Each is independent of the others. The titles were chosen for minimal overlap, and no book in the series requires mastery of any other as a prerequisite for understanding. Of course, where appropriate, the authors have cross-referenced one another for purposes of fuller or more specialized treatment, so that the series, being integrated, offers a common philosophy. Each book is independent yet is also part of a consistent and comprehensive whole.

But the books of this series represent something more than a new format for instructional reading. Each provides an original analysis in depth, relying on recent theoretic advances and bringing to bear the most useful information available. The series is therefore something more than a subdivision and expansion of the typical survey textbook for the first course in speech; each book presents information and theoretical insights not heretofore available to the undergraduate student.

In some cases, it may prove desirable to build a beginning speech course around several topics selected from the series. In others, a single volume may be used to fill a void or to develop a particular topic in greater depth than does the survey textbook. Different sections of the same course may use the same general textbook but study from different volumes of this series in order emphasize topics according to special needs. For many advanced or specialized courses, a particular book of this series may be used as the principal textbook, serving as the point of departure for extensive supplementary readings and special projects. Thus, this series may be used in a variety of ways at many different instructional levels, depending on the needs of the students, the goals of instruction, and the insight and imagination of the instructor.

Theodore Clevenger, Jr.
General Editor

CONTENTS

PREFACE

This book was written for the college student in his first course in speech communication. In our selection of topics, choice of examples, and manner of treatment we have tried to keep that student in mind. Some of the concepts we treat are among those previously reserved for graduate study in speech; but this is an accident of historical development of the field, not a reflection of the intellectually advanced nature of the ideas. High-school instruction has improved so much, and such vast amounts of public communication are now available that most college students will have enough acquaintance with communication theories and their applications to cope with the ideas we present.

This volume is intended to promote understanding rather than develop performative skill, but we have tried throughout to relate theory to practice. We have selected examples not only from public speaking and mass communication but from informal and interpersonal communication as well. We hope this will lead the student to see in speech communication a broad range of phenomena. He should see in it a wide spectrum of speech events ranging from perfunctory comments in the routine of daily living to highly structured, persuasive or artistic, formal "speeches"; and he should understand the key relationships among these different events.

We view communication as a process, and yet we recognize that in describing the parts of the process we risk creating the impression that they can be viewed in a fractionated and static fashion. In Chapter 1 we ask the question, "What is communication?" and suggest a variety of approaches to its study. In Chapters 2 through 7 we present various elements of communication. In Chapters 8, 9, and 10 we describe how these elements interact or work together. Finally, in Chapter 11 we return to the original question as to the constituency of communication and try to answer it by standing back to survey the process in broad outline.

Perhaps we owe the reader some explanation for one departure we have made from the usual practice. Whereas most books about speech and communication present an organizing model of the communication process at the beginning, we present our model at the end. This choice is based on our experience that often students find a model confusing at first, though later they may find it extremely helpful as an aid to organizing what they have learned about the process. Our treatment parallels the history of the field, for "models" came onto the scene rather late in the development of communication study. It was only after a great deal of information and theory had been accumulated that models were introduced as a means of simplifying and unifying our knowledge.

A model is, after all, a very abstract kind of theory. If students are forced to tackle the abstract before they can grasp some of the particulars, a kind of mental indigestion may result. It is true that for the few readers who comprehend the model from the beginning, it promotes understanding of the more specific details developed later; but for most students it seems a trivial and meaningless exercise until they have more concrete ideas from which to generalize. In some ways a model is a kind of summary; in this book we recognize that aspect of our model by presenting it last. We believe this will increase its relevance and utility.

We are grateful to innumerable graduate and undergraduate students, whose reactions to various drafts of chapters of the manuscript have helped us to clarify obscure points; and we also owe a special debt to Dr. Thomas R. King for extensive comments on the final draft.

Theodore Clevenger, Jr.
Jack Matthews

THE SPEECH
COMMUNICATION PROCESS

I.

WHAT IS COMMUNICATION?

The word "communication" has been used to refer to a variety of concepts that at first appear to have little in common with one another. Each meaning of the word reflects a different approach to the subject. We, too, will consider communication from several points of view, some of them more extensively than others.

APPROACHES TO THE STUDY OF COMMUNICATION

In this chapter we will examine briefly six approaches to studying the subject: communication as *culture,* as *language,* as *personal effectiveness,* as *human relations,* as *behavior,* and as *transmission and reception.*

Communication as Culture

The sum total of values, beliefs, and practices of a civilization may be called its culture. Because communication is the primary means by which culture is transmitted from one generation to the next and because it is the medium through which many practices of a civilization are carried out, it is not surprising to find the culture of a civilization revealed in its communication. By studying communication within a society it is possible to enhance our understanding of that society's culture.

One evidence of a high level of culture is the presence of written communication. This level is possible when agricultural and technological advances free some individuals from the burden of daily providing all of life's necessities. Any effort to scale societies according to level of advancement is risky, but one possible gauge is the extent to which a people have developed specialized forms of communication such as poetry, drama, and ceremonial speaking. By examining samples of writing, poetry, drama, and speeches, one may infer the quality of life in a given society, for in such records people leave imprints of their culture in a variety of ways. The written records the Athenians left, for example, bear eloquent testimony to the high value they placed upon justice, truth, and beauty.

Oral communications which pass between individuals during the conduct of routine activities reveal not only the values and interests of a civilization but the patterns of personal relationships as well. Any customary restrictions upon "who speaks with whom about which matters and with what form of address" imply specialization of roles and differences in status between individuals which are an important feature of any culture.

Even the language spoken by members of a society carries the impress of their lifeways. This is perhaps most apparent in differences of vocabulary from one tongue to another. A language will include vocabulary items for those things which members of the society wish to talk about, and these in turn will reflect cultural patterns. Peruvian Indians, for example, have roughly 200 words for "potato," reflecting the great dependence of their economy upon this crop, the special varieties of potato they have developed, and the level to which they have raised the art of potato cultivation. Kinship relations are of paramount importance to the Australian bushman. He must have separate terms to refer to his mother's sister's son, his father's brother's daughter, his wife's father's brother's wife, and dozens of other relatives of varying degree, for his rights and responsibilities differ with respect to each of them. To the bushman it may seem incredible that European languages such as English provide such a sketchy list of kinship terms. Such differences between languages reflect differences between the respective cultures. Indeed some anthropologists assert that language is culture and culture is language.

Because language is communication, we view communication and culture as being very closely related, if not synonymous. The study of culture and the study of communication can proceed hand in hand, each providing a basis for improved insight into the other. However, it is important to note that the description of communication provided by this approach is subject to anthropological bias.

More will be said about those aspects of communication that can be related to cultural variables, and attention will be diverted away from those aspects that are not amenable to description in cultural terms. Not all of what might be said about human communication is encompassed by the cultural point of view. We may study communication as culture, but this is only one of several profitable approaches.[1]

Communication as Language

The most distinctive, and perhaps the most pervasive, forms of communication among people are those which employ language. Although speech and writing are not the sole means of communicating between individuals, they are the most noticeable and the most intensively studied. It is therefore inevitable that the study of human communication should be bound up with the study of language.

All languages incorporate essentially the same general features of design. Of the virtually infinite number of different sounds the vocal organs can produce, no language uses more than a few (though no two languages use exactly the same ones). In each case these are so distributed in the language that it is possible to combine them into a still smaller number of *sets* of sounds (the phonemes, of which we shall say more later). These sounds are strung together in a highly predictable manner to form words, which are in turn strung together in a regular way to produce utterances. Experience with hundreds of languages confirms that these and other general features of structure are to be found in all languages; but much detective work may be required to discover the sound system, the basic structural units, and the combinatorial rules of a newly encountered language.

Having established the structure of the language, one has at hand useful and accurate information concerning the means by which users of the language communicate with one another. Through analysis of the relations of the linguistic units (words, phrases, and sentences in English) to objects and events, it is possible to study the meanings the language is used to convey. Almost invariably these meanings relate to the objects and events that are common and/or significant in the lives of the people who use the language in question, and with their characteristic ways of viewing these objects and events. It is because objects, relationships, and

1. A more detailed discussion of communication as culture can be found in a collection of readings edited by Alfred G. Smith, *Communication and Culture* (New York: Holt, Rinehart & Winston, Inc., 1966).

events will be classified differently from one culture to another that exact translations between the languages of highly discrepant cultures are difficult.[2]

By comparing certain features of language structure and semantics (meaning), it is sometimes possible to detect startling differences in world view between two languages. For instance, in all of the European languages, including English, the typical utterance involves an acting agent (subject), an action (verb), and something which is acted upon (object). "The man threw a stone" is a typical English utterance. It would be quite difficult to express that exact thought in certain other of the world's languages, including the Hopi tongue. To the Hopi, it requires a conscious act of will to think of the situation in terms of a man causing a passive, non-participating stone to be propelled through the air by an action of which he is the sole instigator. It is more natural for him to think of a man and a stone becoming mutually involved in a certain type of event requiring participation by both of them, a relativistic view of the matter that requires a conscious act of will on the part of Europeans. To the English speaker the world proceeds through the action of causative agents upon passive ones; to the Hopi it proceeds through interactions involving mutual participation. This is not to say that the Hopi cannot think in cause-effect terms, and that the European cannot think in interactional terms, but simply that the semantic systems of their two languages are such that each customarily and most easily thinks in his characteristic way. We might on this basis predict some occasional difficulty of communication between native speakers of the two languages, and some difficulty translating from one language to the other. Problems such as these give rise to theoretical questions of great significance for the study of communication, as well as linguistics.[3]

Although the study of language dominates the study of communication, it is not the whole of it. The linguistic approach to communication is limited first of all to those aspects of communication

2. A more detailed analysis of the act of interpreting can be found in Chapter 4 of Hubert G. Alexander's book, *Meaning in Language* (Glenview, Ill.: Scott, Foresman and Company, 1969).

3. At this point it should be apparent that the study of communication as language has much in common with the study of communication as culture. Of course this is because language and culture are highly interrelated. The essential difference between these two approaches is that linguistics deals with the language itself including many aspects that are largely independent of culture, while cultural anthropology deals with all aspects of the cultural system, whether they are reflected in the language structure or not. Much of the common area of overlap between linguistics and anthropology lies in the area of communication. The previously mentioned collection of readings, *Communication and Culture*, contains a number of papers which enlarge this concept.

that involve some sort of structured code, similar to language. (This need not be speech; we might, for instance, postulate a language of gesture having a decipherable code.) But much communication seems to be carried out in the absence of any discrete code. Emotional states are communicated by facial expressions, yet these appear to obey none of the rules of linguistic structuring. Stylized forms of tactile contact, such as the handshake and the kiss, are capable of conveying a wide range of emotional and attitudinal information in context, yet seem to possess none of the characteristics of linguistic structure. The same may be said of nonstructural aspects of vocal pitch, duration, loudness, and quality. It would appear that much communication takes place outside and alongside the language pattern, most of which would be overlooked by an exclusively linguistic approach to communication.

A second restriction upon the linguistic approach is that its sole concern is the language code and its mode of operation. Broader (and perhaps less well-defined) questions of purpose, significance, and effect fall outside the capabilities of linguistic science. It goes without saying that this can scarcely be taken as a criticism of linguistics; within the area it has defined for itself it is remarkably successful. Indeed, restriction of scope is one reason for its success; but just because its scope is restricted we are compelled to note that linguistics does not serve every aspect of the study of communication.

Communication as Personal Effectiveness

One difference between "successful" people and "unsuccessful" ones is that they communicate differently, and sometimes it seems possible to trace success or failure to conspicuously "effective" or "ineffective" communication. If an industrial client who is unwilling to install certain equipment is visited by the equipment manufacturer's sales engineer and subsequently decides to install the equipment, we are prone to attribute the sale to the salesmanship and to conclude that the engineer must have communicated effectively. Conversely, if most of an instructor's students make a poor showing on tests over his lectures, we are prone to believe that his lectures embody poor standards of communication.

Personal effectiveness might be defined as behaving so that the goals one desires are achieved.[4] In the foregoing examples we presume that the salesman wishes to sell the equipment and that the

4. A brief treatment of the ethical problems involved can be found in Chapter 5 of Thomas M. Scheidel's book, *Persuasive Speaking* (Glenview, Ill.: Scott, Foresman and Company, 1967).

instructor desires to impart the lecture content to his students. Their success in accomplishing these objectives is the measure of their personal effectiveness in the selling and teaching situations respectively.

Many of the things people desire call for the understanding, cooperation, or assent of others, and the only way to obtain this assent, cooperation, or understanding is through communicating with those from whom it is desired. Some techniques of communication appear to enjoy greater success in this respect than others, and so may be viewed as instruments of personal effectiveness. To accumulate a collection of such techniques is one approach to the study of communication.

In achieving long-range goals, focus and timing may be extremely important, so that the question of whom to talk to, and when, is sometimes an essential consideration. For instance, in introducing a new farming technique in a developing nation, the ministry of agriculture must know which farmers to talk to and when to talk to them. To approach the wrong villager, or the right one at the wrong season, might sabotage a development program that would otherwise have excellent chances of success. Knowing who is receptive to new ideas and when their receptivity is likely to be highest is important to effective communication in many contexts.

The form in which a written or spoken message is couched may also influence its effectiveness. For example, with respect to long speeches it has been learned that certain principles of speech organization will, if followed, lead to greater retention of information on the part of listeners. Moreover, the same patterns of organization lend an air of plausibility and authority to the speaker and contribute to a more favorable image with his auditors. By learning these organizational principles, a speaker or writer is likely to increase his personal effectiveness in any situation where audience retention of information or the impression of general competence contribute to the achievement of the speaker's or writer's goals.

Because personal effectiveness is highly prized, it is not surprising that much more has been written about communication as personal effectiveness than can be touched upon here. Not only are there many books in the tradition of Dale Carnegie's *How to Win Friends and Influence People,* but a part of the academic training of every college student is directed toward this end. On the whole, for example, business letters written in standard English grammar elicit more favorable responses than letters written in poorer form. In the eye of the reader "incorrect" grammar and word usage mark the writer as a person of inadequate education, intelligence, and/or judgment;

and unless the content of the letter contains some unusually redeeming feature, it is not likely to be treated with respect. Therefore, a study of grammar and word choice increases personal effectiveness in business letter writing by assuring more favorable attention to the letter's content, which is usually consistent with the writer's purposes.

It is apparent from the preceding examples that success in achieving personal goals is highly dependent upon "communication skills." It is also clear that studying the communication behaviors that achieve those outcomes which we most often desire—cooperation, understanding, and assent—can teach us much about communication. In short, the study of communication and the study of personal effectiveness have much in common.[5]

Nevertheless, the kinds of knowledge about communication which can be gained through this approach, though valuable and extensive, are limited by the initial question: "How can one communicate so as to increase his personal effectiveness?" Academic and technical questions that are not directly related to a payoff in some kind of "effectiveness" will tend to be pushed aside. Yet experience in other fields of study shows that it is just such "impractical" questions which often lead to the most important discoveries. For example, it was purely speculative research in animal conditioning that led to the learning theories behind both "programed learning" as now widely used in the schools and "behavior therapy" as practiced in mental hospitals. Unexpected practical benefits became possible in these areas only after a groundwork had been laid in independent theory and research. Thus the study of communication as personal effectiveness is biased by adhering closely to certain desired outcomes of communication.

Communication as Human Relations

If, instead of considering how an individual can maximize his personal effectiveness, we ask how groups can best live and work together in productive harmony, we move from thinking of communication as an instrument of personal effectiveness to thinking of it as a means of enhancing human relations. The study of human relations takes as one of its primary goals discovery of the means of preventing and/or resolving conflict. People relate to one another primarily by means of communication; yet it seems to have been a relatively recent discovery that whenever people are in conflict we may

5. *Interpersonal Communication*, edited by Dean Barnlund (New York: Houghton Mifflin Company, 1968), contains a number of essays which will provide both theory and research data valuable to this subject area.

often find both the source of the difficulty and its remedy in the patterns of communication between the conflicting parties. Analysis of communication is intimately involved in the theory and practice of human relations, and an understanding of many features of the communicative process is enhanced by studying them from this point of view.

Difficulties sometimes arise because people feel that messages of a certain type are being directed to them from an inappropriate source. A small midwestern manufacturing company, plagued by a spate of minor labor disputes, discovered that workers felt that certain information relating to job assignments should be given to them through the union stewards rather than through management representatives as had been the custom. Subsequently, the work climate was substantially improved by channelling job assignments through union representatives so that, insofar as the worker was concerned, the immediate source of information was the steward. As this example demonstrates, people have expectations concerning who will communicate with them, when, and in what manner about what subjects. When these anticipations are violated, conflict may arise if the recipients regard the violation as a threat to their security or a wanton disregard of their interests.

Difficulties may also arise when, without realizing it, people use the same words with different meanings. John Locke reports a long and acrimonious debate among early scientists over the question whether some fluid flows through the nerves. The debate finally ended when each member of the group defined what he meant by "fluid," for then it became clear that there was in fact no disagreement about what happens in the nerves. The apparent disagreement was produced by differences in the conventional use of words; yet for a time the participants in the colloquy thought one another stupid, obstinate, and ill-informed.

Closely allied to the assumption that words mean the same things to everyone is the "but-I-told-you" fallacy. This source of difficulty in human relations grows out of the assumption that the content which A puts into a verbal message to B is the same as the content which B takes away from it. Having "told" B, A assumes that B "knows." If B should later behave as if he did not have the information, A objects, "But I *told* you."

If communication is at the root of much human conflict, it is also true that communication is involved in one way or another in most techniques of conflict resolution other than violence. This is not to say that resolution of conflict always involves increasing the amount of communication between the conflicting parties; indeed it may require just the reverse. "You are a rotten, anti-labor fascist bigot," while it conveys much relevant information, probably does little to foster harmonious thinking. Therefore, sometimes in cases of prolonged labor strife, government negotiators will intentionally constrict the flow of information between labor and management representatives. The parties are separated, and only the negotiator is allowed to serve as a channel of communication between them. Standing thus across the flow of information between the contesting parties, he allows no more than a trickle of carefully chosen and timed messages to flow in either direction, all of which are edited to preserve objectivity and forestall unfavorable emotional reactions. Thus stripped of the name-calling and personality conflicts that often play a major part in prolonged labor disputes, essential information can be exchanged and a settlement brought about.

Though conflict resolution may occasionally require constriction of the information flow between parties, it generally calls for modified and enlarged communication. Through confrontation, discussion, and controlled argument disputants can often be brought to a fuller understanding of one another's positions, appreciation of one another's needs, and awareness of common interests. Some of the techniques human-relations counselors employ are developed from theoretical positions, but perhaps a greater number are empirically discovered techniques which are retained because they work in some cases to bring about good relations.[6]

It is clear that communication is a very important factor in helping people to get along well together; however, the same limitations we discussed concerning the study of communication as personal effectiveness apply with equal force to the study of communication as human relations. Quite clearly, communication involves much more than just human relations, and we cannot limit ourselves solely to this approach.

Communication as Behavior

When people communicate, they engage in behavior; and these behaviors may be studied in relation to the forces producing them. Because a significant fraction of all of the behavior of modern man takes place within a framework of communication with others, the study of communication and the study of behavior share a broad domain of common interest.

6. In Chapter 8 of his book, *Informative Speaking* (Glenview, Ill.: Scott, Foresman and Company, 1968), Thomas H. Olbricht takes the position that informative communication begins to degenerate whenever the integrity of the auditor is violated.

Naively put, the fundamental question raised by a behavioral approach to communication is: "What is it that people do when they communicate with one another, and why do they do that rather than something else?" No specific communicative act has been shown to be common to all mankind, so we may discount the explanation that specific communication behaviors are inherited. But if they are learned, then in all likelihood they are learned in much the same way as other behavior is learned. That being so, we should find it possible to describe and explain the activities involved in speaking, listening, reading, and writing on the basis of the same principles that govern other learned forms of behavior.

Behavioral principles are able to account for a great deal of what happens in communication. For one thing, certain aspects of language have proved amenable to behavioral description. Considered from one point of view, it is profitable to visualize language as a highly complex set of habitual responses developed through stimulation, reward, and punishment and capable of modification by the same means. Such an approach, for instance, makes it easier to understand the process through which one learns a foreign language. At first garbled and peculiar, the sounds of the new language through repeated simulation come to possess identifiable characteristics that distinguish them from one another and from the sounds of English. Then, through repeated trial and comparison with a standard, one gradually learns to produce the sounds himself. His first efforts to utter the new sounds are likely to differ widely from an acceptable standard; but with repeated trials, followed by feedback on his successes and failures, he can approximate "native" pronunciation of the new language as closely as his intelligence, time, and motivation will allow.

The first part of this sequence—that of learning to recognize the sounds of the new language—proceeds according to a principle called *stimulus discrimination,* which applies equally well to language learning and to the process by which a white rat can learn to distinguish reliably between a square and a circle in order to obtain food from a dispensing machine. The second part of the process is carried on by means of "shaping," a name given the procedure of rewarding an organism for successively closer and closer approximations to some desired behavior and so changing behavior gradually in the direction of the desired response. Through shaping it is possible to obtain behaviors of which the organism was entirely incapable at the outset of the shaping process. The same principle that can be used to teach an American to pronounce the vowels of French can also be used to teach a pigeon to play a rudimentary form of table tennis. Though the specific behaviors differ, the principles according to which the behavior is established are identical.

Nor is the operation of behavioral principles in human communication limited to language learning. They also extend to the way a known language is used. This is most clearly apparent in "verbal conditioning" experiments, which demonstrate the possibility of radically altering a person's pattern of language output through reward or punishment. Not only is it possible within a relatively short time to influence the kinds of words one employs (such as doubling the percentage of personal pronouns), it is also possible through judicious manipulation of social rewards and punishments such as attention, approval, and rejection to increase or decrease the amount of time one spends talking about certain topics.

Sometimes it is even possible to account for the fact that people communicate or fail to communicate at all on the basis of considerations such as these. For example, in some places it is customary for people to exchange greetings when passing on a sidewalk or in a corridor even if they are strangers. The newcomer who fails to respond to a greeting in the expected manner will be subjected to social pressure (punishment) until he alters his behavior. If he then carries this communication behavior into a new setting where different ground rules apply, he will be punished for greeting strangers until the habit is extinguished. Thus the decision to communicate or not to communicate in many circumstances can be explained by the same principles as those governing the form and the content of communication.

As the above examples show, the behavioral approach to communication is an extremely powerful one, able to account to some extent for whether people communicate, what they communicate about, and how they do it. However, the approach is limited to dealing with observable behavior; and, moreover, since it describes behavior in terms of the antecedent conditions that produce it, the behavioral approach is committed to those forms of behavior for which antecedents can be found. The search is always for connections between environmental stimuli and observable responses; in a rigorously behavioral approach there is room for nothing else.

Although the behavioral approach to communication has far from exhausted its possibilities for dealing with human communication, it is a very long way from providing a full and intuitively satisfying explication of the whole act of communication in all its rich detail. To begin with, an honest self-appraisal tells us that much seems to occur during communication which is simply inaccessible to observation. The whole cognitive experience of the communication participant is beyond observation, as are his subjectively experienced emotions and feelings. We may be defenseless when told by certain philosophers and behaviorists that those things do not really exist; but the reality we experience is much more compelling than the reality their logic constructs for us. Thus most people refuse to believe that these "internal" events do not play an extremely important role in all of human life, including communication.

Even granted the reality of some "inner life," it would still be possible to argue that all of human experience (including, of course, all of communication) could be encompassed by the behavioral point of view if we could hold that these internal states are always reflected in behavior and always reflected in the same way. We could then search down and analyze the world of experience by noting its influences upon behavior, much as astronomers might establish the location of a heretofore undiscovered planet by studying the perturbations it produced on the orbits of its neighbors. Whether or not such a regular relation exists between subjective experience and behavior is still an open question. Everyday experience tells us that if such a relationship exists, it must be much more complex than anyone has yet imagined. In any case, the major part of the job of establishing such a relationship yet remains to be done; and in the meantime a strictly behaviorist approach to communication fails to account for everything that takes place.

Communication as Transmission and Reception[7]

Although we sometimes speak figuratively of a "meeting of the minds," it is obviously impossible for two minds to come into direct contact. They must interact indirectly by means of messages transmitted by one and received by the other. In order to function as both a sender and a recipient of messages, an individual must have at his disposal both some mechanism for transmitting messages and some mechanism for receiving them.

It is entirely through the operation of transmitting and receiving mechanisms that individuals are able to communicate. In the case of the spoken word, the vocal tract (of the speaker) is the transmitter, and the ear (of the listener) is the receiver; with gesture, the skeletal muscles transmit, and the eye receives.

But what is transmitted and what received? Most of the time we believe that we are communicating ideas; but the vocal tract is in-

7. In this section the authors have been extensively influenced by and have borrowed from the classical *The Mathematical Theory of Communication* by Claude E. Shannon and Warren Weaver (Urbana: University of Illinois Press, 1949). A less technical treatment can be found in Warren Weaver's "The Mathematics of Communication" in *Scientific American*, 181(1949):11–15.

capable of transmitting ideas just as the ear is incapable of receiving them. All the vocal tract can do is set up patterns of vibration, and all the ear can do is detect patterns of vibration; neither is capable of handling thoughts. However, these patterns of vibration transmitted by the vocal tract and received by the ear are not a random assortment. If we examine a very large number of them, we shall discover that (allowing a certain margin for variation) a surprisingly small number of different vibration patterns are produced, and these are repeated over and over again in a great variety of sequences. Moreover, the number of different sequences, though very large, is not infinite; and some sequences of vibratory patterns are repeated many times. The different patterns of vibration represent the various sounds of language, and the sequences of vibratory patterns represent the words. By learning to associate ideas with sound sequences it is possible to use the sounds (which can be transmitted and received) as a substitute for the ideas (which cannot). The system of sounds (language) is then said to be a code, and it is messages in that code, not ideas or thoughts, that are transmitted by the vocal tract and received by the ear.

Ordinarily the situation is even more indirect than the foregoing considerations imply; for usually the transmitting mechanism and the receiving mechanism are not in direct contact with one another, and in speech they never are. In this case, the message must pass through some connecting medium or channel between the transmitter and the receiver.[8] If there are disturbances or distractions in the channel, the message may be lost or changed on the way.

Thus, although we are seldom aware of difficulty in communicating with others, the entire arrangement is a fairly complex and indirect affair. The source must have at its disposal a transmission apparatus; not just any will do, for it must be an apparatus capable of producing the elements of a particular code. Not just any code will do, either. The code must be one that will carry whatever information the source wishes to transmit, and it must be one that will pass through the channel between transmitter and receiver. The destination must have at its disposal a reception apparatus in contact with the channel and be capable of taking from it the elements of the code rapidly and in recognizable form.

According to this view of communication, a message originating at the source is translated into code (encoded) by the transmitter which generates a coded message in the channel. This coded message consists of energy patterns which are propagated through the

8. Strictly speaking, "medium" and "channel" are different things. This distinction is unimportant here, but is explained in Chapter 4 (pp. 48–64).

medium of the channel until they reach the receiver. The energies of the coded message actuate the receiver which retranslates (decodes) the message, making it available at the destination. Of course, the entire system is no more effective than its weakest link. An elegant code will be of no great utility if the transmitting apparatus is unable to produce the code elements speedily and accurately. Even if both of these conditions are met, information transfer will be slow and inaccurate if the receiver is unable to make discriminations rapidly and accurately. Even with an elegant code and ultra-efficient transmitters and receivers, the system will not function well if there are disturbances or obstructions in the channel.

Clearly, the study of message transmission is a vital part of the study of communication. Although it has been most fully developed with respect to the design of electronic communication systems such as telephone and TV, its concepts clearly apply in face-to-face communication as well. There is, however, an important difference which must not be overlooked. In designing communication systems it is irrelevant to inquire into either the origins or the effects of a message, or into the message content.[9] Yet in human terms these are probably the most significant aspects of the whole transaction. In looking at communication as message transmission and reception we are able to examine processes involved in every single act of human communication; indeed, it is because the processes occur so routinely that we tend to overlook them and focus our attention elsewhere. Ordinarily we are aware of the process only when some malfunction calls our attention to it.

INTERRELATIONSHIPS AMONG THE APPROACHES

We have seen that the term "communication" may be used to refer to an aspect of culture, a class of behaviors, the process of message transmission and reception, language, a factor influencing human relations, and an instrument of personal effectiveness. In relation to culture, communication is an embodiment of certain widely shared values, practices, and beliefs; to behavior, an especially rich and complex set of response mechanisms; to transmission and reception, a system by means of which coded messages are passed from a source to a destination; to language, the use of certain types of codes; to human relations, a process which often results in conflict and misunderstanding, as well as an effective means of reducing them; and

9. This topic is considered in detail in Lee Thayer's *Communication and Communication Systems* (Homewood, Ill.: Richard D. Irwin, Inc., 1968).

to personal effectiveness, a set of techniques for achieving one's goals.

Each of these meanings of "communication" represents a different set of ideas about it, a different way of thinking about it, and a different way of relating it to other events and processes. Because communication plays such a vital role in human life, it is not surprising that it has been approached from so many points of view. Because any communication event involving people is so rich in detail, it is not surprising that any one viewpoint fails to comprehend all of it.

To speak of these various approaches to communication as "different points of view" is quite correct, for the same communication event will appear slightly different as seen from each of the vantage points. However, the reader will have noted that these six meanings of "communication" are not independent of one another. Language may be viewed as an aspect of culture and may also enter into human relations. Message transmission may be studied as behavior and as an essential condition of effectiveness. In short, though different, these avenues of approach to communication are not unrelated. Nor is this surprising; for an act of communication is *not* transmission plus behavior plus language plus culture plus human relations plus personal effectiveness. Though it may be analyzed and interpreted from all of these points of view, it remains a whole event possessing an integrity and cohesiveness of its own. Therefore, if a number of different approaches are made to the event, it is inevitable that the resulting analyses should overlap to some extent.

Basic and Applied Viewpoints

The patterns of overlapping concern among the various approaches to communication are neither arbitrary nor random; it is possible to discern a continuum running from "basic" to "applied" interests. In noting this distinction it is necessary also to note—and to discount—the dominant trend in our culture to emphasize "basic" over "applied" studies. This current value, of quite recent origin, is largely a product of the present relationship between basic science and industrial technology. Science is now expanding so rapidly that technological advances are obsolescent almost as soon as they are introduced, whereas "basic" knowledge changes much more slowly. Under these circumstances, technological competence is ephemeral, becoming technological incompetence with each new development. On the other hand, a grasp of basic principles provides a measure of protection against technological change.

However, the relationship between science and industrial technology has no close parallel in those areas of knowledge where human behavior is concerned. There are few notable cases ("programed instruction" comes to mind as the leading recent example) in which it has been possible to develop "human engineering" techniques directly out of basic behavioral research findings. Ordinarily, attempts to apply "basic" social and behavioral research to practical human problems in a natural setting have met at best with partial success. Thus, the value judgments we make about basic science and industrial technology should not govern our evaluations of the various approaches to communication.

If, in order to study communication from a given point of view (A), it is useful to employ theory and technique developed through the study of communication from a second point of view (B); and if the reverse of this is not true, then approach (B) may be said to be more basic than approach (A). Put the other way around, if problems arising during the course of studying communication from one viewpoint (A) may be solved only by recourse to concepts or methods arising from a second viewpoint (B), then the first viewpoint (A) represents an "applied" approach insofar as the second viewpoint (B) is concerned. It is in this sense that we shall use the terms "basic" and "applied" with reference to the study of communication.

In the above sense of the term, the transmission-reception approach to communication is at the "basic" end of the continuum among the approaches discussed, since it proves helpful in dealing with certain problems arising in all of the other five, but receives help from none of them in solving its own theoretical problems. In the same sense, the human-relations and the personal-effectiveness approaches are the most "applied" approaches among those discussed, since they use concepts and methods drawn from the other four, yet contribute concepts and methods only to each other. The behavioral, linguistic, and cultural approaches to communication fall between the two ends of the continuum. In general, they use concepts from the transmission approach, use one another's concepts extensively, and contribute to (but do not draw upon) the human-relations and personal-effectiveness approaches.

In making the distinction between basic and applied studies, one should not make the mistake of assuming that because the basic approach does not draw concepts from the applied one that it is in no way influenced by it. In fact, an applied problem may contain within it the seeds of a profound basic problem. An applied communication problem that has received much attention lately is the effort to produce an automatic speech-recognition system: an arrangement of electronic gear which could, for instance, take in the sound of a human voice and print out a record of what it said. As of this writing the problem remains unsolved except for a few highly restricted examples, because basic theoretical problems of acoustic phonetics and linguistics that are fundamental to the solution have not themselves been solved. What is perhaps most interesting about this situation is that, for the most part, these are basic problems which were unrecognized until the applied problem of building such an apparatus was faced. In fact, until the effort was made, many linguists and phoneticians thought the design of such a machine to be a relatively simple matter. Applied studies contribute indirectly to the basic studies supporting them when they present problems that cannot be solved with existing basic knowledge.

This book concerns itself with that part of human communication which is carried on by means of the spoken word. To take an inclusive view of acts of oral communication we shall examine the subject from a variety of points of view, both basic and applied.

PROBLEMS AND QUESTIONS FOR DISCUSSION

1. What approach or approaches to the study of communication does each of the following examples illustrate? (Note that because the approaches overlap, some examples will represent more than one approach.)
   a. A discussion of the best way to begin a persuasive speech to an unfriendly audience.
   b. A description of the differences in vowel sounds between German and English languages.
   c. A study of the conditions governing the uses of the formal and the informal modes of personal address among French factory workers.
   d. An analysis of the effects of differing levels of noise and the accuracy of communication between pilots and air-traffic controllers.
   e. Experiments dealing with the influence of repeated, strongly expressed disagreement on a student's inclination to discuss controversial topics.
   f. A proposal for establishing community-action councils.
   g. An explanation of the most effective means of promoting international understanding.
2. What are some of the questions about language that would be considered by proponents of the "personal-effectiveness" approach to communication?
3. What are some of the questions about "communication as culture" that would be raised by proponents of the "human-relations" approach?
4. What are some of the questions about "message transmission" that might be raised by proponents of the "behavioral" approach?

2.

LANGUAGE:
THE STRUCTURE OF THE CODE

In Chapter 1, we noted that communication is a complex and multifaceted phenomenon that cannot be explained by any single viewpoint or principle of analysis. Nevertheless, in working toward a comprehensive grasp of speech communication we must begin somewhere; and since wherever we turn in the study of speech communication, we encounter linguistic phenomena, linguistic problems, and linguistic effects, it is appropriate to open our discussion of the speech communication process with an examination of language.[1]

The study of language is almost as rich and complex a subject as the study of communication itself; it is much older, and a great variety of distinctive approaches have been made to it. Because they dovetail with other aspects of the communication process, six of these approaches are of special relevance to communication generally: (1) analysis of the *structure of language,* (2) *language and meaning,* (3) *verbal behavior,* (4) *language and culture,* (5) *language hygiene,* and (6) *linguistic propriety.* The first of these will be discussed in this chapter; the second in the next chapter, and the remaining four will be touched upon at appropriate points in the remainder of the book.

1. H. A. Gleason's *An Introduction to Descriptive Linguistics,* Revised Edition, (New York: Holt, Rinehart & Winston, Inc., 1961) contains an excellent introduction to language structure for the student who wishes to pursue the topic further.

Consider the following sentence, which has been mutilated by replacing certain words and letters with blank spaces:

I __ not going __ to__n and n__ther are __, you may __ __ure.

No adult native speaker of English would have much difficulty replacing all of the missing elements: *am, to, w, ei, you, be, s.* In fact, as we shall see in a later chapter, the replacement or filling-in of missing elements is an essential part of receiving speech in many everyday situations. This is possible because language is highly redundant. In common parlance, "redundant" means "repetitive"; but when we say that all natural languages are highly redundant, we mean that they contain a far greater number of cues than is absolutely necessary for communication under ideal circumstances. Most of this redundancy is something different from simple repetition; it resides in the fact that languages are very highly structured. Although in this short volume we cannot explore language structure in detail, we can gain an appreciation of its meaning by exploring certain broad aspects of the structure of the English language.

PHONOLOGICAL STRUCTURES

In many ways, an English utterance is like a chain in which the order of the links is partly specified by rules governing which links can follow which others; except that when we look closely, we find not one chain but several, so arranged that the larger links are themselves composed of smaller ones. We will begin with the smallest links in the chain and proceed up the scale to the larger ones.

Phones

The smallest links in the linguistic chain are called *phones*. Suppose you read aloud King Richard's famous line, "A horse! A horse! My kingdom for a horse!" Now consider the "s" sound that occurred in the word "horse" each time you pronounced that word. Each of those "s" sounds was a different phone. If you say the line again, you will produce three more "s" phones for a total of six in the two repetitions. *A phone is a single occurrence of a speech sound.* No two phones are quite identical either in the way they are formed or in the sound patterns they produce, although they may sound alike to the human ear.

Phone-Types

With a little training, you could learn to distinguish some "s" sounds from others. For instance, if the Shakespearean line quoted above were to be repeated several times, you might come to distinguish the "s" sound in the first occurrence of "horse" from the final "s" of the line; as the line is normally pronounced, the first "s" is followed by a vowel, while the last one is followed by silence. The vowel which follows the first "s" is sometimes said to "condition" the "s" sound, and make it distinctively different to the trained ear (and to acoustic measuring devices such as the sound spectrograph) from the "s" that is followed by silence. In coming to make this distinction between the two "s" sounds, you would be learning to classify phones as to type. *A phone-type is a group of phones which sound exactly alike to the ear, and are produced in essentially the same way.* Thus, if the foregoing dramatic line were to be read several times, all of the occurrences of the first "s" in the utterance would fall into one phone type, and all of the occurrences of the final "s" would fall into a second phone type. The phones of a phone-type are not distinguishable from one another, but they are distinguishable from the phones of other phone-types.

Phonemes

Having noted that phones are grouped together into phone-types, we must now consider a higher level grouping: the classification of phone-types into *phonemes*.

Consider the words "pot" and "top" as you would usually pronounce them in "pot top" (phrase 1) and "top pot" (phrase 2). The "p" sound at the beginning of pot and the "t" sound at the beginning of top have certain features in common. For instance, both sounds explode with a puff of air, as you can demonstrate by placing a lighted candle a couple of inches in front of your lips as you pronounce the words. These are called *aspirated* sounds.

Suppose we designate the aspirated "p" sound /p'/ and the aspirated "t" sound /t'/. Contrast these aspirated sounds with the "t" at the end of pot in phrase 1 and with the "p" at the end of top in phrase 2. In phrase 2, the "p" in top (call it /p°/) is formed when the lips come together and stop the breath stream. In phrase 1, the "t" in pot (call it /t°/) is formed when the tongue comes to rest against the alveolar ridge above the upper teeth, again stopping the breath stream without any exploding puff of air. A candle flame held in front of the lips does not waver as much on /p°/ and /t°/ as it does on /p'/ and /t'/.

Now, /p′/, /t′/, /p°/, and /t°/ are all phone-types. When all of the sounds of English are considered, there are many dozens of such phone-types: some linguists distinguish more than 200 of them. Yet it is clear that among these 200 types are many groups of sounds that are closely related to one another. Consider, for instance, /p′/ and /p°/. Both are produced by bringing the two lips together, so both are identified as *bilabial* sounds, like "b" and "m." Moreover, both interrupt the breath stream, so they are also identified as *plosive* sounds, like "k" and "t." Thus, the two sounds are *phonetically similar,* but their relationships do not end there. If we find one of the two sounds (say, /p′/) at a certain position in a particular utterance of a certain sentence, then we are quite unlikely to find the other sound (/p°/) used at that same position in any future utterance of that same sentence. We might say that the linguistic contexts of the two phone-types are different; /p′/ occurs at the beginning of an utterance, just prior to the "open" vowel /a/, as in /p′at°/, while the /p°/ cannot occur there, but can occur at the end of an utterance, just after the same vowel, as in /t′ap°/. Because neither occurs in the same linguistic context as the other and because they are phonetically similar, /p′/ and /p°/ are said to stand in *complementary distribution* to one another.

When two phone-types stand in complementary distribution to one another, linguists are inclined to suspect that they are functionally equivalent: that is, that whatever phonetic differences there are between the two sounds are due entirely to the different linguistic contexts in which they appear and are entirely independent of their primary linguistic function. To test this hypothesis with respect to two phone-types, one performs an experiment of the following sort.

Suppose we suspect that /t′/ and /t°/ are functionally equivalent in English. We may take an utterance in which one of the sounds appears and substitute the other sound to determine whether the substitution makes any difference with respect to what is said. Suppose, for instance, that we substitute /t′/ for /t°/ in /p′at°/. The resulting utterance is /p′at′/, and a native speaker of English will tell you that these two sound sequences are essentially equivalent—they "mean" the same thing; and if one is substituted for the other, the resulting pronunciation may sound a little "formal" or "odd" or "artificial," but no linguistically significant change has occurred. When two phone-types pass this final test, they may be said to belong to the same phoneme. Thus, *a phoneme is a group of functionally equivalent phone-types which differ from one another only to the extent that their occurrence in different linguistic contexts produces certain functionally irrelevant differences among them.*

We have observed that /t′/ and /t°/ belong to the same phoneme. Do /p'/ and /p°/ also belong to that same phoneme? Perform the substitution experiment described above for these two phone-types, and you will find that /p'/ and /p°/ are functionally equivalent to one another, but that neither of them is functionally equivalent to /t'/ or /t°/; so the two "t" sounds belong in one phoneme, (t), and the two "p" sounds belong in another, (p). Actually, the (p) and (t) phonemes contain many phone-types in addition to the two variants of each that we have noted here. Out of the many dozens of phone-types in English, linguists have identified just forty-two phonemes; that is, there are forty-two functionally unique elemental speech sounds in English, with each of these forty-two displaying a certain range of variation depending mostly on the nature of the linguistic context in which it occurs.

We have now identified the smallest links in the language chain, the individual sounds. We have observed that they vary a great deal, but that their variation is highly structured; that is, they are reducible to sets of sounds which differ mostly in ways that can be predicted from the position which the sound occupies in the total chain of sounds. Because of the highly predictable nature of this structure, it is possible for purposes of further analysis to ignore differences among the phone-types and deal only with the phonemes. We shall see in a later chapter that this possibility results in a great economy in language usage. For the moment, however, it facilitates immeasurably our further analysis of larger links in the linguistic structure.

Morphemes

If we now envision an English utterance as a string or chain of phonemes, we observe a rather remarkable thing: not all possible orders of phonemes do in fact occur, and some sequences of phonemes occur over and over again. This repetitiveness is further evidence of structure. In developing the following points, we will use conventional spelling for the linguistic elements used as examples. We do so because our brief treatment here has not allowed us to develop the background of information about phonetic transcription we would need for the more precise representation used by linguists in formal language study. Nevertheless, our purposes will be served if the reader bears in mind that what we represent here in standard orthography is in fact a string of *sounds,* and the print will represent the sound with as much fidelity as we could get by using phonetic transcription.

In examining a long utterance in English, we might find several sequences occurring very often: "and," "ing," "go," "ed," "tie," "un," and so forth. Each of these sequences is composed of two or more phonemes, and each might recur with considerable frequency in a long sample of English. Each of these recurring sequences of speech sounds is (when used with the same meaning) a morpheme. *A morpheme may be defined loosely as the smallest linguistic segment that carries specific meaning.* For instance, "g" has no specific meaning, but "go" does have specific meaning. Add "ing" after "go" and you get "going," which has some meaning in common with "go" but seems to have a dimension of meaning added to it. If we add the same "ing" to "tie," we get "tieing," which differs in meaning from "tie" in much the same way as "going" differs from "go." The suffix "ing" then is a morpheme also; so is the prefix "un." We can add it to "tie" and get "untie" but we cannot add it to "go" under the rules of standard English. Even so, the meaning of the morpheme "un" is sufficiently clear that if you were to violate standard usage and say something like, "I wish I could ungo to this party," an imaginative listener would grasp the general significance of what you said, though it would sound somewhat peculiar.

In other words, there are regular ways in which morphemes may be chained together, just as there are regularities about the order of phone-types in a phonetic sequence. There are also variations within morphemes which are similar in many ways to the variations of phone types within a phoneme. For instance, the three sounds that we represent by the letters "ed" in "watched," in "winged," and in "pounded" are in reality three different sounds: the "ed" in "watched" sounds like a "t," the "ed" in "winged" sounds like a "d," and the "ed" in "pounded" sounds like a "d" preceded by a very short vowel sound that lies somewhere between "ih" and "uh." Yet these three different linguistic forms all belong to the same morpheme; they are functionally equivalent, differing only in ways that depend partly on the linguistic environment in which each of them occurs, and partly on other factors having nothing to do with the meaning of the word.

Some morphemes are words, as we noted above. Others are parts of words. The word that is sometimes cited as the longest in English contains the eight morphemes: anti/dis/establish/ment/ar/i/an/ism. With a little analysis, you can determine the contribution of each of these morphemes to the total meaning of the word. Although some linguists do not recognize the word as a legitimate linguistic unit, we shall here regard it as one.

SYNTACTICAL STRUCTURES

As you can determine for yourself by examining any group of words, the order of morphemes in words that contain more than a single morphemic unit is rigidly determined. In the long word above, for example, the "anti" must come at the beginning and the "ism" at the end. The rules governing the order of morphemes constitute another source of structural redundancy. They are the beginning levels of *grammar,* which is concerned with the ordering of morphemes as well as the larger units of language such as words, phrases, and clauses.

Sentences as Linguistic Units

We should pause a moment to consider the sentence as a linguistic unit. In a printed English message there is not much question about what a sentence is—it is whatever is written between one sentence-terminal marker (question mark, period, exclamation point) and another. But the sentence-terminal markers are much more difficult to locate in spoken English, so that some scholars go so far as to suggest that the sentence has no status as a linguistic entity. You may gain some appreciation for this point of view by performing the following experiment. Make an impromptu speech (one which has not been preplanned in any way) on a topic chosen by somebody else, or engage a friend in extemporaneous discussion about any topic. Make a tape recording of what you say and later transcribe your utterance on paper. The odds are very good that you will experience some difficulty in locating the places where one sentence ends and another begins. Now extend your experiment by removing all punctuation and giving the transcript to five or six other people, asking them to locate the sentence terminals for you. Although there will be some consistency, you will be surprised at the variety of locations the different readers choose for sentence terminals.

Phrase-Structure Versus Transformational Grammar

In the preceding analysis of language structure we have deliberately skirted perhaps the most significant issue in modern linguistic theory: Which of several radically different approaches to linguistic structure is most "powerful"; that is, which can best explain the facts of linguistic structure? For the most part, these theoretical differences have little to do with what we have already discussed, since by and large they all recognize phones, phonemes, morphemes, words, phrases, and sentences as legitimate elements of linguistic structure (though certain approaches put more emphasis on some of these elements than do others). But the theories differ sharply on *how* we are to account for the fact that some strings of linguistic units form valid meaningful sentences while others do not. The issues raised by this controversy are so important that no discussion of language structure would be complete without some mention of them.

The significant fact behind the controversy is that we produce grammatical sentences without understanding how we do it. Anyone with a good command of English can distinguish readily between "grammatical" and "ungrammatical" sentences. As used here, "grammatical" does not mean elegant or admirable, but simply allowable by the rules of the language. We make such distinctions easily because we have internalized the rules as part of learning the language. But exactly what *are* the rules? And by what strategy can we best go about discovering them?

Now these two questions—what are the rules, and how can we best discover them—may at first seem like nonsense. After all, we just said that everybody learns the rules as part of learning the language; so if we all know the rules, why don't we just write them down? According to this viewpoint, no one would have to study grammar to know grammar, since everybody who can speak the language already "knows" all the grammatical rules; otherwise, he would not be able to "use" them in speaking and in listening to speech.

Clearly something has to be wrong with the foregoing analysis. Without formal training, very few people can state any grammatical rules (let alone all of them); and as we noted above, linguists are undecided among themselves about just how the rules should be stated. The trouble with the analysis, of course, is that we are using the word "know" in two very different senses. In one sense we are talking about mastery of a psychomotor skill—speaking—while in the other sense we are talking about conscious awareness of the detailed structure of that skill; and these are very different things. In the first case we refer to doing; in the second case we refer to *understanding* and to *talking about*. You can talk intelligently about many things that you cannot do; but you can do even more things that you cannot talk intelligently about.

Mastery of language behavior versus awareness of structure of behavior: an experiment. You can demonstrate the difference between mastering language behavior and being consciously aware of the structure of that behavior by means of a simple experiment. Take eighteen small cards (3 × 5 or so) and on each one make a separate geometric figure according to the following rules. One third of the cards are to be triangles, one third squares, and one third circles. One third of each group will be colored blue, one third red, and one third black. For each color-figure combination, one figure will be large and one figure small. Thus, you will have a large red square, a small red square, a large blue square, and so on—one card for each of the possible combinations of size, color, and shape.

Now assign each card a name according to some system such as the following: all large figures are given a name that begins with MAH, all small ones a name beginning NUH. The next sound in the name will refer to color: S for reds, SH for blues, NG for blacks. The final syllable will refer to shape: TAW for squares, KI for triangles, PO for circles. Thus, MAHSHKI is a large blue triangle; NUHSPO is the small red circle, etc.

One more step and you are ready to begin the experiment. Take out six representative cards, and designate them a "test" set. Select them so that you have half large and half small figures; one third blue, one third red, one third black; and one third of each shape. Now you have a very simple artificial language for naming your geometric objects. You will use the remaining twelve cards to "teach"

FIGURE 1
Sample Cards

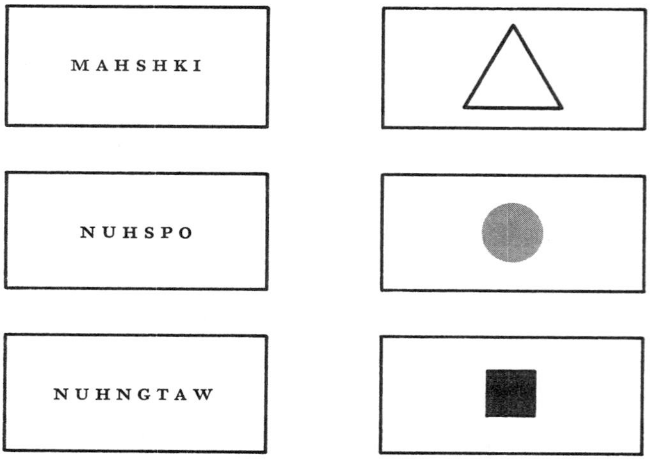

the language to somebody else (without telling them the "rules" of the language, of course), and then you will present the six test cards to determine how well they have learned those rules.

Teach the language to your subject by presenting the twelve cards one at a time and pronouncing the name for him. The next time through, ask him to try to remember the name. If he can't recall it (as he won't at first), repeat it for him. Continue through the twelve cards as many times as necessary until he can name all of them correctly without prompting. (For most college students, this should take between fifteen and thirty minutes.) At this point he can be said to have "learned" the language, in the sense that he can name all of the cards that have been taught to him. But has he "learned" the rules in the sense that he can apply them in a new situation? To test for this ability, present the six "test" cards, and ask him to name them. You will be surprised to find that your subject will be able to name all six objects with very few errors, and these will usually be minor ones. This proves that he has internalized the rules of your artificial language since he can apply them in a novel situation.

But now ask your subject to describe the language to you as precisely as he can. The odds are better than 50–50 that he will describe the rules imperfectly. Following his stated rules, some of the cards would be given "improper" names—that is, names that do not conform to your rules—even though he may have named those same cards correctly at an earlier time! He has "learned" your language in the sense that he has mastered the behavioral skills required; but he has not "learned" it in the sense that he can give an accurate description of what he is doing.

Learning how versus learning about. Realization that one can do something well without knowing what he is doing comes as a rude shock to most educated people. We tend to believe that one first learns *about* a task, then uses this information to learn *how* to do it. In language it usually is the other way around: we first learn *how*, then (if we have time and are so inclined) learn *about*. Thus, it is not at all surprising that people who have known for years how to use language should argue about how to describe it. In the case of the artificial language in the experiment above, imagine what it would be like to arrange a confrontation between two subjects representing different "schools of thought" about the structure of the language. Multiply the complexity of the problem a thousandfold, and you have the situation confronting linguists—except of course that they have no one to tell them which theory is "right."

Criteria for evaluating grammars. In the absence of an acceptable arbitrator for their differences of opinion, linguists resort to the language itself and ask the question: Which theory has the greatest explanatory power? In the case of syntactic rules (the part of language theory that we are concerned with now) this explanatory power refers to two things: (1) How many ungrammatical sentences will this theory generate? (The fewer generated, the more powerful the theory.) (2) How many grammatical sentences will this theory fail to generate? (The fewer it fails to generate, the more powerful the theory.) The trick, obviously, is to create a theory that will generate all grammatical English sentences, but will not generate any sentences that are ungrammatical in English. Since not all of the possible English sentences have yet been spoken, this is certainly asking a great deal of a theory; yet this is precisely the goal of syntactic theorists, and represents the yardstick against which their work is measured.

Two of the most important theories that are currently being measured against that yardstick are "phrase-structure" and "transformational" grammars. Neither phrase-structure nor transformational theory can be said to represent a syntactic theory; each represents a broad *approach* to thinking about the structure of language, and a number of distinct theories have been developed under each approach. We cannot attempt here to cover either phrase-structure or transformation theory in detail, but we can examine briefly some major points of difference between them.

Phrase-structure grammars. Phrase-structure grammars are based on a method called "immediate constituent analysis." Using this approach, the linguist tries to invent a set of categories for language units that will permit him to divide a sentence into a very small number of units (usually just two—a noun phrase and a verb

FIGURE 2
Immediate Constituent Analysis

the cat	chased	the mouse
NOUN PHRASE	VERB	NOUN PHRASE
	VERB PHRASE	
SENTENCE		

phrase). Each of these units is then divided into smaller units until we arrive at the individual words (sometimes the individual morphemes) of which the sentence is composed. Thus, the sentence "The cat chased the mouse" would be divided into a noun phrase (the cat) and a verb phrase (chased the mouse); the verb phrase would then be divided into a verb (chased) and a noun phrase (the mouse). This analysis of the sentence could be represented by the diagram in Figure 2.

Ideally, every sentence could be reduced to such a diagram; and indeed it appears that every grammatical sentence can be represented in this way by phrase-structure grammar. But it has always been known that some sentences are ambiguous in the structural sense, in that they can be represented by different diagrams. Consider, for example, the following sentence: "We are cutting edges." It may be taken to mean, "We are cutting some edges," or "We are edges of the kind called cutting edges." The first meaning of the sentence is represented by Figure 3, and the second meaning by Figure 4. One problem with phrase-structure grammars is that they

FIGURE 3
A Possible Sentence Diagram

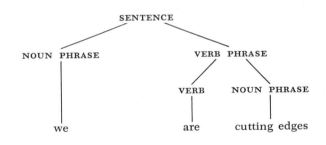

FIGURE 4
An Alternative Sentence Diagram

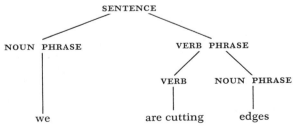

provide no rules for removing the ambiguities from this sentence; that is, the grammar itself gives us no way of distinguishing between the two different meanings of the sentence.

Transformational grammars. In a response to this and other problems that arise in connection with phrase-structure grammars, some linguists have advanced transformational theories of language structure. Rather than beginning with immediate constituents, transformational grammars begin with "kernel sentences"—usually simple declarative sentences in the active voice—and then provide transformational rules for changing these and combining them into longer and more complex sentences. Kernel sentences are viewed as basic units of meaning, such as "The man walks," "They read books," "The secretary types," and "Hurricanes come in summer." Simple transformation rules specify how these kernel sentences are altered to express past tense, passive voice, negation, qualification, and other aspects of meaning. Further rules specify how the kernel sentences are altered in combination to produce such sentences as "They have read all of the books that his secretary typed," or "When hurricanes come in the summer, nobody walks on the beach."

It is not much of an oversimplification to say that phrase-structure grammars begin with the surface features of the sentence and work back toward the meaning, while transformational grammars begin with simple units of meaning and work out toward the surface features. In some instances this procedure of generating sentences from kernels by the application of strict transformation rules can remove ambiguity in cases where phrase-structure grammar would be powerless to do so. Consider the sentence in Figures 3 and 4 as a case in point. If we say that "We cut edges," "We are edges," and "Edges cut" are kernel sentences, then we might specify one transformation rule that will convert "We cut edges" into "We are cutting edges" in the sense of Figure 3, and another transformation rule to convert "We are edges" plus "Edges cut" into "We are cutting edges" in the sense of Figure 4. Since the kernel sentences and the transformation rules are different in each case, the transformational approach has accounted for the ambiguity of this sentence, which the phrase-structure approach could not do.

An added benefit of transformational grammars is that, for the most part, the essential meaning of a kernel sentence is preserved through the transformation. It is for this reason more than any other that transformational grammars have been so fascinating to those who are interested in how it is that we *understand* language. To comprehend in detail how we could understand a complex sentence seems an almost impossible task. But to comprehend how we understand a simple "kernel" sentence does not seem so formidable. If indeed it should prove possible to generate all possible English sentences from a relatively small set of kernel sentences by means of a relatively small set of exact transformational rules, then we may look forward to the day when we can grasp how it is that we assign meaning to any sentence, however complex it may be.

Although this cursory view of language structure has not provided a detailed picture of any level of language analysis, it does serve to provide substance to the assertion that language is structured in many levels and is therefore redundant. Of all of the possible sounds that the human vocal tract is capable of producing, a given language uses only a couple of hundred—the phone-types. Moreover, these are grouped into sets which are functionally equivalent—the phonemes—with the various phone-types distributed in a regular and predictable way among the variety of linguistic contexts in which the phoneme occurs. Phonemes are strung together into chains, and again not every possible chain of phonemes in the language is actually used. Recurring strings compose morphemic units, with many of the morphemes displaying a range of variants depending to some extent on the linguistic context in which the morpheme occurs. Morphemes may be strung together to make words, words to make phrases or clauses, and phrases or clauses to make sentences. At each level of linguistic analysis we find a defined set of alternative units. These are combined in some way to form units of the next larger size. But at each level there are rules of combination that specify which units may occur in a given context. These rules introduce redundancy which, among other things, makes it possible to replace missing or mutilated parts of an utterance. They also provide the framework by which language carries meaning.

We have observed that knowing structural rules in the sense of being able to produce grammatical sentences provides no guarantee that one understands the rules in the sense of being able to describe them accurately. Linguists have set for themselves the task of specifying the rules of language. Two radically different approaches to finding linguistic rules are phrase-structure grammar and transformational theory. Each is very powerful, in the sense that both seem able to account for most grammatical English sentences. However, transformational theory seems better able to deal with structurally ambiguous sentences, and it holds greater promise of allowing us someday to comprehend how it is that people understand complex sentences.

PROBLEMS AND QUESTIONS FOR DISCUSSION

1. Perform the experiment referred to on page 20, in which a candle is used to distinguish between aspirated and unaspirated sounds. Report your results, and compare them with the results obtained by other students.
2. Perform the experiment calling for an impromptu speech described on page 24. Compare your results with those of your classmates.
3. Perform the experiment referred to on pages 26–27, in which you teach someone an artificial language. With three of your classmates, test two subjects each, and pool your results for a joint report.
4. In your own words, describe the difference between transformational and phrase-structure theories of syntax.
5. What is the difference between a letter and a speech sound? Are all speech sounds represented by a single English letter? Do all letters represent a single sound?

3.

MEANING IN LANGUAGE[1]

In exploring the method of establishing phonemes in the last chapter, did it occur to you that one convenient test of "functional equivalence" of two phone-types could be based on a test of meaning? If two words, identical in all ways save for the single phone-type being tested, have the same meaning, then the two phone-types could be called equivalent. If the words have different meanings, then the phone-types are not equivalent and belong in different phonemes. Many field linguists employ just this procedure; thus, the notion of "meaning" lies at the very heart of linguistic science; it is even related to such mechanical details of language as the definition of the individual phonemes.

Some linguists have tried to devise tests of functional equivalence that bypass the question of meaning altogether. Some even try to define the morpheme without reference to meaning. By contrast, we have defined the morpheme as the smallest linguistic unit that carries specific meaning.

Why would one go to such lengths to circumvent the question of meaning? It turns out that this term "meaning" cannot be given a scientifically satisfying definition that covers even a majority of the

---

1. A more detailed analysis of meaning prepared for the student of speech is Hubert G. Alexander's book, *Meaning in Language* (Glenview, Ill.: Scott, Foresman and Company, 1969).

ways in which the term is regularly used. When a term cannot be defined explicitly, the tendency is to drop it; but, in the case of "meaning," this poses much difficulty. Most of what we know about language grows in some way out of the fact that linguistic events are meaningful. Indeed, much of our motivation to study language stems from our desire to understand this meaningfulness more fully. In this chapter, therefore, we will simply ignore the scientific and philosophical problems that surround the term, and assume that we all know from intuitive experience that it refers to something real in human terms. Proceeding on that act of faith (or common sense if you prefer), we will then try to understand some of the more important aspects of meaning as it relates to communication.

CONTENT WORDS

Most discussions of meaning deal largely, if not exclusively, with words like "cat," "table," "red," "quickly," "run," "beautiful," etc. One popular way of putting it is that words such as these (nouns, adjectives, adverbs, and verbs) carry most of the content of an utterance. These form classes often referred to as the *content* words, and are distinguished from words like "to," "and," "therefore," and "the," which are sometimes called *form* words. We shall discuss form words later. For the moment, we can begin our examination of meaning at the most common point—with the content words.

Content words may be thought of as having meaning by virtue of standing for classes of objects, events, or aspects of experience. Just what is meant by saying that a word "has meaning" is not easy to describe. However, it is reasonably clear that the meaning of a word does not reside in the word. Rather, the word has the power to arouse the meaning in the mind of a human being. This leads some semantic theorists to claim that "meanings are not in words; meanings are in people." [2] In a sense, this is true; but whether exactly the same meanings could be aroused in people without the words to stimulate them is a moot question. Actually, insofar as linguistic meanings are concerned, it seems reasonable to say that meanings are neither in people nor in words, but rest in a special kind of relationship between words and people. Thus, when in this chapter we refer to the meaning of a word, we refer to the meaning that word stimulates in people.

2. This point of view is well developed in Chapter 7 of David Berlo's *The Process of Communication* (New York: Holt, Rinehart & Winston, Inc., 1960), 168–188.

Advantages of Content Words

Content words confer at least three great advantages on their users: convenience, abstraction, and manipulability.

Convenience. To begin with, content words allow a short and convenient symbol to stand for or represent a much more cumbersome thing. When one wishes to make some reference to Mt. Whitney, it is generally more convenient to say "Mt. Whitney" than to take one's conversational partner to a place where the mountain can be seen and point to it. The convenience of being able to refer to objects which are not in immediate view enables language users to operate with vastly increased flexibility: anything that has been given a name can be thought (and talked) about at any time.

Abstraction. Secondly, content words allow the formation and preservation of abstractions, one of the most useful (and one of the most dangerous) inventions of the human mind. Abstractions are extremely varied. Some of them permit us to refer to a group of things by a single label. I may wish to say something about mountains in general—not just Mt. Whitney, but all or many or the majority of mountains. The word "mountains" permits me to perform this operation; and, moreover, it permits me to retain the abstract concept of mountains in mind for future use in other statements. Eventually, I may build up quite a store of knowledge, beliefs, experiences, and attitudes about mountains, all of which will be more or less linked together by the common label. Without language, this sort of abstract reference and storage would be impossible.

Another kind of abstraction deals with "things" which never exist in isolated form. Nobody, for example, has ever seen "red." We see red cars and red shirts and red flowers, but we never see red by itself, in isolation. We cannot point to redness. We can only point to red objects. Yet aided by language, we can isolate the characteristic of redness conceptually from the objects of which it is characteristic, and can then deal with it as a separate entity, independent of the specific objects to which it might be attached.

Still another kind of abstraction is concerned with "things" that are never present in visible form. Nobody has ever *seen* "freedom," or "waste," or "intelligence." Each of these things is a complex attribute, a property of objects or events which is composed of many ingredients. Each of the ingredients of "waste" might be ascertained by direct observation, but the attribute of "waste" itself is not observable; it is a perceived pattern of relationships among all of these elements. The abstract character of content words thus permits us to refer to many objects with a single label, to deal with properties which could not be physically isolated, and to conceptualize and deal with complex relations that are not directly observable.

Manipulability. In addition to convenience and abstraction, words also allow for manipulability. A simple and compelling illustration of the value of symbolic manipulation is the final short sentence from a kitchen recipe: "Slowly fold in the beaten egg whites and pour into a nine-inch spring pan." All that has been manipulated in the above sentence is symbols; yet, anybody who knew those symbols could perform the physical manipulations described, for the words in a sense perform the manipulation symbolically. Moreover, he could also explore the possibilities of alternate courses of action without actually manipulating ingredients or utensils: What would happen if the eggs were beaten in rather than folded in? How about folding them in quickly rather than slowly? Why a spring pan? Why not a seven-inch pan or a ten-inch one? Thus, even if it were possible to have an expert cook lead one through the motions described, the expression of the process in words allows one to explore other possibilities more quickly and conveniently, and thus to be more flexible in behavior. This possibility of symbolic manipulation is a great advantage, particularly, as we shall see in a later chapter, when it comes to problem-solving.

Connotative Meaning

Most people would agree to what has been said up to this point about the meanings of content words; many, however, would point out that thus far our discussion has been limited to a single dimension of meaning—denotation. They would urge that in addition to denotative meanings, words also carry connotations. One of the reasons why the question of connotative meaning has proved such a fertile source of argument among students of language is that we use the distinction between denotation and connotation to cover not just one, but several quite different distinctions. Three of these distinctions will help us to gain considerable insight into the richness of meaning carried by content words: they are the distinctions based on *extensionality, publicity,* and *saliency.*

As we explore these distinctions below, keep in mind that we do not intend to substitute any of these for the distinction between denotation and connotation. Instead, we hope to show that the notion of connotative meaning is vague and ambiguous, and that what we mean by the term varies markedly from one occasion to the next. The distinctions based on extensionality, publicity, and saliency are more useful for distinguishing among the varieties of meaning. We will discuss the first two of these distinctions here and the third later in the chapter.

Extensionality. Often when one talks about a distinction between denotation and connotation, he is trying to distinguish between *extensional* meaning (which is then called "denotative") and *intensional* meaning (which is then called "connotative"). Extensional meaning might in one sense be called "logical" meaning. It is the meaning of a word which "points to" some object, event, characteristic, or state of affairs. Thus, when I speak of "magnolia trees," I can point to one or more objects of the kind in question to indicate what I mean by the term. Even in the case of a relatively vague term, such as "beautiful," I can point to a range of objects—flowers, equations, girls, fence-rows, poems, etc.—which, in my judgment, display the trait. In short, whenever I use content words, I am (or may be) pointing to something in the environment which you and I both share.

It would appear, however, that few if any of our experiences remain uncolored by our emotions and values; and so it is with words. Whatever we have a name for, we also have some feeling toward. When we refer to the intensional meaning of a term, we refer to the feeling we have about that word or what it represents. Thus, "snake" has not only an extensional reference—a range of objects to which it applies—but also, for some of us, the word carries strong negative implications. If we wish to put someone down, we may refer to him metaphorically as "a snake," and most people will understand thereby that we hold him in extremely low regard.

It is apparent then that as we talk, the content words we use serve not only to point to certain objects, events, relations, etc. in the environment, but also serve to express for the speaker and arouse in the listener emotional reactions of varying intensity. What and how strong those reactions are, will depend upon the nature of one's experiences with the words and the things to which they refer. They may not be quite the same for both speaker and listener—but this topic will be discussed in greater detail later.

Publicity. When we distinguish between denotation and connotation, we sometimes have in mind the difference between *public* meaning (which is then called denotative) and *private* meaning (which is then called connotative). The public meaning of a word refs to that meaning which is shared among all or most of the members of a particular language community; the private meaning is that which is peculiar to one or a few.

It should be apparent that these two dimensions of meaning, extensional *versus* intentional and public *versus* private are in fact independent of one another, and that the two taken together create not just two categories of meaning, as the denotative-connotative distinction would lead us to suppose, but four: public-extensional, public-intensional, private-extensional, and private-intensional.

Measurement of Meaning

Perhaps the significance of this four-way classification can be clarified further by examining two ways in which meaning can be "measured": (1) extensional agreement index and (2) semantic differential.

Extensional agreement index. The "extensional agreement index" is a measurement based on the proportion of agreement among a group of people in a certain language community concerning which items among a very large set of items should be included within the definition of a particular term. "Chair" is a good example of a word having a very high extensional agreement index (which is why it is used so often as an example in discussions of language and meaning). If we were to look at a very large array of objects, almost all of us would agree in almost every instance as to whether a given object were a chair or not. Of course, agreement would not be perfect. Some would call the seat of a school desk a chair; others would not; perhaps a few would include milking stools, chaises longues, and cobbler's benches; some might exclude opera seats and thrones. But for each of us, our extensional meanings for "chair" would in the overwhelming majority of cases fall within the public meaning of the term. Those objects on which we individually disagree with predominant public usage would constitute for each of us our private meanings for "chair"—either extensional or intensional.

For some words, the extent of public agreement on extensional meaning is very low. One example of such a word is "liberty." Individual extensional meanings for the term differ so much that this word has very little public extensional meaning; on the other hand, we tend to agree to a remarkable extent that liberty is a good and desirable thing. The word "liberty" (in modern Western civilization) has almost exclusively positive emotional attachments; so much so that we would be inclined to think of anyone who thought of liberty in a negative light as distinctly peculiar, if not an outright crackpot. It is a word with high intensional agreement.

Semantic differential. One way to measure whether a person's emotional reactions to a word are positive or negative is to use a measuring device called a "semantic differential." [3] There are many such devices, but all of them call for evaluation of the word or concept on a set of scales running between bipolar, adjectival "values," like the following:

FIGURE 5

A Sample Semantic Differential

"LIBERTY"

	7	6	5	4	3	2	1	
good :	:	:	:	:	:	:	:	bad
fair :	:	:	:	:	:	:	:	unfair
desirable :	:	:	:	:	:	:	:	undesirable
kind :	:	:	:	:	:	:	:	cruel
beautiful :	:	:	:	:	:	:	:	ugly

One indicates his reactions to "liberty" on such a test by checking the blank which most accurately reflects his views on each of the scales. The average response on the five scales in the above test yields an "evaluative factor score," which is a measure of the direction and intensity of a person's evaluative response to the concept being rated. On such a test, "liberty" would score very close to 7.0 (the most positive possible score) for most of us: the test would show that there is high public agreement on the intensional meaning of "liberty." [4]

But how about the word "chair," on which we found such high extensional agreement? Would evaluative meanings for "chair"

3. Charles E. Osgood, George J. Suci, and Percy N. Tannenbaum, *The Measurement of Meaning* (Urbana, Ill.: University of Illinois Press, 1967).

4. For further information concerning the semantic differential see Raymond G. Smith, "Validation of a Semantic Differential," *Speech Monographs,* XXX (March, 1963): 50–55.

display such regularity? Probably not. Emotional meanings for the term would probably not be very strong for most individuals, but they would probably vary over a wider range than our reactions to "liberty." Thus, we have seen that it is possible for a word to have much agreement on extensional meaning with little agreement on intensional meaning (like "chair"); or to have much agreement on intensional meaning with little agreement on extensional meaning (like "liberty"). In short, extensional meaning and intensional meaning are independent aspects of meaning; the components of each may be described as public or private along a continuum of relative agreement.

There has been a tendency in the past for investigators to be interested in both the public aspects of extensional meaning (dictionaries devote much of their space to cataloging extensional public meanings), and the private aspects of intensional meaning (peculiar emotional reactions to words are used in psychological evaluation of individuals). This accident, as much as anything else, contributes to the confusion of these two dimensions of meaning under the denotative-connotative dichotomy.

Salient and latent associations. The same dichotomy also covers another distinction: sometimes we use "denotative" to refer to the *salient associations* of a term, and "connotative" to refer to its *latent associations.* "Winter," for example, refers to a particular season of the year. We associate it with a series of months on the calendar and, depending on geography, a certain kind of weather. These are primary associations which may be said to be salient because they are very often thought and spoken of in connection with winter, and so lie very close to the surface of our meanings for the term. But for each of us there is also a variety of further associations with the term which lie deeper beneath the surface: semester examinations, sleigh rides, the smell of wood smoke, the hiss of snow under skis, etc. These are the secondary associations which may be said to be latent because they are thought and spoken of less often in connection with winter and are therefore usually aroused only by special circumstances.

Both latent and salient associations are part of the meaning of a term, and language is often used in such a way that latent associations carry the primary burden of communication. Much poetry is written in such a way as to arouse latent associations, but such associations may play a key role in more mundane activities as well. For instance, William Jennings Bryan in a famous speech referred to the gold standard by saying, "You shall not press down upon the brow of Labor this crown of thorns." The "crown of thorns" concept carries latent associations of martyred righteousness and nobility. Thus, the statement in its context conferred an aura of these characteristics upon Labor, elevating it by indirect implication to a highly favorable position. This was accomplished more effectively through latent associations than it could have been through more direct reference.

We have seen that content words carry several types of meaning, not simply denotative and connotative. The denotation-connotation distinction, in fact, covers three distinctions among types of language meaning. The first of these is the distinction between extensional meaning, which points to something in the common environment of speaker and listener, and intensional meaning, which refers to the emotional or valuational reactions of speaker or listener or both. The second distinction is between public meaning, that which is shared by all or most of the members of a given linguistic community, and private meaning, that which is peculiar to one or a few. The third and final distinction is between salient associations, those used most often and therefore most easily aroused, and latent associations, those which are used less often and tend to be aroused mostly by special circumstances.

STRUCTURE WORDS

We may agree that content words have meaning in the sense of labeling or referring to objects, events, qualities, and the like; but when we come to the structure words of a language, it is difficult to make such a case. It is not easy to see what "the," "of," "a," "and," and "for" stand for. It is even hard to see what the most common verb "is" could possibly stand for in the same way that "chair" stands for chairs and "red" stands for redness.

Moreover, the difference between content and structure words does not stop with this qualitative difference: there are dramatic quantitative differences as well. First of all, there are vastly more content words in any language than there are structure words. In English there exist tens of thousands of content words (from "aardvark" to "Zulu"), but only a few hundred structure words (such as "that" and "not"). This remarkable difference in the number of different words of each kind is enough in itself to set the two types apart from one another. It is even more significant when taken in conjunction with a second quantitative observation: although the structure words are few in number, they are remarkably high in frequency of occurrence.

In fact, the structure words are far and away the most frequently occurring words in any utterance. Consider the following statistics from a speech by a university student on the subject of elementary education. A list was made of all of the different words the student used in the speech, then the frequency of each word's occurrence in the text was counted, and this frequency converted to a percentage of the total number of words in the speech. The ten most commonly occurring words, along with their percentage of the total wordage of the speech, are presented in the table below:

Table I

*Relative Frequencies of Occurrence of
Ten Words in a Speech*

Word	Percent
the	5.0
of	3.0
a	2.5
and	2.4
for	2.3
is	2.2
not	2.1
that	2.0
in	1.7
can	1.6
Total	*24.8*

Nearly one fourth of the total number of words in the speech is accounted for by only ten different words, and all ten of them are what we have described as structure words. It is not until we come to the eleventh word in the rank frequency list that we find a content word, "child," with a relative frequency of 1.5%; the thirteenth word is "education," with a relative frequency of 1.2%. In a speech about education, it is natural that these two words should have relatively high frequencies; but even they, which lie at the very heart of the speaker's subject, are overshadowed in relative frequency by the structure words.

Thus, we find two striking statistical differences between structure and content words. In English we find a large number of different content words but a very much smaller number of different structure words. At the same time, there is an impressive discrepancy between the high frequency of occurrence of the structure words and the much lower frequency of occurrence of content words. These facts taken together suggest that content words and structure words must perform quite different functions in the language. This difference is simply that the meaning of structure words lies not in their reference to objects, events, and the like, but in the relations which they establish among other words.

For example, "and" is sometimes used as a sort of instruction to perform a simple kind of addition or cumulation among linguistic units of any size. "Water is composed of hydrogen *and* oxygen." "Surfing at Waikiki *and* bowhunting in Alaska are both exciting." "You should wait here *and* I should go in to look for her." "And" in these sentences has no reference outside the sentence in which it is used; it is simply an instruction to put two linguistic units together in an additive way: words in the first case, phrases in the second, and clauses in the third. This sort of adding-together is an important aspect of symbolic manipulation. Other structure words perform different manipulative functions. If the structure words did not make such manipulation possible, content words would be of much less value in both thought and communication.

ADDITIONAL FACTORS OF MEANING

We have given our primary attention to the word as the unit of meaning; but it is apparent from our examination of the meanings of structure words that meaning in an utterance extends over units that are much more comprehensive than individual words. We shall now turn our attention to four additional factors of meaning: *linguistic context, paralinguistic features, source effects,* and *social context effects.*

Linguistic Context

It is sometimes claimed that individual words have no meaning in themselves, but derive whatever semblance of meaning they have from the contexts in which they are used in sentences. However that may be, it is clear that we cannot get an entirely satisfactory understanding of meaning from any examination of individual words. We must consider also the way words are put together into larger units of discourse, as well as other factors having to do with nonverbal features of the utterance and of the situation in which the utterance is made.

Consider the following sentences:

"The student *failed* the course."
"The transistor *failed* after 5,000 hours of continuous use."
"I *failed* to leave a forwarding address."
"He *failed* in life."

The word *failed* "means" something quite different in each of the foregoing sentences: both extensionally and intensionally, and in terms of both salient and latent associations. To be sure, all of these meanings have a little in common with one another, but the differences seem to overshadow the similarities.

As the foregoing example demonstrates, to be accurate we cannot think of words as though they had single fixed meanings; rather, we must regard a word as if it had several possible meanings. Which of these meanings is aroused by a particular usage of the word will be a function of the other words in the utterance and the way they are related to the word in question. "Failed in life" and "the transistor failed" have little in common.

Paralinguistic Features

In addition to the structure of the utterance, meaning is also influenced by intonation, rate of utterance, voice quality, and other aspects of vocal delivery, as well as by gesture and facial expression. These factors taken together are sometimes called "paralinguistic" features of speech. Without much dramatic ability, you could say the sentence, "The student failed the course," so as to convey a wide range of implications, such as:

"So he says, but frankly I doubt that it is true."
"And isn't it a shame?"
"Believe it or not!"
"The idiot!"
"And that is the end of the matter."
"Just why is a mystery to me."
Etc., etc., etc.

Each of the other sentences listed at the top of this page could also be delivered in a variety of ways so as to convey different "implications" or meanings. In some cases these implications may constitute the sole purpose of utterance, and may carry essentially all of the information which passes from speaker to listener. You and I may both know that the student failed; yet in an effort to express your incredulity to me, you may say, "The student failed the course! (*Oh, you must be kidding!*)." The meaning that will be of greatest concern to us in analyzing this expression will lie not in the verbal elements themselves, but in the details of vocal and facial expression and the other aspects of delivery.

Source Effects

Beyond the question of what is said and how it is said, the receiver of a spoken message may interpret a dimension of meaning based on his knowledge of the source of the communication. You probably know some individuals whose meaning for the sentence above would contain the implication: "And there you have another example of how irresponsible young people are these days," or "No matter what you do, the system is bound to get you down." In short, how a given assertion fits into the listener's previous experiences with the speaker adds something to what is being said. The practical consequences of this interpretation of meaning on the basis of prior knowledge of the source are hard to overestimate. In the civil-rights controversy which has occupied the public attention for so long, one finds ample evidence of such interpretation of meaning in terms of the source. To take just one example, "individual freedom" means something different to extremists on both sides of the controversy, so that whether one agrees with the statement, "The most important task of government today is to preserve and extend individual freedom," will depend entirely upon who the listener is and whom he knows the source of the statement to be. In the abstract, of course, the statement is unexceptionable, because its public intensional meaning is very strongly positive, and its extensional meaning is extremely vague. Specify a source, and you specify more precisely the extensional meaning of the sentence; it then becomes very acceptable to some people and very unacceptable to others.

Social Context Effects

In addition to the nature of the communication source, the meaning of an utterance is affected also by the context in which the sentence is uttered. Depending on the total situation in which two people are involved, the sentence "You're crazy" could mean "You're very entertaining," "You're loathsome," "You're quite admirable," "You need help," "I hate you," or "I love you."

In later chapters we deal in somewhat greater detail with these extralinguistic factors of meaning. The important point to remember, however, is that they are not simply factors of social interaction which are "added on" after the meaning of a word or a sentence has been received; they are part and parcel of the meaning itself.

We have seen that content words and structure words carry different kinds of meaning in language. Content words for the most part refer to real or imaginary events and objects in the world outside the speaker and the listener (extensional meaning) and to the feelings and attitudes of the communicator (intensional meaning). They have the advantages of convenience, abstraction, and manipulability. These meanings, both extensional and intensional, may be public (shared among a community of language users) or private (unique to the individual speaker or listener). We have examined the extensional agreement index and the semantic differential as ways of "measuring" meaning.

Differences between "denotation" and "connotation" are profitably recast as questions of the degree to which a given meaning is extensional *versus* intensional, and the extent to which it is public *versus* private, and also as a question of saliency or latency of associations. Using these three yardsticks, a more precise discrimination among meanings is given than the simple "denotative" *versus* "connotative" dichotomy.

It has been noted that structure words, which are few in number but which occur with remarkably high frequency in language, perform a very different function in speech. They serve not to point to things within or outside the speaker or listener, but for the most part to set up relations among other words and larger linguistic units.

Beyond the individual words themselves, we have observed four additional sources or factors of meaning: (1) the linguistic context, (2) paralinguistic features, (3) effects stemming from the communication source, and (4) effects attributable to the social context. These four variables account for much of the meaning which a speaker intends and which a listener receives.

PROBLEMS AND QUESTIONS FOR DISCUSSION

1. Taking the typescript of the impromptu speech that you prepared for Problem #2 at the end of the preceding chapter, make a list of all of the different words that you used. Note the frequency with which each word was used in the speech, and rank-order the words according to their relative frequencies, the most commonly occurring word at the top of the list, the second-ranked word next, and so on, according to the pattern in Table 1.
   a. Compare your results with those of at least two other students in your class. In what ways are your lists similar? In what ways different? Can you account for the similarities and differences?
   b. How many of the top-ranked words in your list are content words?

How many are structure words? Are any of the words that occur only once structure words? Can you account for any content words that occur high on the rank-frequency list? Can you account for any structure words that occur only one time? Why do you think some structure words occurred with higher frequency in your sample than did others?

2. Try to write your own definition for the word "meaning."
3. Why do the distinctions between denotation-connotation, extension-intension, public-private, and salient-latent not apply to structure words?
4. From a speech or editorial, select five words that you feel are very important to the communication of the speaker's message. Analyze each word in terms of the three distinctions presented in this chapter for content words.
5. Practice saying the line "The student failed the course" so as to distinguish between the six different meanings on page 44. Give this list of meanings to another student and ask him to choose which of the six meanings you intend by each "rendition" of the line. If you fail to get a perfect score with the first subject, try to improve your ability to give the line different meanings, and try again on another student. Continue this procedure until you register a perfect score with at least one subject. Discuss the problems you encountered and the results you obtained, comparing your experience with that of other students in your class.
6. Report on at least one instance in which the source or context of a statement caused you to reinterpret its meaning differently than you ordinarily would. The incident might have to do with an ordinarily positive statement that took on negative meaning because of who said it or where it was said; or it might refer to a usually negative statement rendered positive by source and/or context; or, it might refer to a statement that simply implied something altogether different than it ordinarily would have, due to its source or context.

4.

VOICE:

ENCODING THE SPEECH SIGNAL

The physical basis of speech communication is a band-width of acoustic energies lying roughly between 20 and 20,000 cycles per second. Because speakers can produce a wide variety of different sounds within this range, and listeners can discriminate among them, speech serves as man's principal mode of communication the world over. In this chapter we will discuss the way the vocal sound is originated, and note certain characteristics of the voice signal that make speech such an effective means of communication.[1]

THE VOCAL TRACT

Those organs and bodily structures involved in the production of vocal sound are collectively labelled "the vocal tract." Figure 6 shows the vocal tract in simplified outline. Roughly in the order they are used in producing speech sound, the principal parts are: (1) the *diaphragm*, a thin sheet of muscle bent up to form a low, flat dome separating the abdominal cavity from the chest cavity; (2) the *lungs* which, from a speech point of view, serve only to hold a volume of air; (3) the *bronchi* and (4) *trachea* (windpipe), which channel air

1. For a more detailed presentation, see Grant Fairbanks, *Voice and Articulation Drillbook* (New York: Harper & Bros., 1960). Also see Donald Ecroyd, Murray Halfond, and Carol Towne, *Voice and Articulation: A Handbook* (Glenview, Ill.: Scott, Foresman and Company, 1966).

FIGURE 6
The Vocal Tract

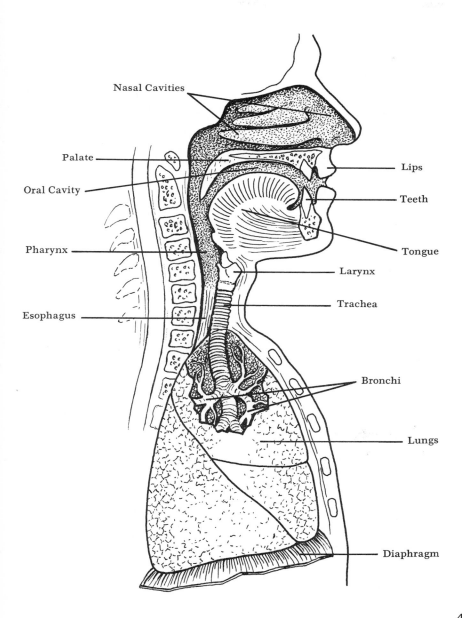

Nasal Cavities

Palate

Oral Cavity

Pharynx

Esophagus

Lips

Teeth

Tongue

Larynx

Trachea

Bronchi

Lungs

Diaphragm

into and out of the lobes and sacs of the lungs; (5) the *larynx* (voice-box), a complicated structure of bone, muscle, and cartilage holding the vocal folds; (6) the *pharynx,* (7) the *oral cavity* and (8) the *nasal cavities,* which work somewhat like the sounding-box on a guitar; and (9) the *lips,* (10) *teeth,* (11) *tongue,* and (12) *palate,* which combine to produce the individual sounds of speech.

Before exploring how these components make speech sounds, we should notice that none of the structures in the vocal tract acts solely (or even primarily) as an organ of speech; all of them serve more fundamental biological functions. The diaphragm, lungs, bronchi, trachea, and nasal passages are important parts of the respiratory system, by which land vertebrates exchange oxygen for carbon dioxide in the metabolic process. The lips, teeth, tongue, and pharynx comprise that portion of the digestive system by which food is ingested. The larynx serves as a sort of valve in the breathing mechanism at the point where the respiratory and digestive systems separate. These two vital systems share the mouth and throat, but branch at the larynx into two tubes: the esophagus, running to the stomach; and the trachea, running to the lungs. So speech is what is called an *overlaid function*—one that is superimposed on an assortment of biological apparatus designed primarily to serve more basic needs. What we have called "the vocal tract" is in fact not an intact system from a physiological point of view, but is seen most appropriately as an assemblage of components "loaned" from other, more basic systems.

This "overlaid" or "on-loan" feature of the vocal tract shows itself quite clearly when more fundamental biological operations come into conflict with speech. In all such cases the biological function takes precedence. You cannot simultaneously eat and talk intelligibly. Speech will be interrupted by a belch (or the effort to repress one). After twenty or thirty seconds of talking (which may be thought of as a particularly noisy exhalation), even the hardiest chatterbox will pause to inhale. Heavy breathing due to violent exercise interferes with speech. In short, when more pressing respiratory or digestive needs do not occupy the so-called vocal tract, it is free for use in speech making; but when these more basic functions intervene, the digestive tract and the respiratory tract revert to their primitive functions.

SPEECH PRODUCTION

Human vocal sounds are made by a four-stage process involving *respiration, phonation, resonation,* and *articulation.*

Respiration

Speech sounds are normally produced on the exhalation phase of the breath cycle. During inhalation, the diaphragm contracts, pulling downward, thus increasing the vertical dimension of the chest cavity. At the same time, the intercostal muscles, which are laced between the ribs, pull the rib cage outward, thus increasing the chest's diameter. This causes an increase in the volume of the chest, lowering the air pressure in the lungs and creating a partial vacuum. Air rushes into this vacuum through the nose and/or mouth, through the pharynx and the larynx, down the trachea, and through the bronchi into the lobes and sacs of the lungs. When the air pressure inside the lungs finally equals that in the surrounding atmosphere, the inhalation phase of the cycle ceases, and the exhalation phase is ready to begin.

Phonation

To understand what determines whether vocalization occurs during exhalation calls for a discussion of the larynx in somewhat closer detail. The larynx is the structure of cartilage, muscle, and bone sitting on top of the trachea at the base of the throat. You can feel its notched front ("Adam's apple") just below the point where your chin joins your neck. Inside the larynx are the "vocal cords": two tough, muscular folds joined at the front and (when at rest) lying along the sides of the larynx in such a way as to form a triangular opening, the glottis, through which air flows freely in or out. As this triangular opening is narrowed by bringing the edges of the vocal folds closer together, it restricts the air flow more and more. In fact, the vocal cords can be pressed so tightly together that they stop the air flow completely, as sometimes occurs when we lift heavy weights or engage in other strenuous physical effort. Whether or not vocalization occurs depends on how close together the vocal cords are during exhalation.

As the diaphragm gradually relaxes upward, and a second set of intercostal muscles slowly squeezes the rib cage inward, the volume of the chest cavity decreases, the air pressure inside the lungs goes up sharply, and air seeks to escape through the only opening— the trachea. On its way out, the air must pass the vocal folds. If they are approximated, but not jammed so tightly together as to prevent all air flow, the friction of the air past the vocal folds sets them into vibration, along with the column of moving air above them. It is this vibration that accounts for the basic voice sound. The process is called *phonation*.

Resonation

The raw vocal sound produced by phonation bears little resemblance to the voice we hear. Before it reaches our ears, the vocal tone is shaped and reinforced through the process of *resonation*. The pharynx, oral cavity, and nasal cavities selectively amplify certain components of the laryngeal tone, producing the rich and distinctively human sound of the voice. Let us briefly examine three important aspects of this statement: (1) the fact that the vocal tone is made up of numerous components, (2) the process of amplification through resonation, (3) and the idea of selective amplification.

Components of the vocal tone. From the engineering point of view, the simplest sound is a *pure tone*—that is, one whose cyclic pattern rises and falls in the smooth curve of a sine wave. In the case of a one-thousand-cycle tone, this pattern repeats itself one thousand times every second. A one-thousand-cycle pure tone sounds like a medium-pitched whistle.[2] The difference between such a tone and the sound of a human voice is simply a matter of complexity. The laryngeal tone is a complex tone—that is, one whose cyclic ups and downs follow an extremely complicated pattern that does not look at all like a curve. Such a complex tone consists of many pure tones of different frequencies, superimposed on one another and presented or "sounded" simultaneously. The components of a complex tone are the simple pure tones of which it is composed; and although the limits of measuring equipment make it impossible for us to break down a vocal tone into all of its individual pure tones, we can identify many of its components and measure how strong or "loud" they are with respect to one another.

Amplification through resonation. Now let us look for a moment at the phenomenon of amplification through resonation. Blow across the mouth of a bottle or jug, and you can cause it to sound a tone that is low-pitched for big jugs and high-pitched for small bottles. This tone is the resonant frequency of the bottle's cavity. If you set some physical body into vibration at this same frequency, and bring it close to the mouth of the bottle, the column of air inside the bottle will begin to vibrate in tune with the vibrating body. This sympathetic vibration is called resonance. Moreover, the resulting sound will be louder than the sound of the vibrating body alone.

---

2.   In the fifth section of this chapter, pages 59–60, there is a brief discussion of acoustic measurement.

Through the process of resonation, the bottle will amplify the sound produced by the vibrating body.

Selective amplification. Suppose that the bottle in the preceding experiment has a resonant frequency of 500 cycles per second (cps); in other words, it resonates most strongly when it is caused to vibrate at that frequency. At frequencies that are close to 500 cycles, it will still resonate, but less strongly. As we move farther away from 500 cps, the amount of resonation drops off until finally (perhaps at 300 cps on either side of the resonant frequency—that is, below 200 and above 800 cps) the bottle will not resonate at all. Now suppose that we make a vibrating body that will produce a complex tone composed of ten tones, the lowest at 100 cps, and the other nine spaced 100 cps apart up to 1000 cps. Suppose also that none of the pure tones is any stronger or louder than any of the others. And suppose further that we now set this device into vibration and bring it close to the opening of our bottle. What will happen?

The 500-cycle tone will of course be strongly amplified by the bottle's resonance. The 400- and the 600-cycle tones will be somewhat amplified, but not as strongly as the 500-cycle tone. The 300- and the 700-cycle tones will perhaps be very slightly amplified; and the bottle may not resonate at all to the 100-, 200-, 800-, 900-, or 1000-cycle tones. In short, the bottle will amplify the various components of the complex tone *selectively*—that is, some more than others, and some not at all. The resulting tone—after amplification—will sound quite different qualitatively than the original one. Not only will it be louder overall due to the resonant amplification, but it will also have quite a different balance of tones or general quality, since the 500-cycle component will now stand out much more than it did in the original. Thus, the quality of a complex sound can be changed by selectively amplifying its components.

What happens in the resonation cycle of speech production is very much like what occurred in the foregoing example. The vocal cords represent the vibrating body producing a complex tone of many frequencies; and the pharynx, oral cavity, and nasal cavities resemble an interconnected maze of odd-shaped bottles and jugs. The vibrations set up by the vocal folds are an extremely rich and varied mixture of acoustic energies. Each individual resonating chamber picks out of that mixture its own characteristic frequencies, amplifies them, and thus boosts their amplitude or loudness relative to other components of the laryngeal tone.

Because no two people have resonating chambers of exactly the same size and shape, no two of us have exactly the same vocal quality. In fact, recent developments suggest the possibility that the acoustic pattern of one's voice may be sufficiently distinctive to be used for personal identification in much the same way as fingerprints are presently employed. As of the time of this writing, "voiceprints" are admissable as legal evidence in some states, and several companies are at work on voice-operated locks that will open a door or vault when actuated by command from a "recognized" voice.

Being lined with bone and cartilage, the nasal passages have a fixed size and shape; but within limits, the pharynx may be expanded or contracted, the tongue can be moved around inside the mouth to change its interior shape, and the soft palate can be raised or lowered so as to open or partly close off the nasal passages. As you might suspect, by changing the size and shape of these modifiable resonating chambers, any one person can make quite a variety of distinctively different sounds. Some of these changes in the resonating chambers are reflected in what we call voice quality: lower your soft palate and you add a more "nasal" quality to your voice; open the pharynx wider and you add the "pear-shaped tone" of the old-school voice coach. Other changes in the size and shape of the resonators account for the differences among the vowel sounds of the language. For instance, if you start from the position for making an "AH" sound, and gradually hump the middle of the tongue forward and up toward the hard palate (the roof of the mouth), you will find yourself moving from "AH" to "EE." In changing the shapes and relative sizes of the linked resonating chambers in the front and the back of the mouth, you will have changed from one vowel to another.

Articulation

Resonation is the process of selective amplification that converts the relatively weak laryngeal tone into the strong, distinctive sound of the human voice. The final stage of speech production, whereby the breath stream is modified to produce the individual sounds of speech, is *articulation*. As we have just seen, in the case of the vowel sounds, resonation and articulation blend into one another: we might say that where vowel sounds are concerned, correct articulation consists of moving the articulators (in this case, mostly the tongue and the lips) so as to cause appropriate patterns of resonance. However, when we speak of articulation, we usually are thinking about the production of consonant sounds. In most languages the consonants outnumber vowels four or five to one, and they require the most rapid and sophisticated movement of the articulators.

CLASSIFICATION OF CONSONANTS

In general, the consonants of English are distinguishable from one another on the basis of three distinctive features: (*a*) voicing, (*b*) "place" of articulation (that is, which articulators are used to make the sound), and (*c*) manner. Although this is not the place to discuss consonant production in detail (an in-depth treatment is worth a short book [3]), a brief look at these three distinctive features will improve our understanding of articulation as a process, and of the incredible coordination required to produce everyday speech.

Voicing

The first distinctive feature of English consonants is voicing. Most of our consonants come in pairs, identical in all aspects except that one member of the pair is *voiced* and the other is *voiceless*. This is the distinguishing factor in the difference between "f" and "v," "t" and "d," "s" and "z," "p" and "b," and several other pairs. To get a feel for the difference between a voiced and an unvoiced consonant, place your fingers lightly on your "Adam's apple"—the notch at the front of the larynx. First, take a deep breath and exhale: you will feel no vibration. Now take another breath and say "Aahhh": you will feel a slight, buzzing vibration in your throat, due to phonation. Once you have learned how to feel this vibration, you are ready for an experiment. Alternately make the isolated sounds of "d" and "t"; then try "s" and "z," and go on to "p" and "b." On "d," "z," and "b" you should feel evidence of phonation; but on "t," "s," and "p" you should feel none: you are feeling the difference between voiced and voiceless consonants. There are some voiced consonants that have no voiceless counterpart—for instance, "l," "r," and "w"—but every voiceless consonant has paired with it a voiced consonant that is almost identical in all respects, save for the voicing distinction.

Place of Articulation

The second distinctive feature of English consonants is place of articulation. To label this feature of speech sounds, early scholars used Latin roots: *labio* for lips; *lingua* for tongue; *dental* for teeth; *velar* for soft palate (sometimes called the velum), and *alveolar* for the front edge of the hard palate, just behind the teeth. Two articulators are used to make each speech sound—usually a movable articulator (lips or tongue) against a fixed one (teeth, alveolar ridge,

3. See Fairbanks, *op. cit.*

palate, or velum). Using this terminology, the combination of articulators that form a consonant can be identified; and, because of the fixed geography of the mouth, the place of articulation can also be identified. For example, a lingua-dental sound is one using the tongue against the teeth (such as "th"); a lingua-velar sound is one using the tongue and velum (such as "k"); a bilabial sound is one using both lips (such as "b"); a labio-dental sound is one using lips and teeth (such as "f"), and so on. Following this system of classification, how would you label "t" and "d"? Since they use the tip of the tongue against the alveolar ridge, they are lingua-alveolars. One of them is voiced; the other is voiceless. (Do you remember which is which? If not, review the preceding two paragraphs before going on.)

Manner of Articulation

The third distinctive feature of English consonants is manner of articulation, and the most basic distinction is between *continuants* and *stops*. Continuants are sounds that push the breath stream through a relatively stationary constriction; stops are sounds that halt the breath stream entirely against a complete obstruction. Stops are sometimes called "plosives" because when the temporary obstruction is opened, these sounds terminate in a little puff or tiny explosion of air. (Usually when a plosive comes at the end of a phrase, the obstruction is not released in this way, so that no explosion occurs. That is why the term "stops" is usually preferred for this class of speech sounds.) A good rule of thumb for distinguishing between continuants and stops is that a continuant can be "continued" for as long as you wish, but a stop is always of very short duration— it cannot be artificially extended. Using this criterion, how would you identify each of the following: "g," "p," "z," "h," "m," "d"? (In order of presentation, they are stop, stop, continuant, continuant, continuant, stop.)

With these three distinctive features in hand, one can easily classify almost all of the consonants of English. One common way of organizing the complete label is to refer first to voicing, second to placement, and third to manner. Thus, the voiceless bilabial stop is "p." Now try your grasp of these principles on the following: (See the footnote on page 58 for correct answers. [4] If you miss more than two, review this section before going ahead.)
1. What is the voiced bilabial stop?
2. What is the voiced labio-dental continuant?
3. What is the voiced lingua-alveolar stop?
4. Does English have a voiceless lingua-velar continuant?

5. How do you classify the "k" sound?
6. How do you classify the "p" sound?
7. How do you classify the "f" sound?

Thus, we have seen that some of the speech sounds are produced by a combination of resonation and articulation, whereas others are produced entirely within the mouth and depend in no way on the *voice* (that is, the action of the vocal cords) as such. All of the vowels and the voiced consonants make use of the vocal cords and phonated sounds, but the voiceless consonants are produced by various kinds of friction in the mouth itself. When you consider that the typical speech sound lasts no longer than a tenth of a second, it is apparent that the voicing apparatus must be able to "cut on and off" with amazing speed and in perfect synchrony with the movements of the articulators. From the phonetic point of view, even very poor speech is a virtuoso performance.

ADVANTAGES OF THE SPEECH SIGNAL

If one were to try to invent an effective and efficient means of communication among animals constructed like human beings, he would be hard pressed to improve upon speech. Because we use it almost from birth, we are inclined to overlook its elegance from a purely technological aspect. For just a moment let us look at the advantages and disadvantages of speech communication from a bio-engineering point of view.

To begin with, the apparatus required to transmit the speech signal adds nothing to the weight, size, or complexity of the organism. As we noted earlier, speech is an overlaid function that uses biological equipment already "installed" and in use for other purposes. Note, however, that these other functions use the apparatus only part-time or intermittently, so that the vocal tract is free most of the time for communication purposes. Moreover, the use of this equipment for speech purposes costs very little effort. The whole system burns only a few calories per hour even under continuous use. From the biological point of view, then, the speech-signalling system costs nothing to install and very little to run.

Another point with regard to efficiency is that operating the speech system does not interfere with other activities. Except for swimming or hard running, locomotion and speech are possible simultaneously. During speech the hands are free for other work (except, we are told, for the Italians). Sometimes during intense or difficult speaking or listening, one's attention will be so completely absorbed in the communication process that all other activities are suspended; but as any professor knows who has lectured to a class of knitters, doodlers, or textbook-underliners, it is often possible to talk and listen effectively while engaged in other simultaneous but unrelated activities.

In addition to these purely biological considerations, the acoustic signal itself has certain built-in advantages. It can be used in the dark of night, around corners, over or through barriers and obstacles, and in other circumstances where line-of-sight communication is out of the question. It will carry over a considerable distance, and can be "broadcast"—that is, transmitted homogeneously through an entire volume of space—even when the exact number and location of receivers is unknown. The signal itself can be generated at sufficient strength to overcome most other noises, making it suitable for use under virtually any environmental conditions.

Finally, the channel in which the signal is propagated is capable of carrying a great deal of information per unit of time. To the language-using species as a whole, this makes possible a choice between different types of codes: those which enable the user to say a lot in a short span of time, or those which are redundant enough to overcome the likelihood of decoding errors. As we will shortly see, ordinary language strikes a balance between these two extremes, sacrificing some speed of communication to accuracy-improving redundancy. Even so, due to the vast information capacity of the acoustic channel, speech transmits reliable information at a prodigious rate when compared to any other biologically feasible mode of communication.

True, speech does not fly with the speed of thought. If human beings were built of transistors, diodes, and similar hardware, we could communicate with one another by means of high-frequency electromagnetic signals, thus greatly expanding the channel capacity. So equipped, we could probably "talk" as fast as we can think— perhaps even faster. But considering the quantity of ill-conceived and half-digested talk one hears already, the potential benefits of this improvement seem doubtful. As matters stand, we find ourselves equipped with a communication system that calls for no peripheral

4.   Answers to phonetic classification questions:
(1) voiced bilabial stop is "b"; (2) voiced labio-dental continuant is "v"; (3) voiced lingua-alveolar stop is "d"; (4) No, English does not have a voiceless lingua-velar continuant; but German, Hebrew, and certain Eastern European languages do. You can make the sound by forming your mouth as if to make a "k" sound, but instead of stopping the breath stream, push it continuously through the constriction formed by the back of the tongue and the velum. (5) "k" is the voiceless lingua-velar stop; (6) "p" is the voiceless bilabial stop; (7) "f" is the voiceless labio-dental continuant.

gear, uses very little energy, is almost always available, interferes little with other activities, can be used anywhere under almost any conditions, and transmits information at what appears to be an optimum rate. On the whole, no invention of communication technology is half so good; and while we may extend its range in space with radio broadcasting equipment and in time with magnetic recorders, we are not likely to improve upon the basic system in the foreseeable future.

REDUNDANCY IN THE SPEECH SIGNAL

In Chapter 2, we noted that structural rules specifying the allowable combinations of language symbols introduce redundancy into every natural language. On one hand, this requires that we take a little longer to say what we have in mind; but on the other hand, we gain resistance of our messages to mutilation through error, interference, or misunderstanding. Syntactic structure is not the only source of redundancy in language. When we look at the individual sounds of speech, we find that the signal itself is much richer in information than it strictly needs to be; and just as in the case of syntactic rules, we find this acoustic redundancy contributes to accuracy of communication under less than ideal conditions.

Acoustic Measurement: Frequency and Intensity

Let us try to understand just how redundant the voice signal really is. In order to do so, we will have to make a brief side trip into the elements of acoustic measurement. The two most important characteristics of a pure tone are its *frequency* and its *intensity*. Frequency is measured in cycles per second.[5] In general, frequency corresponds to the pitch of a tone: the greater its frequency, the higher pitched it will sound. Amplitude is measured in decibels (db) relative to a standard reference point. In standard acoustic measurements this reference point is usually established at .0002 dynes per square centimeter. A dyne is the unit of physical energy that can alter by one centimeter per second the velocity of a weight of one gram. This is a very small unit of force indeed, so two ten-thousandths of a dyne spread over a square centimeter exerts an al-

5. Modern electronics has changed the semantics of acoustic measurement somewhat, and now describes frequency measurements in "Hertz" units, usually abbreviated "hz." One hz equals one cycle per second, but for purposes of clarity and consistency with other explanations in this book, we shall retain the older term, cps, which continues to be both accurate and descriptive.

most infinitesimally small force. Yet so little physical energy is involved in even the mightiest sound wave that it is measured in these tiny units. The amplitude of a sound wave corresponds roughly to its perceived loudness: the lower the amplitude, the softer the sound.

Earlier we noted that the voice signal operates in the frequency range between 20 and 20,000 cycles per second. But now we must also take into account the amplitude of these sound waves. For each of us there is a threshold of detectability below which any sound of lower amplitude will simply not be heard. Moreover, this threshold of detectability is found at different amplitudes for different frequencies. Thus, most people have a low threshold—very acute hearing—for sounds around 3000 cycles per second, but the threshold is much higher for sounds of 1000 and 6000 cps, and goes up even more sharply for sounds of higher or lower frequency. On the other end of the loudness range, as intensity approaches 140 db, one experiences first a tingling sensation in the ears, then discomfort, and finally acute pain. The practical range of intensities available for communication, then, lies between the variable threshold of detection and the threshold of discomfort or pain. Taken together the frequency range and the intensity range of hearing constitute the *audible area,* which is pictured graphically in Figure 7. Note that while sound pressure (amplitude) is displayed in *equal* units along the vertical axis, frequency is represented *logarithmically* on the horizontal axis. This reflects the fact that frequencies grow harder to discriminate from one another as they move up the scale. One has no trouble distinguishing between a 50-cycle and a 60-cycle tone, but two tones of 1050 and 1060 cps are indistinguishable from one another, and at very high frequencies it requires more than 1000 cycles separation between two tones for the listener to distinguish between them. This decreasing discriminability between adjacent tones is reflected in the logarithmic scale.

Complexity of the Speech Signal

Within the audible area there are about 1600 distinguishably different frequencies and roughly 350 distinguishably different intensities. One voice scientist has estimated that all told there are about 340,000 discriminably different pure tones to be found within the audible area. It is hard to imagine 340,000 sounds, each distinctively different from all of the others. If you were to listen to each for just one second, it would take you four days to hear them all just once. In speech, of course, we do not use pure tones, but complex tones made up of dozens of pure tones combined. Therefore, the num-

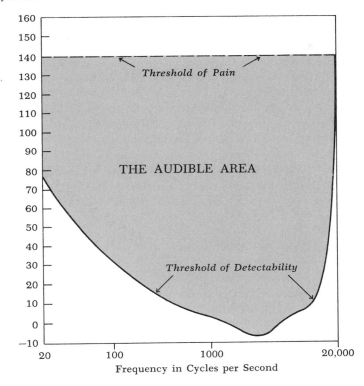

FIGURE 7

Frequencies and Intensities
Audible to Normal Human Subjects

ber of different complex tones possible within the audible area is vastly larger than the number of pure tones.

Moreover, the foregoing considerations disregard the question of time. Quick changes in vocal tone are not only possible in speech; they are the rule. Supposing that we are able to transmit and receive ten acoustic patterns per second (in fact, we can do much better than that when we try), it is obvious that the capacity of the vocal channel is truly immense.

Of course, we do not use anything like all of this capacity. Of the millions of different sound-wave patterns that we might use for

Voice: Encoding the Speech Signal   61

communication, we use in fact only a few (four dozen or so), and these are so distributed among the whole range of possibilities as to minimize the likelihood that one of them will be mistaken for any of the others. They are also distributed so that talkers do not have to produce signals to very close tolerances: if the speaker comes reasonably close to the target sound, the listener will usually interpret him correctly.

It is a mathematical certainty that we could achieve greater speed of communication if we used a greater variety of different speech sounds—if, for example, the language had seventy or eighty phonemes instead of forty-two or so. We could unquestionably get more said in less time, because we would have to use fewer phonemes per word. But this increase in channel efficiency would cost something in return: speech would not be nearly so resistant to mutilation as it is with the present arrangement. Under ideal conditions, we would communicate more rapidly; but we would also make many more errors in interpreting the speech of others; and we would encounter many more occasions when noise, distance, or other environmental factors would make it difficult or impossible to be heard.

REDUNDANCY AS RESISTANCE TO MUTILATION OF THE SPEECH SIGNAL

When the acoustic redundancy of the speech signal is combined with syntactic redundancy in the language, the resulting speech is exceedingly resistant to mutilation. We will close this chapter with some examples of what can be done to speech without significantly impairing its intelligibility. This should give some idea of how much redundancy there is in our language, and how useful it can be.

Frequency Mutilation

One group of experiments produced some remarkable results with regard to the frequency range necessary to hear and understand speech. When all frequencies below 1900 cps were completely removed from the signal, speech was highly intelligible; such speech sounds tinny, like a very old phonograph, but it is quite easy to understand. Perhaps even more remarkable, when all of the frequencies *above* 1900 cps were eliminated, the speech was still intelligible. It sounded rather like someone talking in a rain barrel, or like a radio that has been tuned to deep "bass" on the frequency selector, but it could still be understood. In other words, you can completely dispense with a large portion of the signal's band-width, either the high or low frequencies, and retain speech intelligibility. This confers a great advantage on speech as a means of communication, for it retains its utility even when many of the frequencies are masked by environmental noise, or when the listener's hearing is poor over a great part of the frequency range. This is valuable because most people over forty years of age suffer from a significant impairment of hearing, usually in the higher frequencies; but they seldom notice it in communication because the language has more than enough redundancy to compensate for the loss.

Interruption Mutilation

Another way to mutilate a speech signal is to interrupt it, cutting out small segments of the utterance. When these interruptions are of relatively short duration ($\frac{1}{20}$ of a second or less), we can understand speech when as little as half of the original is left. In other words, over half of the time used in ordinary speech is attributable to redundancy.

In recent years, voice scientists have exploited this fact for educating the blind. A device called a speech-time compressor is applied to a tape-recorded lecture or other instructional material, cutting out very short segments of the signal at rapid intervals, and piecing the remaining segments together on a shorter tape. As much as fifty percent of the signal can be deleted in this way without impairing comprehension of the message content, so that an hour's lecture can be played in thirty minutes. To the blind student, whose braille reading rate may be little more than twenty-five or thirty words per minute and whose fastest information input is "talking books" and other recorded materials, speech-time compression comes as a great boon. It can increase his "reading" (that is, listening) rate from perhaps 150 words per minute to as much as 300 words per minute or more. He can use the time saved to hear the lecture a second time, review, or cover collateral or enrichment materials.

In this chapter we have described the main features of the vocal tract, discussing implications of the fact that speech is an overlaid function. We have seen how the vocal tract operates to produce speech through the interlocking processes of *respiration, phonation, resonation,* and *articulation.* Some attention has also been directed to classification of consonants on the basis of voicing and place and manner of articulation.

We have noted that from an engineering point of view the speech signal is remarkably effective and efficient. It calls for no special equipment, uses little energy, is almost always available, interferes little with other activities, can be used anywhere and under almost any conditions, and transmits information at an optimum rate.

The speech signal is highly redundant. Of the hundreds of thousands of sounds that could be discriminated by listeners, only a few dozen are actually used in speech. When this acoustic redundancy is added to the syntactic redundancy of the language, it imposes definite limits on the speed at which information can be transmitted through normal speech processes.

Redundancy has been noted not merely as a factor that limits the rate at which speech can be transmitted, but as a major source of strength in the speech signal. Because it is highly redundant, the speech sound does not have to be produced to close tolerances and is readily understood even in the presence of environmental noise or when the listener is handicapped by considerable hearing loss. It also makes possible time-compressed speech for special educational purposes.

PROBLEMS AND QUESTIONS FOR DISCUSSION

1. Some of the sounds of English were deliberately left out of the discussion of articulation in this chapter. Consult another speech book, such as *Voice and Articulation: A Handbook* by Donald Ecroyd, Murray Halfond, and Carol Towne (Glenview, Ill.: Scott, Foresman and Company, 1966), and identify the phonemes that were left out of this discussion. Why were these phonemes omitted from our consideration of articulation?
2. Practice reading aloud a page or so of simple printed prose, working to get your rate to the fastest possible. When you have achieved as rapid a rate as you can, time yourself over the passage and calculate your speaking rate in words per minute. Next, have a friend time your rate during a regular classroom speech, and compare the two rates of utterance. Can you draw any conclusions from the difference?
3. Why do we say that speech is an overlaid function? Would the vocalizing of animals be considered an overlaid function? Why?
4. In the case of the vowel sounds, why is it so difficult to separate resonation and articulation processes?
5. When we label a speaker's voice "nasal," are we commenting about the resonation or the articulation process?
6. What advantages would humans enjoy if they communicated by means of radio waves rather than speech? Would there be any disadvantages?

5.

HEARING AND PERCEPTION: DECODING THE SPEECH SIGNAL

A conventional view of the speech communication process provides for a talker-speaker and a hearer-listener, both differing greatly in activity level. We recognize that sending out a speech signal is an active process requiring intent, planning, and more or less continuous effort and control; but we tend to think of receiving the signal as simply a matter of being present when the message is sent, with effortless, automatic processes somehow taking care of the rest. This view of the receiving process is obviously too simple. When we consider more carefully, we see *two* receiving processes at work rather than one. First, the listener must take in the sound of the speaker's voice; second, he must select from that complex signal certain information that will be useful in formulating his response. The first of these processes is what we usually call *hearing,* and the second is what we usually call *listening.*

We may think of hearing as the passive phase of speech reception, and listening as the active phase; for in principle, hearing and listening may be separated on the basis of *purposiveness* and *modifiability.* Generally, we think of hearing as biologically determined and hence not subject to modification through either experience or psychological factors; on the other hand, we usually think of listening as a psychological process guided and controlled by both habits and conscious intentions. More specifically, we think of hearing as the process that provides the raw material on which the listening process operates. As we explore hearing and listening below, we will find that this distinction, which is useful in principle, is in some cases difficult to maintain, and that the interface between hearing and listening is very complex indeed.

HEARING AND PERCEPTION

In everyday thought, hearing is associated with the function of the ear. If the ear is damaged, hearing is impaired; if the ear is healthy, hearing is free of human error—or so we think. However, as we shall see below, hearing may be divided into two distinct phases, *transduction* and *auditory perception;* and only the first of these takes place in the ear.

Transduction Phase of Hearing

This first stage of hearing converts an acoustic signal into nerve impulses. "Transduction" refers to any process whereby energy in one form is converted or transformed into energy in another form. Three kinds of energy are involved in hearing, and these pass through four stages of transduction.

For our present purposes, the schematic drawing in Figure 8 represents the principal parts of the ear. The outermost organ is the *tympanum,* or eardrum—a thin, tough membrane stretched across the end of the auditory canal. The eardrum is attached to three delicate bones, or *ossicles,* that form a chain through the *middle ear.* At the superficial end, closest to the surface of the body, one of these ossicles attaches to the eardrum; at the other end, deeper inside the skull, the third ossicle fits into the *oval window,* which serves as the entry into the *cochlea.*

The cochlea is the main organ of the inner ear. It is a spiral structure somewhat like a snail shell, filled with a fluid called *endolymph.* Inside the spiral lies a sensitive structure called the *organ of Corti,* which performs for the ear a function somewhat similar to that performed by the retina for the eye. Rising from the organ of Corti, a profusion of tiny hair cells extend into the endolymph. These hair cells are like the retina's rod and cone cells; each will emit an electrochemical impulse when appropriately stimulated.

The main function of this entire system is to transduce acoustic signals into electrochemical ones. An acoustic wave strikes the eardrum, causing it to vibrate. The vibration is transmitted via the os-

FIGURE 8
Gross Anatomy of the Ear

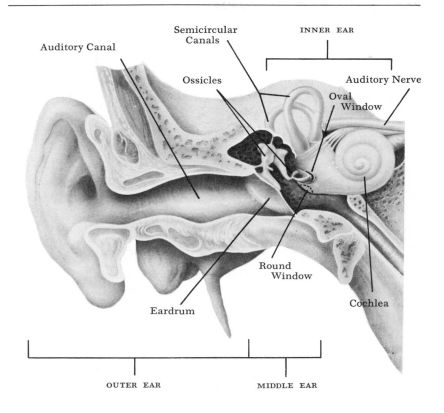

sicles through the middle ear to the oval window, and the resulting vibrations of the oval window set up acoustic waves in the endolymph within the cochlea. As these waves move through the cochlea, they disturb the hair cells. Depending on the frequency and amplitude of the acoustic wave, some cells will be disturbed more than others. If a given hair cell is stimulated above its threshold, it "fires"—that is, it emits one or more electrochemical impulses, the number and rapidity of the impulses depending on the intensity of the sound. The transduction of acoustic energy to electrochemical nerve impulses is now complete. The sum total of neural impulses coming from the cochlea is the raw material from which the brain constructs a representation of the sound.

Certain features of this process deserve special note. First, three forms of energy are involved: *acoustic* (first in the air and later in the endolymph), *mechanical* (first in the tympanum, the ossicles, and the oval window, and later in the hair cells), and *electrochemical* (in the hair cells). Moreover, four stages of transduction are involved: (1) acoustic-in-air to mechanical-in-eardrum, (2) mechanical-in-oval-window to acoustic-in-endolymph, (3) acoustic-in-endolymph to mechanical-in-hair cells, and (4) mechanical-to-electrochemical within the hair cells.

Auditory Perception

We have seen how the ear operates as a complex transducer to make an acoustic signal available to the brain in the form of electrochemical nerve impulses. However, it is clear that there is more to hearing than transduction. When the neural representation of a stimulus sound leaves the cochlea and begins its journey up the acoustic nerve, it leaves the physical world behind and becomes part of the activity of the nervous system. What happens to it there is only partly a result of the physical characteristics of the sound. It is also a result of the condition and ongoing activity of the nervous system, particularly the brain.

Factors influencing auditory perception in the brain. The influence of the central nervous system upon hearing is particularly striking in certain cases of brain damage, such as temporal-lobe epilepsy. A victim of this condition is able to hear pure tones quite clearly; and, if given the usual kind of hearing test, he may pass with flying colors. However, he will be unable to distinguish one vowel or consonant from another. Because of temporal-lobe malfunction his brain does not process the neural representation of the acoustic signal so as to synthesize recognizable speech sounds. To ask, "Does the patient *hear* the speech sounds?" merely invites another question in reply: "What do you mean by 'hear'?" In such cases as this, the distinction between hearing and listening breaks down, and another distinction becomes more useful: the distinction between *reception* and *perception*. The temporal-lobe epileptic is able to receive the speech signal, as demonstrated by his performance on a pure-tone hearing test; but he is unable to perceive the speech sounds, as demonstrated by his inability to distinguish among them. Most audiologists would say that the patient's hearing is normal; but insofar as hearing speech is concerned, he might as well be deaf.

Even when the ear and the brain are intact, one may be unable to hear certain sounds. If you have never spent much time in the forest, you can demonstrate this to yourself by spending a few hours there with an experienced woodsman. It will soon become apparent that he can hear sounds you are unable to detect, even though his hearing is essentially no better than yours. He will hear a squirrel running through the branches or a deer moving through the brush where you will hear nothing at all. As you approach a running brook, he will hear it long before you do. The same sound waves are striking the woodsman's ears and your own, and similar patterns of neural impulses may be transmitted from his cochlea and from yours. However, your auditory perceptions will differ markedly, for he has learned to process the information in a way that is better adapted to the woodland environment than yours is. If you spend enough time in the woods, you will find that one by one these formerly inaudible sounds suddenly become quite plain. A new set of auditory habits will improve your adaptation to this new environment.

The foregoing example illustrates that the arrival of a signal at the tympanum constitutes no guarantee that the signal will elicit an appropriate percept in the brain.[1] To a considerable extent we hear what we have learned to hear. Speech therapists recognize this fact; and in retraining children with articulatory defects, they sometimes devote considerable time to "ear training"—teaching the patient to hear the difference between the "incorrect" pattern that underlies his speech defect and the "correct" sound that constitutes acceptable speech. Teachers of foreign language also recognize the relevance of auditory habit in speech recognition. They know that the habits of speech perception that the student was forced to develop in order to communicate effectively in his own language will prevent him from hearing the relevant characteristics of speech sounds in the new language, at least in the beginning. They realize that he will not be able to produce the sounds of the new language accurately in his own speech unless he first learns to hear them correctly.

Selectivity in auditory perception. We have seen that hearing (in the sense of auditory perception) is influenced by habit, but it is also influenced by momentary purpose and intent. You can demonstrate this to yourself right now by putting down this book for a moment and listening to the noises around you; listen carefully and you will hear a number of sounds that were inaudible to you only a

---

1. This point is developed in an interesting fashion by Paul D. Holtzman in his book, *The Psychology of Speakers' Audiences* (Glenview, Ill.: Scott, Foresman and Company, 1970).

moment before. Is there a clock ticking or a fly buzzing nearby? Can you hear traffic on the street? Is somebody playing a radio or phonograph? Can you hear footsteps or voices in a nearby room? Is the wind blowing or the rain falling? Can you hear a dog barking or an airplane passing overhead? Listen only a moment and you will see how rich your acoustic environment is in information about your surroundings, both immediate and remote.

Now, where were all these sounds earlier when you were reading, before you started listening? The acoustic signals were present, of course. They were causing your eardrum and the ossicles in your middle ear to vibrate; they were engendering some electrochemical patterns in your auditory nerve, and it may even be that they were synthesized and in some subconscious way "recognized" by the brain; but somehow they were rejected or suppressed before they reached the level of consciousness. Your attention was elsewhere, and they went unnoticed until you chose to listen to them.

This ability to screen out auditory stimuli is not absolute, and happily so; if it were, none of us would be here today, for all of our ancestors would have been destroyed by predators as they sat with their attention riveted on other things. Even now, if an extraneous stimulus is particularly loud, sudden, or significant, or if your attention lapses momentarily, auditory perceptions will crowd into consciousness. If one of those stimuli touches on a matter that is more immediately compelling than what you are doing now—your roommate coming down the hall with a midnight snack, the cat mewing to be let out, someone rapping at the door, the ringing of the telephone—then you will lay the book aside and transfer your full attention to the interrupting stimulus. Powers of concentration are most valuable, but so is the ability to be interrupted. When it serves our purpose to do so, we can attend to a single stimulus to the virtual exclusion of all others; but this voluntary attention can be overridden by involuntary attention to strong or unexpected stimuli, or to stimuli that are associated with purposes that take momentary precedence over the purpose that commands our voluntary attention.

One way to describe the phenomena that we have outlined above is to say that auditory perception is selective. From all of the information that the ear makes available, the central nervous system selects that which fits best with its perceptual habits and immediate activities, and it discards the rest. In the case of speech perception, this is strikingly apparent in the auditory phenomenon known as "the cocktail-party effect." This effect takes its name from the fact that in a noisy gathering, such as a cocktail party, one can with a little effort follow a single voice, even though it is weaker than the surrounding noise. It is even possible to eavesdrop on the faint voice of someone in a neighboring conversational group while ignoring the much louder voice of one's own conversational partner. However, if the latter suddenly says something very interesting—for example, if he pronounces your name—your attention will involuntarily be drawn away from the neighboring conversation and back to your own.

The physiology of neural inhibition. Granted that we can observe the effects of such selective perception of sound, the question arises: How is it possible? What sort of physiological apparatus will allow the listener to operate on an incoming sound signal so as to suppress a part of it, even the strongest part? Partially, at least, the answer seems to lie in the activity of *inhibitory neurons,* which are distributed throughout the central nervous system.

Ordinarily when we think of neural activity, we think of the action of excitatory neurons. When such a neuron is stimulated, it discharges an electrical impulse along all its fibers or dendrites. At the end of each dendrite is a synaptic bulb which rests against another nerve cell. When the electrical discharge of the first cell reaches the synaptic bulb, it squirts a very small quantity of electrically active chemical into the synapse or gap between the two cells. This electrochemical change in the synapse ordinarily causes the second cell to discharge also, and in this way a neural impulse may be propagated rapidly through many nerve cells, one after another. But the excitatory neurons tell only part of the story. The flexibility of the nervous system is greatly enhanced by the presence of inhibitory neurons which perform in exactly the opposite way. The chemical substance secreted from the synaptic bulb of an inhibitory neuron has the effect of neutralizing any impulses arriving at the same time from excitatory neurons; that is, the inhibitory neurons block the transmission of neural impulses.

Some of the possible effects of such inhibition are diagrammed schematically in Figure 9, where E1, E2, E3, E4, and E5 are excitatory neurons and I1, I2, I3, and I4 are inhibitory neurons. Suppose that a nerve impulse representing some aspect of an acoustic stimulus is transmitted across the synaptic gap to E1. Under usual circumstances, E1 will discharge an electrical impulse that will stimulate both E2 and E3; E2 will discharge, causing E4 to do likewise; and E3 will discharge, causing E5 to do likewise. The signal will divide into two identical branches. However, if I3 discharges at about the same time as E1, then E2 will be inhibited so that no impulse will be transmitted to E4; and what we have here pictured as the upper branch of this pattern of neural impulses will be blocked, so that only the lower branch, through E3 and E5, will carry a signal. Conversely, if I4 discharges at the same time as E1, it will inhibit E3, and the neural signal will pass through E2 and E4. Complete inhibition of this entire component of the sensory signal can be prevented by the discharge of either I1 or I2; and in this case, neither the upper nor the lower branch will transmit any signal.

Thus, we have seen that a component of a sensory signal can be either blocked or rerouted by the action of inhibitory neurons. But what is it that causes an inhibitory neuron to discharge in the first place? Some of them perform an automatic feedback-and-control function for reflexes that synapse in the spinal column. These are triggered by receptor action. Others seem to be subject to cortical control. These enable the brain to exert some measure of control over its own inputs, suppressing some signals before they are processed, and routing others for processing in particular locations. We may visualize perceptual habits, momentary sets, and purposes as

FIGURE 9
Schematic Representation of
Excitatory and Inhibitory Neurons

(Shaded neurons are inhibitory; unshaded are excitatory.)

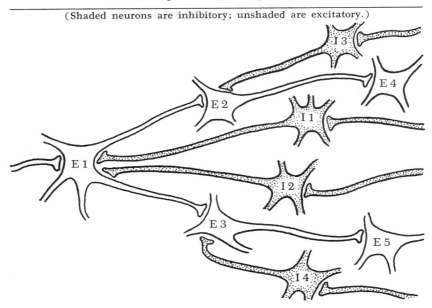

patterns of brain activity, whose function may be to activate inhibitory circuits so as to screen out unwanted information, presenting to the consciousness only that which best fits with established patterns or serves present needs.

SPEECH RECOGNITION

Of all the functions of auditory perception, the most remarkable is perception of speech. Without doubt, the speaking voice generates the most complex and elaborately patterned signal in our acoustic environment. From it the auditor is able not only to reconstruct the verbal content of a speaker's utterance, but also to make judgments about the speaker's character and personality, his sincerity and confidence about what he is saying, and his emotional condition at the time of speaking. In some cases the auditor may also be able to make reasonably good guesses about his geographical origin and social class. Even so, the auditor never makes use of all of the information in the voice sound, for there is simply too much of it. Without a very sophisticated set of habits for selecting relevant features and rejecting others, the listener would be overwhelmed by the sheer quantity of information pouring into his brain over the acoustic nerves.

This is the situation that confronts an infant when he hears talk. It is not that the child hears too little, but probably that he hears too much, and has not yet learned which aspects of the voice sound to attend to and which to ignore. By the time he is a few months old, he is able to detect certain gross emotional qualities in the voice, such as playfulness, sympathy, love, impatience, and anger. But it is not until he is four or five years old that the child has acquired most of the auditory habits that enable him to recognize the content of speech. By that age, he is already well launched into the verbal world, though his ability to listen to speech will continue to develop as he acquires broader experience with new words, with new ways of putting words together, and with new ideas.

In the next few pages we will explore some of the auditory habits that contribute to speech recognition. At this time we will not consider the perception of mood, emotional tone, sincerity, or other incidental information that is carried by the voice signal. Rather, we will be concerned only with the perception of those elements which permit the listener to reconstruct the verbal content of the speaker's utterance.

Sequential-Order Theory of Speech Recognition

It must be admitted that at this time very little is known about the electrochemical processes by which the brain accomplishes this feat. However, on the basis of psychological evidence we can say that speech recognition must provide for at least three subprocesses: *First,* some method must be available for identifying short trains of neural impulses as phones and classifying them as phonemes. *Second,* some process must be available to analyze strings of phonemes into individual words. *Third,* there must be some way that meaning is assigned to utterance on the basis of both the individual words and their structural relations to one another, which implies that there must be a neurological process by which structural relations are recognized.

At first glance, it seems most reasonable to suppose that these three subprocesses are arranged in serial order: first, neural representations of acoustic waveforms are analyzed into phonemes; second, phonemes are analyzed into words; and third, grammatical structures are analyzed and meaning assigned to them. In fact, when engineers first tried to design automatic speech-recognition systems (such as voice-operated typewriters), they followed this model of the speech-recognition process. They tried to design one subsystem that would analyze sound waves to identify phonemes, another that would analyze strings of phonemes to identify words, and a third that would "parse" word strings—that is, recognize the grammatical relations among the words and divide them into units: phrases, clauses, sentences, and the like. It was generally agreed that if any such system could be made to work, we might assume it to be at least possible that the human brain operated on the speech signal in a similar, stepwise fashion. The best of these systems almost worked; but even when coupled to very large computers, none of them reached the level of speech recognition of a five-year-old child.

Why did they fail? The theory of serial or stepwise arrangement of speech-recognition subprocesses is based on an idea that works very well for many other processes, both natural and manmade. In building an automobile or a television set, for example, small units are fabricated first; these are combined into larger components; and, in turn, the larger components are assembled into the finished product. Obviously, you cannot assemble the finished product until the components have been fashioned, and the components cannot be built until the basic units have been fabricated. Moreover, the subprocesses in the manufacture of such an item are entirely independent of one another. The steps involved in building a TV amplifier out of transistors have nothing to do with the steps involved in manufacturing the transistors themselves, except that the amplifier assembly uses components produced by the transistor-manufacturing process. We can visualize the manufacture of such a product as a hierarchical arrangement of subprocesses proceeding in a fixed order from smaller units to larger ones. This idea works very well to describe many manufacturing processes as well as certain natural ones, such as synthesis of certain organic compounds in the living cell; but it does not seem to be an accurate description of speech recognition.

Consider, for example, the problem of phoneme recognition. We know that some reliable process must be available for recognizing phonemes because the change of a single phoneme can change the whole meaning of an utterance, and thus affect subsequent behavior. The words *ban, can, Dan, fan, Jan, man, Nan, pan, ran, tan, van,* and *than* are identical except for the first phoneme in each. If there were not some means of recognizing differences among phonemes, the differences among these twelve words would be hard to learn and difficult to recognize, and this would have profound behavioral significance. If you tell me to call Jan and I call Dan instead, your intent has miscarried. If you ask for the can and I hand you the pan, you will be frustrated. If you tell me to order a fan and I order a van, undesirable complications will result. I must be able to discriminate phonemes if I am to understand what you say and respond accordingly.

It is a mistake to assume that I must be able to discriminate every phoneme you utter in order to understand your utterance. This has been demonstrated experimentally by mixing speech with high-intensity noise that completely masks out some of the weak consonant sounds such as "s," "sh," "t," and "p." If these sounds are presented individually to the listener's ear and are mixed with enough noise, they will be unintelligible. If the same sounds are used in words that are familiar to the listener and these words are presented with noise, the listener will hear many of the words correctly, and may even report that he heard the masked sounds. If the words are then combined into easily-comprehended phrases, and the phrases are presented in noise, the listener will hear a very high percentage of the words correctly. If the stimulus phrases instruct the listener to perform simple and unambiguous operations with materials that are before him, he will make fewer errors still. If the listener is allowed to read through the list of stimulus phrases sometime before they are read to him, he will make virtually no mistakes at all. In short, we can find many situations in which speech can be understood perfectly well even though many of the individual sounds of which it is composed cannot be heard.

If larger components (words) can be "heard" even when the smaller units of which they are composed (phones) cannot, then it is impossible to account for speech perception and recognition on the basis of operations that process an acoustic signal according to a fixed hierarchical sequence. On the contrary, the listener seems actively to reconstruct the speaker's language, filling in the missing pieces on his own initiative when they fail to appear in the acoustic signal.

Analysis-by-Synthesis Theory of Speech Recognition

At present, our best guess as to how this reconstruction is carried out rests on an idea called the "analysis-by-synthesis" theory, represented schematically in Figure 10. This theory suggests that we use "hints" from a variety of sources to generate entirely within the brain a matching signal—a sort of guess as to the verbal content of

FIGURE 10
Schematic Representation of
Analysis-By-Synthesis Theory of Speech Recognition

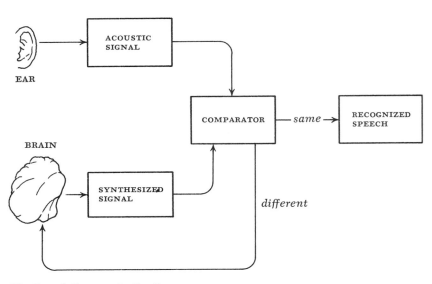

the utterance. This matching signal is then compared to the sensory signal from the ear. If the match is close enough, the sensory signal is "recognized." If it is not, the matching signal is modified, and another trial comparison is made. If no satisfactory matching signal can be generated, the listener finds the utterance unintelligible. According to the analysis-by-synthesis theory, this matching can be conducted at any language level: phoneme, word, phrase, or other utterance. Often an utterance can be recognized (that is, reconstructed) even though some of the phrases in it are unintelligible. A phrase may be recognized even though some of the words in it are unintelligible. A word may be recognized even though some of the phonemes in it are unintelligible. The information that makes possible the reconstruction of a partially unintelligible speech signal comes from a variety of sources. Most of these can be classified under three general headings: (1) *experience* (or learning), (2) *situation* (or context), and (3) *expectation* (or set).

Learning, context, and set as factors in speech recognition. It is easy to arrange a simple experiment to demonstrate the effect of experience on speech perception. To prepare for the experiment, make up a list of one-syllable nonsense words that are similar to but not quite identical with English words, syllables such as ZDROL (which is similar to "stroll"), LANP (similar to "lamp"), SPEESH, and similar items. Mix a half-dozen or so of these with an equal number of ordinary one-syllable English words to form a single list arranged in a random order. Practice reading the list until you can read the nonsense words easily and naturally. Then get two or three of your friends to serve as experimental subjects. Have them sit with their backs to you at a distance of twelve to fifteen feet, and tell them that you are going to read to them a list of one-syllable words and that you want them to write down each word as they hear it. Read the words naturally, without overly precise articulation and without emphasizing the nonsense words. (A little practice will overcome the tendency to emphasize the "incorrect" sound in the nonsense words.) Give your subjects time to write each word after you have said it. You will find that almost every one of your listeners will in at least some instances "recognize" the English word in place of the nonsense word that is similar to but not quite identical with it. This experiment provides a well-known example of "perceptual distortion." Because his experience has taught him that "lamp" is a frequently-recurring verbal pattern in English, and because he has no experience with -NP as a word-ending, your subject is likely to hear M for N in LANP.

You can increase the probability of perceptual distortion in a slightly different version of the foregoing experiment. Instead of using words in isolation, place each word in an appropriate sentence or phrase: "I am going for a ZDROL," "Please turn off the LANP," "She is majoring in SPEESH." Now your subject will distort his perception of the nonsense word almost every time, hearing its English counterpart. In this version of the experiment, we can see learning and context working hand-in-hand to produce perceptual distortion. In addition to the tendency to perceive a learned pattern, the subject also has a larger context in which the distorted perception makes much better sense than does the actual utterance.

Having performed both of the foregoing experiments with different subjects, you can now demonstrate the effects of expectation or set by performing still another version of the same experiment on a third subject. Use basically the same instructions given for the other experiments, but vary them by telling your subject that some of the words will not be pronounced correctly and that he should listen carefully and record exactly what he hears. In this version of the experiment you will find that the proportion of perceptual errors will be lower, and many subjects will not make any errors at all. The difference between the results of this experiment and the former one can be attributed to differences in *perceptual set*. In the first two experiments, the subject was led to expect ordinary words, and so was not searching for errors. In the last experiment, the subject was expecting errors, and hence found them.

As the third experiment shows, expectancy or set can increase the accuracy of speech perception; however, it can also interfere with speech recognition. Almost everyone has had an experience that demonstrates this point in a dramatic way. You are dialing a friend's telephone number and somehow get the wrong connection. You are expecting to hear your friend's voice saying "Hello," but instead a different voice answers with the name of a commercial company. In all probability you will not hear the name of the company at all —it will be an incomprehensible sound. If you had been calling that company, or even if you knew that the response would be unpredictable, you could have heard correctly; but because you were anticipating something quite specific and entirely different from what you heard, you were unable to decode the utterance.

Benefits of Perceptual Distortion

We have seen that auditory perceptual distortion can be a serious source of error. However, it is a source of strength rather than weakness in recognizing speech. For instance, consider the problem of listening to a speaker with a foreign accent or with a dialect different from your own. Without considerable tolerance for error in speech recognition, you would never be able to understand him. Pronounce the following aloud: FAHT ESS DEE METTAIR VIT HYOO? Almost any English speaker will recognize that you have said, "What is the matter with you?" Yet from the standpoint of phonemic content, the two utterances do not have a great deal in common: the "correct" pronunciation has fifteen phonemes (in general American); the "incorrect" one has eighteen, and only eight of the phonemes are common to both versions. Still, in spite of these discrepancies, the "foreign accent" version is recognizable as English.

Anyone who has ever flown in a private airplane is familiar with a second example of the utility of perceptual distortion in speech recognition. As the plane is approaching the landing field, your pilot identifies himself to the control tower and asks for landing instructions. Suddenly the radio speaker comes alive; but instead of a crisp voice relaying landing instructions, it emits a few syllables of unintelligible gibberish almost completely obscured by heavy static. Unruffled, your pilot says, "Out," hangs his microphone back on the instrument panel, and brings the plane down. How could he have heard his landing instructions, when in all probability you could not identify even a single word in the gabble that came through the radio? The answer lies in perceptual distortion—the pilot's, not yours. First of all, learning was at work: the pilot knew the limited and specialized vocabulary of control-tower jargon; second, context and expectation were operating: the pilot understood the situation and could anticipate what landing instructions he probably would receive. Both of these factors contribute to his ability to decode the control tower's instructions; without either advantage, you must rely exclusively on the acoustic signal for information, and it is too heavily overlaid with static to be decoded by an untrained ear.

Thus, the same factors which contribute to perceptual error under one set of conditions contribute to super-efficient auditory perception under another set of conditions. When the symbols being transmitted are common, anticipated, and appropriate to their context, the auditory habits of the listener will enable him to reconstruct the symbols even though they may be distorted or overlaid with noise that would ordinarily prohibit reception. On the other hand, when the symbols being transmitted are unusual, unanticipated, or unsupported by their context, the auditory habits of the listener will lead him to misperceive them. In particular, if the symbols are similar to other symbols that are more common, more anticipated, or better fitted to the context, the listener is likely to respond inappropriately to the context, and to "hear" something quite different from what the speaker intended to say.

In this chapter we made a preliminary distinction between hearing and listening. As a working hypothesis we tentatively identified *hearing* as an automatic biological process not modifiable according to the purposes or experiences of the auditor, and *listening* as a flexible psychological process that could be directed according to the habits, attitudes, and intentions of the listener. We warned that this distinction would not stand up under close examination, and it has not.

For one thing, the biological-psychological distinction fails because the psychological processes in fact occur in the central nervous system. For example, selective perception of speech, which we have viewed as a psychological phenomenon, is thought to rest upon neural inhibition, a physiological process. Moreover, instead of a dichotomy between unmodifiable, automatic hearing processes and flexible, purposeful listening processes, we have found a continuum along which it is possible to identify at least three different degrees of conscious control. In the case of speech *reception* we have seen that the events in the ear and the acoustic nerve are mostly beyond the speaker's control. In the case of speech *perception* we have seen that speech recognition depends not merely on reception, but also on habits which can be modified by experience or training, and which, once learned, operate more or less automatically. In the case of message *selection* (as in the "cocktail-party effect") we have seen that the listener may voluntarily direct his attention to one of several competing message sources, so as to perceive that particular one and virtually screen out the others.

Finally, we have observed that accuracy of decoding is strongly affected by experience, context, and expectancy. Under one set of conditions these factors work to enhance the decoding accuracy; under another set of conditions they lead to decoding errors.

PROBLEMS AND QUESTIONS FOR DISCUSSION

1. What are the main differences between transduction and the other phases of the hearing process? Are there similar distinctions which can be made in regard to the process of seeing?

2. For one day, keep a record of the times that your attention was distracted by an auditory stimulus from something to which you were paying attention. Report on the situation at the time of interruption, the characteristics of the interrupting sound, and your interpretation of why this particular stimulus was able to attract your attention away from what you were doing at the time.

3. With a group of your classmates, try the following experiment: Out of the hearing of the rest of the group, have two members practice telling about some interesting personal experience—a different experience and a different story for each of them. They should practice telling the stories together at the same time so that they can do so without hesitation. Now invite other members of the group in one at a time to serve as listeners. Have the listener sit between the two story-tellers, and listen to both stories simultaneously. Instruct one of the listeners to listen to one of the stories, a second listener to the other story, and a third listener to try to get as much as possible of both stories. Afterwards, have each listener (out of hearing of the others) repeat as much as possible of *both* stories. How much could each of the first two listeners repeat of the story he was supposed to listen to? Could he remember anything at all of the second story? How much could the third listener recall from each of the stories when compared to the first two? (*Note:* The experiment can be improved by recording each story on one track of a stereo tape recorder, then playing back the combined tapes through a stereo headset.)

4. Why are computers unable to recognize "running" speech at the present time?

5. Show how the "analysis-by-synthesis" approach to speech recognition helps to account for recognition of English spoken with a foreign dialect.

6. In the light of the concepts presented in this chapter, how would you evaluate a parent's report that his child "hears what he wants to hear"?

7. Discuss possible relationships between "the generation gap" and auditory perception.

6.

LISTENING TO SPEECH

Considered from the viewpoint of hearing, speech perception is the end of a long and complex process; but from the standpoint of personal and social utility, speech perception is only the beginning. Under most circumstances we assume that the hearing processes are functioning normally, and our attention is focused not on the verbal content but on the semantic content of speech—not on the words, but on the meanings. We listen to talk because we expect to make use of it in some way. We have seen that many aspects of the hearing-listening process are not under the conscious control of the listener; in this chapter, however, we will consider some aspects that are. For present purposes we will define "listening" as the processing of the speech signal more or less under conscious control for a particular purpose. We will explore briefly three different kinds of listening: (1) *listening for retraining verbal-auditory habits*, (2) *listening for comprehension and recall*, and (3) *listening critically*.[1]

RETRAINING VERBAL-AUDITORY HABITS

Earlier we discussed two cases in which listeners must learn to hear speech differently than they have heard it before: the student learning a new language, and the speech-handicapped child learning to

1. For a detailed consideration of the role of the listener in the communication process, see Paul D. Holtzman's *The Psychology of Speakers' Audiences*.

eliminate an articulation error. In both of these situations the learner must modify his habitual way of hearing (or listening to) speech sounds. These two examples by no means exhaust the situations in which one must retrain his verbal-auditory habits. Auditory rehabilitation for the partially deaf requires developing a new set of auditory discriminations; and, as we shall see, each of us faces a similar task whenever we encounter a new word for the first time.

Most theories of auditory retraining specify that the most efficient way to retrain old verbal-auditory habits or to acquire new ones is to raise speech discrimination, ordinarily an unconscious process, to the conscious level. New discriminations and recognitions are first acquired through consciously directed active listening, and then are made habitual and unconscious through repetition and reinforcement.

Consider, for instance, the problem of learning to hear a new word. On first thought this seems extremely simple. Having heard a word once, we should be able to distinguish it from all other words and recognize it again. That some sort of verbal-auditory learning must occur, however, is obvious if one considers such words as "polyunsaturated" and "chlorophyll." Once learned, neither word presents any difficulty; but on first hearing, either of them can cause considerable confusion. Even an adult, if he has not heard one of these words before, is likely to be doubtful about whether it is one word or two words or three, to fail to hear some of the sounds in the word, and to hear some of them incorrectly. In learning to hear a new word, three techniques seem to be especially useful: *division, contrast,* and *imitation.* A fourth technique, *graphic representation,* is sometimes useful in supplementing these. The same four methods are also useful in other auditory retraining problems.

Division

The easiest way to learn a new word or sound is by division. For maximum effectiveness, the new word is divided into the largest units that are already in the learner's verbal repertoire. In the case of "polyunsaturated," for example, most high school students would already know "poly-" and "un-" as affixes, and would also know the word "saturated." Such a listener could readily learn to hear the new word if it were pointed out to him that it consisted of these three parts. Note that this represents a division into morphemes and not a division into syllables: "poly-" contains two syllables and "saturated" four. But if these morphemic units are already known (that is, if the listener is able to hear them in connected discourse), then they can serve as components for building the larger word. The word "chlorophyl," on the other hand, would probably have to be broken into syllables for auditory comprehension by the average listener, because there are no larger components of the word that are already in his repertoire. Learning either of these two words could be enhanced by graphic representation—that is, by showing the word printed or written out and divided into its component parts. Pronouncing dictionaries follow this approach.

The technique of division can also be applied to learning new speech sounds. Most speech sounds are produced by the complex coordinated activity of several parts of the vocal tract. By dividing the whole pattern into those functions performed by the tongue, vocal folds, velum, etc., and describing the order of each in the sequence, it is possible to draw attention to each component of the sound in turn.

Imitation

The division technique is especially useful in teaching new sounds when it is combined with the technique of imitation. Indeed, in retraining children with articulatory disorders and in teaching students to speak a foreign language, auditory training and articulatory training often proceed hand in hand. The student is not simply asked to repeat the new sound, for often he will be able to do no better than to pronounce some sound he already knows that is close to the new one, and thus will learn nothing. Instead, the student not only hears the new sound, but he is also provided with a detailed articulatory description of how it is produced (that is, the sound is divided into articulatory units). Especially in the early stages of training, his ability to pronounce the new sound and his ability to hear it accurately are evolved more or less concurrently, although typically he will be able to hear it accurately for some time before he can pronounce it correctly.

Again, graphic representation may supplement division as a technique in teaching new sounds. A diagram of the parts of the vocal apparatus and their mode of action during the production of the sound is often helpful to the learner in grasping the interrelations among the parts and the sequence of action (see Figure 6, page 49).

Contrast

A final technique that is useful in learning new words or sounds is to contrast the new symbol with others that might easily be confused with it. "Polyunsaturated" might be contrasted with "unsaturated" to emphasize the "poly-" component. "Plantar" is easily confused auditorily with both "planner" and "planter"; thus, when "plantar" is introduced to a listener, the speaker does well to show the contrast between it and the other two words. Once the contrast has been established, the listener will recognize the difference and will hear "plantar" more accurately.

The technique of contrast is one of the methods sometimes used in the auditory rehabilitation of those having handicapped hearing. Phoneticians have established that there are appreciable differences in the characteristics of most vowel sounds depending on what consonants they follow. "O" in "cone" is different from the "O" sound in both "bone" and "tone." Even though the difference is noticeable, it is one that we do not ordinarily learn to hear because usually it is of little value in communication; because we can hear the preceding consonant sounds, there is no need to discriminate among these three different kinds of "O" vowel. Hearing loss frequently impairs the ability to distinguish among consonants, but it often allows the victim to distinguish among vowels. If the hearing loss is not too severe, an audiologist may train a partially deaf person to hear the differences among vowels which reflect the consonants preceding them. In this way, the trainee learns to "infer" the presence of a particular consonant from the traces it leaves on the following vowel, in effect partially restoring speech discrimination. The development of these new auditory habits usually requires procedures that contrast vowels on the basis of their preceding consonants: first the patient learns to hear differences among vowels, then to associate them with particular consonant sounds.

In the foregoing examples, we have assumed a speaker or trainer whose purpose was to change some aspect of the auditor's verbal-auditory habits. He accomplished this by inducing the auditor to listen for details of the speech signal that would otherwise have been ignored. But the same procedures may often be employed by the listener on his own initiative, particularly if he has opportunity for repeated exposure. He may try to divide, contrast, and imitate if he finds the auditory pattern confusing and is motivated to perceive it more accurately. But whether he initiates the procedure himself or has it performed for him, his verbal-auditory retraining will proceed by paying conscious attention to new features of the acoustic pattern. The new recognitions are made first by a conscious exertion of effort; through repetition and reinforcement they eventually become unconscious, relatively effortless, and habitual.

LISTENING FOR COMPREHENSION AND RECALL

By convention we use the word "comprehension" to refer to one's immediate grasp of some idea or fact at the moment when it is presented to him. We use the word "recall" to refer to his ability to remember the item at some later time. Immediate comprehension is no guarantee of subsequent recall; however, the two obviously are related since it seems impossible to recall an idea that was not originally comprehended. This relation is a useful one, for it has proved impossible so far to construct a real test of comprehension. All so-called "comprehension tests" are in fact tests of immediate recall. Typically, an informative message such as a speech is read to an auditor; and when it is over, the auditor is given an objective test over its content. Such a test measures comprehension only indirectly. We can infer that (except for the intervention of chance factors) the auditor will not be able to answer questions concerning items that he did not comprehend; and since the test occurs immediately following the message, we assume that he will not have forgotten a great deal of what he did comprehend. This latter inference is not equally justified in all cases, so we know that these immediate recall tests are imperfect measures of comprehension. Nevertheless, evidence strongly suggests that the same factors that affect comprehension also affect long-range recall (as measured after the lapse of several days or weeks following the hearing of the message). Several of these factors are under the conscious control of the listener, and so fall within the province of listening skills.

Listening with a Purpose

The first of these factors is listening with a purpose. If at the outset of the listening experience the auditor has clearly in mind the particular use he can make of the informative content of the message, he can increase the relevant comprehension-recall by a sizeable factor. For example, if the listener knows that he will be able to use the information in answering questions on a test following the speech, he will do much better than if he does not know he is to be tested. If he knows just what questions will be asked, he will do even better. If he knows that following a lecture on "Cleaning the M-1 Carbine" he is going to have to clean one, he will learn much more about how to do it from the lecture than if he does not expect to use the information in this way. In short, the more specific his purpose, and the more clearly he sees it, the more he will seem to comprehend and recall. Of course, only part of this effect is real; the rest of it is attributable to selective perception. The listener is able to economize his effort by focusing on those aspects of the presented information that he expects to use, and ignore "irrelevant" information. Nevertheless, if the information is being presented for some specific purpose, the auditor who is aware of that purpose will be more successful as a listener than the auditor who is not. Knowing that this is so, effective public speakers often build into the introductions of their speeches "motivating" materials that explain to the listener just how he will be able to use the information he is about to be given. If the speaker succeeds in establishing that purpose, the auditor will acquire more information from the speech and will retain it longer.

Forming an Organized Image

A second factor contributing to comprehension and recall is an organized image of the content of the message. If the listener is able to pick out a small number of key ideas and relate these to the rest of the information in the speech, the supporting relationships among the ideas will enhance retention of all of them. Thus, effective listeners always give special attention to main points, transitions, and to any hints about how one idea links up to another. Even if the speaker should fail to provide him with any guidelines, such a listener will at least partially organize the material in his own mind, drawing relationships and linkages where the speaker has failed to do so. Of course, the effective speaker, knowing that an organized picture is understood and recalled more easily than a disorganized one, ordinarily makes every effort to provide the listener with guideposts and landmarks; and the shrewd listener uses these to advantage.[2]

Relating to Experience

A third factor that contributes to comprehension and recall is relating the content of the utterance to previous experiences. Any information that fits conveniently into what we already know is retained more easily than is information standing in isolation. If the content of a message is such that the listener is easily able to supplement it with related information from his own memory, he will find the content easier to comprehend and recall. It is partly for this rea-

2. This point is discussed in greater detail in another book in this series, Thomas Olbricht's *Informative Speaking*.

son that public speakers try to select examples, illustrations, comparisons, and other supporting materials for their speeches from areas which touch upon the experience and knowledge of their listeners. But the motivated listener need not rely on the speaker to provide these materials; he can draw the relations for himself as the speaker develops his main ideas. Whether this relating is accomplished by the speaker or by the listener, it will serve in either case to increase comprehension and recall.

CRITICAL LISTENING

One can listen critically to speech in a number of different ways. One can criticize the speech as an artistic performance, or analyze it from a formal point of view. One can attempt to discover the speaker's underlying ethical presuppositions and evaluate them for their correspondence to some criterion of excellence. But ordinarily when one talks about "critical listening," he is talking about analyzing the adequacy with which the discourse supports its intended point of view or conclusion. The critical listener in this sense operates very much like a debater who is going to take the other side of the question. A full account of critical listening would entail a textbook on argument; but in general the critical listener looks for assumptions, tests for flaws in argument, evaluates evidence, and tries to think of contrary cases.

Listening for Assumptions

No line of argument is without some assumptions. If I say, "You should not use insecticides on your garden because you will destroy birds as well as insects," I am assuming that there is something desirable about preserving birds; and I might also be suggesting that it is more desirable to preserve birds than to destroy insect pests. Either of these issues is at least potentially debatable, but in the argument stated above I have chosen to ignore them and to assume that they are true, or at least acceptable to my listeners. Other assumptions are harder to spot, but some auditors have trained themselves to look for these hidden issues in argument. To become really proficient at listening for assumptions, one must undergo rigorous training. A little practice, however, will show almost anyone that he has considerably more talent in this direction than he customarily uses and that, when so motivated, each of us sometimes listens for assumptions.

Listening for Fallacies

Suppose I say, "The communists want to have Red China admitted to the U.N., and that is precisely the position that Senator X takes; therefore, it is clear that he is a communist." In this argument there are no hidden assumptions, but the argument is unsatisfactory because one cannot go logically from the premises to the conclusion. It is possible that Senator X is indeed a communist, but the argument does not prove it, for not everyone who takes the communist position on admission of Red China to the U.N. is necessarily a communist himself. Such logical flaws in argument we call "fallacies," and there are many different kinds of them. This particular fallacy is an instance of an undistributed middle term; if the argument were valid, the major premise would have to provide that "Everyone who believes that Red China should be admitted to the U.N. is a communist." It would then be logical to argue that because Senator X wants admission, he is therefore a communist. But this new premise is so clearly false that the argument, when properly stated, never gets past the first step. Such fallacies are common in everyday arguments and very often are found in formal speeches. The critical listener looks for these and thus tests the strength of the speaker's arguments as he listens to them.

Listening for Bias

Most messages that seek to convince or persuade use arguments based on some kind of evidence. In arguing for a federal drivers' examination, for instance, I may contend that the highway death toll is rising at an alarming rate. If I do so, you will probably want some evidence that the contention is true—authoritative opinion, comparative statistics, charts, etc. Much of this evidence is subject to bias, and the critical listener is alert to this possibility. He must consider that the information source may not have enough facts at his disposal to form a valid judgment. Statistics on traffic fatalities from the National Safety Council are based on comprehensive nationwide surveys with cooperation from state and municipal officials; but statistics on the same subject from an automobile corporation, even a very large one, are based on partial evidence, since private profit-making corporations cannot obtain such information nearly so readily. The listener must also be aware that the information source may be inclined to view the available data from a biased viewpoint. If I am writing a shocking exposé of auto safety standards, it clearly is to my advantage to find as many hazards as possible in automobile design, and to place the worst possible interpretation on each of them. On the other hand, if I am an auto manufacturer, it is clearly to my advantage to overlook these same factors whenever possible, and to minimize hazards where they cannot be entirely overlooked. The critical listener tries to be alert to such personal interests and to discount evidence when such biasing factors are present.

Considering Contrary Implications

Finally, the critical listener tries to think of contrary cases. In order to illustrate a principle or prove a point, the speaker generally will offer specific examples to illustrate the meaning *he* intends, the point *he* wishes to establish. An uncritical listener will allow the features of these specific cases to exert undue influence on his judgment, and will go along with the speaker's tacit assumption that the principles that govern the cases he has presented will serve to govern all similar cases. However, by thinking of cases with contrary implications, the critical listener protects himself against any tendency that the speaker might have to overgeneralize on the basis of too few cases.

Hearing and listening to speech form a continuous and integrated process. However, in the interest of simplicity we considered in this chapter several separate aspects of the hearing-listening process that are more or less under the conscious control of the listener.

Consideration was given first to listening for the purpose of establishing new verbal-auditory habits. Four techniques especially useful in this type of listening are *division, contrast, imitation,* and *graphic representation.*

A distinction was made between comprehension and recall. Several factors contributing to comprehension and recall were noted: listening with a purpose, building an organized image of the content, and relating content to familiar, known experiences.

Critical listening was identified primarily as listening to analyze the adequacy with which a discourse supports its intended point of view or conclusion. It was pointed out that the critical listener looks for assumptions, tests for flaws in argument, evaluates evidence, and tries to think of contrary cases.

PROBLEMS AND QUESTIONS FOR DISCUSSION

1. The next time you hear a polysyllabic word you are not familiar with, write the word down and learn how to pronounce it. Check your pronunciation and your spelling in the dictionary. Report on (a) the circumstances under which you heard or read the word, (b) the method you finally used to "learn" to speak and to hear it, and (c) the errors you made in the process.

2. Persuade an advanced student of some foreign language (one you do not speak) to teach you one of the sounds of that language that is not present in English. Report how your informant tried to "teach" you the sound, how you finally learned it (if you did), and how rapid and satisfactory your progress was. Did your mentor use the techniques discussed in this chapter? Did he use any others? If so, how useful were they?

3. In one of your other courses, take thorough notes on the lecture for one day or one unit of instruction. After your notes are complete, organize them in outline form, arranging the points in a different order than the lecturer's, if the reorganization improves the clarity of the outline. What was the effect on your learning of (a) listening to take notes, and (b) trying to organize the material as logically as possible?

4. During a lecture in another course, make brief notes regarding points that were unclear, or questions that remain unanswered after the lecture is concluded. Did the plan to look for such questions make you listen more carefully to the lecture? Discuss the merit of this technique as a general strategy for learning from mass lectures.

5. In a political speech or newspaper editorial, try to identify all of the hidden premises that you can find. What proportion of them do you regard as debatable? What proportion of the intended hearers/readers probably would regard each premise as debatable?

6. Find a similar speech or editorial that uses examples as a means of proof or persuasion. Can you think of contrary examples? Are the speaker's examples or the contrary examples more representative? How does this affect the validity of the argument? Do you think most people accepted it?

7. Choose two editorials or speeches, one that you agree with and another that you disagree with. You should base your agreement and disagreement on your immediate reactions, not detailed or careful analysis of the discourses. Now try to listen to each (or read each) as critically as possible, using the techniques described in this chapter. Which task was more difficult? Which did you enjoy most? Do you now feel differently about either than you did before you began the exercise?

7.

VERBAL AND NONVERBAL MESSAGES

All communication concerns sending and receiving messages, and the most ancient of communication theories—linguistics and rhetoric—deal largely with message structure and content. Yet the term "message" is one of the most elusive words in communication theory. In use it leads to confusion at least as often as to understanding.

In this chapter we will explore the idea of messages in general, with special emphasis on verbal messages and on nonverbal communication as it relates to the spoken word. First, we will consider the general idea of "the message" from three different points of view. Next we will examine verbal messages in terms of content, overall structure, and effects, and in the process, notice certain striking features of nonverbal communication as it usually operates in the speaking-listening situation.

MESSAGE AND VIEWPOINT

Three Views of the Message

We usually think of a message as something that is "sent" *from* some source *to* some destination *through* some channel. Indeed, it is due to this general conception of the nature of messages that Shannon's transmission model of communication, discussed in Chapter 1, has been so persistently applied to communication in all its guises, both human and nonhuman. But, also, as we noted earlier, the language *sent . . . from . . . through . . . to . . .* can easily lead our thinking astray; for this language suggests that what is "sent" is the same thing as what is "received," and a moment's thought reminds us that this is never true. We must emphasize that the *sent* and the *received* messages are not merely different versions of the same elements in the communication process; they are altogether different elements. Thus, when one is trying to think clearly about communication, to speak of "*the* message as *it* was sent and received" is inexact and usually confusing. Terminology like "the" and "it" suggests a single message that merely takes a somewhat different form at the transmission end and at the reception end of the communication chain. Actually, these two "versions" are entirely different events. Remember first of all that they occur at different points in space, located sometimes even thousands of miles apart. Secondly, since passage through a channel is never quite instantaneous, they occur at different points in time. These simple physical facts alone should serve to remind us that sent and received messages are not—and can never be—identical.

We need, then, to make a basic distinction between these two messages: the one that was *sent by the source* and the one that was *received at the destination*.[1] In any complete communication transaction, both events are present. As you will recall from Chapter 1, the degree of correspondence between the two is the measure of "fidelity" of communication: the more the received message has in common with the message sent, the greater the fidelity of communication. We will say more about fidelity when we discuss message content in the next section of this chapter.

For the moment, however, we need to recognize a very important third point of view with regard to messages, one having nothing to do with either senders or receivers. Often when we talk about messages, we are thinking not so much of either the message the speaker sent or the one the listener received, but of the message as *observed by a third party* to the transaction, one who tries as much as possible to stand outside the transaction in order to describe it from neutral ground. This is the difference between the communication participant and the communication analyst.

At this point we need to recall another item from Chapter 1, namely the distinction between *message* and *signal*. You will recall that the signal is a physical event, such as a sequence of acoustic

---

1. The message received by the destination-listener is given considerable attention in a component book in this series, Paul D. Holtzman's *The Psychology of Speakers' Audiences*.

vibrations, while a message is a symbolic event representing an interpretation of the physical occurrence. Signals pass through channels in the environment, but messages occur only at source and destination. Still, it is possible for an observer who has access to the signal to construct from it a message of his own and to analyze that message to make inferences about the source, predictions about the destination, or judgments about the process.

Advantages of the Objective Viewpoint

Such message analysis by observers can be quite useful. Indeed, it accounts for a good deal of what we know about communication. Consider, for example, the fields of logic, poetics, and certain aspects of rhetoric such as stylistics and the theory of organization. All of these branches of communication study, which have contributed enormously to our understanding of and skill in speaking and writing, take as their point of departure the message as observed. Usually they begin with a poem, an essay, a story, or the written record of a speech. They then try to understand it, describe it, and draw principles from it that can be extended to other examples of the same kind. All of this is undertaken not from the point of view of the writer or speaker, nor from the point of view of any particular reader or listener, but from a broader perspective.

Conclusions and principles derived by studying communication in this way are designed to be useful to speakers and writers *in general* (that is, to all or most of them) for the improvement of their communication skill, and for readers and listeners *in general* for the improvement of their understanding and appreciation of verbal messages. Often the objective of training in these skills is to induce the student to incorporate communication *analysis* into his communication *behavior*. When such training succeeds, the student devotes part of his attention during communication to analyzing the messages he is receiving and/or those he is about to send, in much the same way as he would if he were an outside observer.

Probably the simplest case of this kind is logic. When I press my point in a discussion with you, probably I feel intuitively that my arguments add up to a reasonable conclusion. If you disagree with me, you will be equally sure that they do not. But the theory of argument allows anyone to examine the reasoning supporting our conflicting points of view, and to evaluate both for validity. Obviously, anyone expecting to spend much time in verbal argument would do well to study its principles in order to test his own positions for soundness before exposing them to others, and then to construct verbal arguments reflecting that validity. Obviously, too, anyone who expects to read or listen to much verbal argument would be wise to study those principles so as to detect the fallacies in unsound arguments, as well as to appreciate and place greater confidence in sound arguments when he hears them. Indeed, we have seen in Chapter 6 that this is an important aspect of critical listening.

The foregoing examples should make it clear that both speakers and listeners can use ideas about communication gained from the viewpoint of observers who are themselves outside the main flow of communication. Perhaps the strongest motivation for studying communication from this angle is to provide useful information for speakers, writers, readers, and listeners. But such analyses of communication must begin from an "objective" standpoint. For instance, when we say that a speech by the national president of SDS to a local chapter contains three non sequiturs in a single passage, we are saying nothing at all about either what the speaker intended to say or what his audience heard him say, but only about the logical analysis of the speech as received by an observer.

Now, what makes it so easy for us to forget all of this and to speak of *the* message is that when we are not playing the role of the speaker (in which case *the* message is the one we intended) or of the listener (in which case *the* message is the one we heard), we are playing the role of the critic (in which case *the* message is the one we reconstructed for the speaker or the listener or both). When observing communication, it is very difficult *not* to believe that what we are observing is (except for the speaker's or listeners' own errors of perception or want of understanding) very much like what both the speaker and the listener are experiencing. But when observing the communication of others, we need to be cautious about claiming any special validity for our perceptions of the message.

Often the observations of an objective third party will be useful to speaker or listener or both. Moreover, the flexibility of both speaker and listener is improved by training that enables them to take the "objective" view of their own behavior and that of their communication partners. But a balanced view of the process cautions us to recognize that although the observed message is different from both the sent message and the received message, it is not inherently superior or more valid than either.

MESSAGE CONTENT

Since most of what is known about messages in regard to content, structure, and effects grows out of the objective viewpoint, throughout the remainder of this chapter we will be looking at the message primarily as an observed event. When necessary, we will call special attention to sent and received messages; but unless we specifically note otherwise, it will be understood that these principles are developed from the standpoint of the message as reconstructed and analyzed by the nonparticipating observer.

The Relativity of Content

Undoubtedly the most vexing problem in studying message content is knowing where and how to look for it. Startlingly different views of what constitutes the content of a message and where it can be found come to us from different schools of communication study.

The linguistic level of content. Sometimes the content of a message is defined as the string of symbols one can decode from the signal. If a listener can properly convert the signal into the symbols that the speaker uttered (and that an observer is able to confirm), then the listener is said to have received the content of the message. On other occasions, the content of the message is said to lie in the meanings of the symbols, particularly in the ideas they convey. (Note the difference between saying that the content is in the meaning, as we do here, and saying that the meaning is in the words—a position we rejected in Chapter 6.) On still other occasions, the message is thought to consist of further interpretations or elaborations of this immediate ideational content.

The ideational and implicational levels of content. Suppose, for example, that you hear a girl say to a boy, "No, I'm sorry, I can't go to the Art Festival with you on Saturday." At the first level of analysis, the message consists simply of the string of words reproduced in the foregoing sentence, and the boy would be said to have received the message if he simply decoded the signal into that symbolic string. A phonetician or a telecommunication engineer might be satisfied with the fidelity of communication if the boy could faithfully reconstruct the symbols from the signal. A rhetorician, however, would want to go further and be sure that the boy understood that the girl had said that she was not going to go with him to this particular event—that is, that he grasped the idea involved in her statement. But the student of human interaction (for example, a clinical psychologist) might be interested in another kind of message altogether. Putting the statement itself—together with certain nonverbal behaviors such as vocal tone, facial expression, and physical movements—into the context of the immediately preceding statements and the previous relationship between the parties, he might observe an altogether different message. In his terms, the girl might be saying, "I want to be persuaded," or "You know I don't like to be asked at the last minute," or "Can't you see I'm not interested in going out with you?" All of these are perfectly legitimate messages which the girl might send (intentionally or unintentionally) and which the boy might receive (accurately or inaccurately).

At which of these three levels—the linguistic, the ideational, or the implicational—should we say the content of the message is to be found? Obviously, the answer is at all three. Clearly, any message is a complex event that can be interpreted and analyzed in many different ways. Each of these modes of analysis contributes something different to our understanding of messages, and each is especially useful for some particular purpose. If you want to design and test electronic communication systems, you will find it more profitable to consider message content at the phonetic level. If you want to improve the abilities of speakers and listeners to communicate ideas, you would probably concentrate at the ideational level. And if you were interested in improving interpersonal interaction, you would focus on fidelity at the implicational level. In each case, you could claim that you were interested in the content of the message; but since linguistic, ideational, and interpersonal content are made manifest in somewhat different ways, your attention would be directed to different aspects of the message in each case.

We can see, then, that the term "content" is a relative one; for where and how one looks for the content of a message will depend on his reason for examining the message in the first place. Now, in saying that "content" is a relativistic term, it is important to recognize that we are *not* declaring thereby that it is vague, but merely that it is ambiguous. A vague term is one that is imprecisely defined; an ambiguous term is one that has a number of definitions, each of which may be more or less exact. Because there are so many different reasons for analyzing communication, the number of levels and types of message content are much greater than the three examples listed above. But what we mean by "content" need never be unclear if we are always sure to specify which level or type of content we mean in each case.

Content and Organization

One level of content that has proved endlessly fascinating to students of speaking and writing is the level that is reflected in the overall organization of the message. Later in this chapter we will take a closer look at message organization or structure, but for now it is worthwhile to notice the close relationship between a certain kind of message content and its organization.[2]

When we examined language in Chapter 2, we found that part of the meaning of an utterance is to be found in the arrangement of words and phrases within it. So it is with content and organization in the framework of longer messages: some of the significance of the content is to be found in the way it is organized.

The outline as the principal organizational tool. According to the most widely accepted theory of speech organization (one that can be traced back more than 2000 years), a well-built speech can be represented as a hierarchically arranged network of ideas.[3] The principal or most important ideas are subdivided into less important ones; these in turn are divided into still smaller units, and so on to the smallest units. The principal ideas are the main points; the ideas supporting them are the subpoints, and so down to the level of the ultimate "supporting materials" of the speech: the examples, illustrations, comparisons, quotations, and other concrete data that enliven, clarify, or prove the points that the speaker wants to make. According to the theory, the best speeches—that is, the clearest, most convincing or persuasive, and the most pleasing—can be represented by such a structure pointing toward a *single* idea often referred to as the thesis, purpose sentence, or central focus of the speech. Such a speech can be visualized as a pyramid, with the central idea at the top; the main points spread out at the next level below it; the subpoints spread out below the main points, and so down to the supporting materials at the base of the triangle. (Note the similarity of this structure to the phrase-structure diagrams of Chapter 2, page 29.)

No one seems to have investigated just when the formal outline was invented as a means of representing this kind of organization, but for a very long time the outline has been regarded as the principal instrument of organization. A speech that can be thoroughly and faithfully outlined is recognized by everybody as a well-organized speech, one in which the content units appear to be chosen and arranged in a coherent way. Sometimes a well-organized speech fails

2. Brief summaries of research studies investigating the relationship between organization and effectiveness can be found in Wayne Thompson, *Quantitative Research in Public Address and Communication* (New York: Random House, Inc., 1967).

3. Aristotle, *Rhetorica*, trans. w. Rhys Roberts, in *The Basic Works of Aristotle*, ed. Richard McKeon (New York: Random House, Inc., 1941).

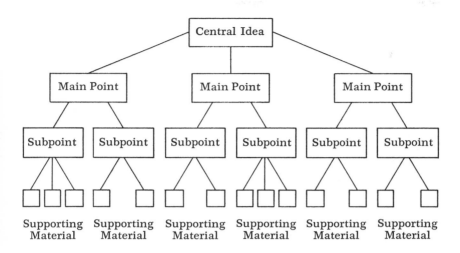

FIGURE 11

Representation of Pyramid Structure of Speech Organization

to reach its objective, and sometimes a poorly-organized one succeeds; but usually this occurs for other reasons, and the great contribution that good organization makes to clarity and effectiveness of communication can scarcely be questioned.

Organization as a factor in message potency. A moment's reflection tells us that this commonplace observation covers a remarkable circumstance. As speakers, listeners, readers, and writers, we use organization principles so much and so automatically that we never give any thought to *how* they work. What is even more remarkable is that nobody has published any research into the reasons why organization works as it does. Does organization capitalize on some structural or dynamic principle of the brain? Does it reflect some as-yet-undiscovered principle of language? It is based on a deep-lying property of the culture that is somehow built into each of us as we grow up in Western civilization? Or is it simply an indirect result of training in the schools? Whatever the reason, the effect of organization on a listener's or reader's reception of a speech or written message is so profound that a part of everyone's education is devoted to studying how to produce organized messages, and learning how to analyze the organization in messages one hears and reads in order to better comprehend them. To this end, we will have something more to say about organization later in the unit on message structure.

It is obvious from our discussion in the preceding section of this chapter that not everything we might call "content" in a message is captured in its organizational outline. We will further emphasize this point when we consider content analysis below. But because of the pervasiveness of the theory of organization, and because of the psychological impact of organizational patterns on the receivers of messages, most of the time spent talking about the content of a speech will concern the network of ideas that can be represented in an outline of it.

Content Analysis

Any systematic procedure for examining messages so as to describe significant features of their content may properly be called "content analysis." Of course, the specific type of content we find in a message will depend very much upon our purpose for examining it in the first place. There are many different methods of content analysis, but most of these fall into a small number of major categories: *source, style, vocabulary,* and *attitude.*

Source. First of all, content analysis is often used to make judgments about the communication source: who he is, how he feels in general or about particular things, or how he is likely to behave. Each of us has a distinctive style of discourse that is probably as unique as his fingerprints (or his voiceprints). What we talk about, the vocabulary we use, the syntactic forms we prefer, and the way we organize our discourse are highly variable from one person to another. Given a message from an unknown source, we often find it possible to identify its author by methods of content analysis. For example, a public speech, delivered more than two thousand years ago to an Athenian assembly, and whose authorship had been disputed by scholars and experts for hundreds of years, was finally attributed to Demosthenes on the basis of content analysis. Research showed that Greek orators of the period differed from one another in the relative frequency with which they used two short, one-syllable words. The frequencies of those words for the disputed speech were very close to the average frequencies in speeches known to have been made by Demosthenes, and far removed from the frequencies used by other speakers of the period. In a famous kidnapping case, police were able to distinguish telephone calls from the kidnapper from those of "cranks" on the basis of vocabulary and sentence length.

And perhaps you are already familiar with the continuing line of research on the "true" authorship of the plays of Shakespeare. Each new piece of content evidence—word frequencies, figures of speech, dominant themes, rhyme patterns, etc.—points toward the conclusion that the plays were all written by a single author, and that his style was significantly different from that of Bacon, Johnson, Marlowe, and others of the period to whom the manuscripts have sometimes been attributed.

The significant thing about this kind of content analysis is not simply that literary detective work is possible—that is just an interesting technological application. What is ultimately most important is the revelation that individual language habits are to a considerable extent unique, and that they differ in ways that can be described by simple (if sometimes time-consuming) methods of analysis.

Style. Not only does each of us have a more or less unique verbal style, but that style is affected by our attitudes and moods. This is especially true of spoken language. Under stress, the frequency of "hesitation phenomena"—repetitions, false starts, unplanned pauses, and vocalized pauses ("uh," "ah," and the like)—increases very noticeably. For a given individual, the amount of verbal disruption is roughly equivalent to the level of stress, so that the frequency of hesitation phenomena is sometimes used as a measure of the amount of stress an individual is experiencing in a communication experiment. And of course all of us unconsciously use this kind of evidence in evaluating the emotional state of our friends and acquaintances in everyday contacts.

Vocabulary. As speakers, our vocabularies reflect our moods, too. Social workers in Chicago found that they could gauge a client's progress by a simple kind of content analysis of his comments in interviews. No matter *what* the client talked about in the interview, the case worker could calculate the interviewee's "discomfort-relief" quotient by counting the number of his words reflecting a positive evaluation (relief words) and the number reflecting a negative evaluation (discomfort words). This "DRQ" proved a predictor of progress: clients whose ratio of relief words increased steadily over a period of time showed a degree of improvement.

Attitude. Content also reflects one's attitudes toward specific persons and things, often without his intending to express an attitude. All of us are accustomed to making judgments about people's attitudes on the basis of their verbal behavior, and such judgments are often surprisingly accurate. Indeed, we find it almost impossible to talk about anything for any length of time without revealing our feelings about it. If we wish to conceal our attitudes about a particular object, person, or event, we instinctively try to avoid talking about it at all. This natural evaluative quality of language is the basis of an elaborate method of content analysis called "evaluative assertion analysis." The objective of evaluative assertion analysis is to arrive at a precisely quantified measure of attitude toward some attitude-object. The measure is based on a painstaking method that assesses the degree of positive or negative attitude toward a given person, nation, proposal, etc., as expressed by a message source in each individual assertion the source makes about that attitude-object. These individual assertions are then averaged over a message or series of messages in order to arrive at an overall measure of attitude. In all probability, the whole complex procedure merely quantifies what most of us experience qualitatively as we listen to or read the message.

Coupled with other information, knowledge of a source's expressed attitudes may help us to predict his future behavior. Except for our closest friends, few of us would ask acquaintances how they intend to vote in a coming election; but we can make fairly good predictions of voting behavior from a surprisingly small sample of their comments on the parties, candidates, and campaign. In international relations, predictions based on such evidence are extremely important, and world powers spend vast sums on the collection and analysis of the verbal output of other nations. In the U. S. State Department, for example, groups of analysts are constantly at work scrutinizing the news releases, state speeches, official communiques, and texts of broadcasts of foreign powers. Most of this information is collected and analyzed so as to improve our ability to predict the course of international events. Sometimes the analysis is very minute. For instance, at one stage of the talks, the State Department predicted a softening of the "hard line" of the North Vietnamese government in Paris peace negotiations, largely due to the *absence* of a formerly prevalent phrase from a speech by the leader of North Vietnam. Thus, in a particular context, the absence of an expected content element may be quite significant, especially when we are trying to predict the source's future behavior.

In addition to telling us about the speaker, content analysis may also help us to make judgments or predictions about the listener. Since most of what content analysis can tell us in this regard consists of predicting various effects of the message on him, we will defer further consideration of this point to the forthcoming chapter on message effects.[4]

The Content of Nonverbal Communication

Under most circumstances, we prefer to receive messages from others in face-to-face interaction rather than in any other form. The reason for our preference lies partly in the fact that experience has taught us that considerable information may be conveyed by the nonverbal behavior of the person addressing us. To interpose a telephone line is to remove the visual parts of the message. To reduce the message to writing further deprives it of the nonverbal vocal content in rate, pause, force, inflection, and the other paralinguistic elements. In cases where we prefer some mode of communication other than face-to-face, it is usually because we specifically wish to avoid receiving these nonverbal message components: we want to save time by stripping off the nonessentials, or we want to avoid the embarrassment or discomfort we expect to accompany the expression of some emotion. Thus, both our usual preference and the everyday exceptions to it underline the fact that nonverbal behaviors communicate.

Nonverbal communication as an indicator of attitudes and emotions. But what does nonverbal communication communicate, and how does it do so? The "what" is somewhat easier to answer than the "how"; for what nonverbal behavior communicates most clearly and universally is feelings and attitudes, but precisely how it does so is not easy to say. For instance, most of us have from early childhood been able to tell very quickly and with great certainty whether someone liked us, even though overt verbal expressions of like or dislike are socially taboo, and rarely occur. Of course, these clear impressions result from the nonverbal communication behaviors directed to us by others. In fact, if someone were to express verbally a like or dislike for us, we would attach very little credibility to the statement if it conflicted with the nonverbal cues he supplies. Yet, even though we were sure enough of our conclusion to discount the overt verbal expression, we might have trouble identifying precisely what our impression came from. In this way nonverbal communication is not very different from language (remember the arti-

---

4. A comprehensive treatment of content analysis can be found in *The Analysis of Communication Content,* edited by George Gerbner, Ole R. Holsti, Klaus Krippendorff, William J. Paisley, and Philip J. Stone (New York: John Wiley & Sons, Inc., 1969).

ficial language experiment); but in another way, nonverbal cues are very different from words; for it is characteristic of nonverbal communication that it operates around the fringes of our conscious awareness.

Where attitudes, feelings, and moods are concerned, nonverbal communication is thought to carry a high percent of the content of a message. We have already referred to hesitation phenomena as an indicator of speaker anxiety or stress. Other manifestations of anxiety and of habitual or momentary insecurity are fidgetiness and self-manipulation (such as hair twisting, hand wringing, ear pulling, and the like). The next time you have a chance, watch closely someone you think is anxious or insecure. You will find that almost all of the cues on which your judgment is based involve nonverbal behavior, and most of them will consist of visible signs.

Researchers in kinesics and related disciplines are at work deciphering the nonverbal communication codes, especially the significance of visible bodily positions and movements.[5] Each new discovery brings to light additional information that can be conveyed through the nonverbal channels. For example, posture and directness somehow interact to convey information about liking and perceived status. The more we like the person we are talking to, the more we tend to lean toward him and the more inclined we are to look into his eyes. When talking to someone you like and trust, you will be neither tense nor overly relaxed, but will display a moderate level of tension in your posture and muscle tone.

But the perceived status of the receiver is also a factor in posture and directness. If someone fails to relax when talking to you, it may be because he dislikes you; or it may be because he perceives his status as being lower than yours. We tend to relax around persons of equal or lower status, but to "tense up" around persons of higher status. We show contempt (i.e., express feelings of vastly superior status) by extreme relaxation. Does someone impress you as being insulting and disrespectful? Very probably he ordinarily talks to you in a more relaxed manner than you think appropriate to your relative status, and does not face you directly when talking to you. He is reflecting peer or perhaps even superior status in his nonverbal behavior, causing you to feel that he has overstepped the bounds of propriety.

Gestures. Somewhere between the broad emotional and attitudinal content outlined above and the relatively specific content

5. See Edward T. Hall, *The Silent Language* (New York: Doubleday & Company, Inc., 1959).

conveyed by the verbal part of a message lies the kind of information conveyed by those specifically patterned movements we call "gesture." By long tradition, gestures are divided into two categories, *descriptive* and *expressive;* and these categories prove helpful in considering this aspect of nonverbal communication.

Descriptive gestures provide specific information about a topic, and may occur alone or in combination with verbal behavior. Pointing to a person, place, or thing—either as an isolated behavior or in conjunction with a verbal reference—is an example of a descriptive gesture. Other examples are such graphic gestures as making a circle with the fingers when referring to something round; indicating with the hand "so high" or "so big"; or demonstrating relative placement, such as "Tampa is here (gesture) to the northeast, and St. Petersburg is here (gesture) to the southwest." Another kind of descriptive gesture is enumeration or counting by holding up the appropriate number of fingers.

Expressive gestures are used to express specific moods, or for emphasis. President Truman used a chopping gesture of the hands for emphasis. President Nixon most often uses a vigorous nod of the head for the same purpose. Both gestures arise from the same impulse and convey the same information. Most of us probably employ a larger number of expressive gestures than descriptive ones, especially the expressive gestures that emphasize key words and phrases. It is from such gestures that the listener gains an impression of the speaker's vigor, enthusiasm, and sincerity. The gestures unconsciously direct his attention to those specific verbal elements of the message that are (to the speaker) most significant. Emphatic gestures are almost always timed to coincide with the emphasized syllable of the key word in the phrase or utterance. When a speaker's gestures are not so timed, we intuitively feel that he is insincere, ineffectual, or somehow emotionally disturbed.

The next time you are talking with someone who impresses you as unusually dynamic, unusually apathetic, or slightly peculiar, analyze his pattern of physical movement, including posture, directness, descriptive gestures, and expressive gestures. You will frequently find that many of the cues leading you to the impression that this is an unusual person come directly from his bodily movement, and from the way it relates to the content of his speech. You will also find that what you construe from what he says is conditioned by these elusive nonverbal cues.[6]

6. The student wishing to explore nonverbal behavior in greater depth is referred to *The Rhetoric of Nonverbal Communication* by Haig A. Bosmajian (Glenview, Ill.: Scott, Foresman and Company, 1971).

MESSAGE STRUCTURE

Just as a sentence has a syntax that describes the structural relations among its individual components, longer messages—speeches, lectures, essays, and magazine articles—display structural relations among their parts. It is possible to talk about this structure in three different ways: (1) the *relationships among ideas in the speech,* (2) the *order or sequence in which the elements are presented,* or (3) the conformation of the speech in terms of *standard organizational patterns.* All three approaches can help us to better understand the message.

Relationships Among Ideas Within the Speech

Even in speeches prepared by untrained speakers, the sentences are never merely isolated assertions. Usually some of them bear some kind of more or less logical relationship to one another, and in general the better the speech, the more consistent this logical relation will be. In almost any speech produced by a rational person, adjacent sentences will make some kind of connection with each other, and there will be loose connections across some of the larger segments of the speech. Sometimes the speaker may seem to wander off into irrelevancies, unexpectedly change subjects, and make many false starts and digressions. On the other hand, the sentences and larger parts of a well-made speech hang together in a fully consistent way. We are likely to attribute differences of this sort to the mentality of the speaker and/or to his knowledge of the subject on which he is speaking. This judgment is not altogether wrong; for, in general, bright and well-informed people produce much better structured messages than dull or ignorant ones. However, we should bear in mind that the immediate source of our impression is not the speaker, but the speech. What we notice when we make such judgments is the extent to which the ideas in the speech bear some recognizable relationship to each other.

"Some recognizable relationship" is a term that covers a lot of ground, for the variety of relationships among ideas is very large. In the classical theory of invention, a fairly long catalog of such relations was presented as a sort of check-list for orators in the preparation of speeches. By considering each of his main ideas in turn, and going through the list of standard relations, the speaker might discover many more ideas which could then be considered for inclusion in the speech. These relations were very general ones, such as cause, effect, example, similarity, difference, exception, and so on.

In any given speech, only some of them would be fully applicable; and in most instances, the standard relationships alone were not sufficient to analyze the topic in depth. Often, however, they did provide a fruitful starting point, and their use continued into the twentieth century. Their discontinuation as a standard resource of the educated speaker seems to have coincided with the proliferation of knowledge. As the number of special fields grew, the standard general relations accounted for less and less of what most speakers were called upon to say, so that a speaker who relied too heavily on them would appear shallow, trivial, and uninformed.

Clearly, there exists a multitude of ways in which ideas can relate to one another, and it would be useless to try to list them all. But readers and listeners readily respond to the presence or absence of such relations, and the speaker who fails to make the relations clear will present a speech that strikes the listener as disorganized, incoherent, and lacking in structure. Conversely, the speaker who fits everything he has to say into a clearly defined structure (that is, one in which the relations among the ideas are all clear and logical) will strike his listener not only as organized and coherent, but as more intelligent and informed as well.

Sequence of Elements Within the Speech

The structure of relationships among the ideas of a speech is most accurately thought of as a simultaneous arrangement in which none of the ideas can really be said to come before the others. However, in speech or writing, the ideas cannot be presented all at once; language being what it is, they will have to be proffered one at a time. For the speaker this introduces the problem of sequence: in what order should the ideas be presented? The sequence problem actually breaks down into two parts—coherence and emphasis.

Coherence. Coherence is effected by putting related ideas as close together as possible in the speech, and by using transitions, parallel forms, and other rhetorical devices to point up the relationships and to compensate for the occasional need to place related points at some distance from one another.

Suppose, for instance, that you are talking about how to keep your pet healthy and happy. You want to cover three points: diet, keeping the pet free from parasites, and exercise and play. To insure that the audience understands, you will list the three main points somewhere in the speech and clearly delineate them by using definite transitions. If you present the list in the introduction of the speech, before you have developed the points, it is called a "partition." If you present it in the conclusion of the speech, it is called a "summary." By using partition, transitions, and/or summary, you can be reasonably sure that your listeners will be able to understand the relationships among the ideas as you understand them yourself.

Emphasis. The emphasis problem is more difficult to solve: where in the speech should one place material that he wants to receive special attention from the audience? Two well-established psychological principles conflict in their application to this problem: the *primacy* principle states that whatever is presented first will have strongest impact and be best remembered; but the *recency* principle holds that the most recent (that is, the last) material will hit hardest and stick longest. There is research supporting both principles, so the choice is not a simple one.[7]

In fact, the safest conclusion at the present time is that both the first and the last parts of the speech are places of strong emphasis, and which of the two is more emphatic may depend on context. Some peculiarity of the topic, the audience, or the occasion may give the clue as to whether the natural point of emphasis is the beginning or the end of the speech. Successful speakers often try different arrangements of ideas (i.e., different sequences of points). By placing themselves in the shoes of what they imagine to be a typical auditor, they try to determine by intuition and trial and error which arrangement "works" best; that is, which results in the clearest understanding of the entire speech. When they try, most speakers find they can make surprisingly accurate predictions of audience response in this regard.

Conformation of the Speech to Standard Formats

Certain overall, general patterns of arrangement have proved to be so widely useful in message organization that they have been formulated in detail and are widely studied as standard formats. Examples of such standard formats are *time sequence, spatial order, problem-solution sequence, cause-effect order,* and the like. Most textbooks on composition and speech making list several such standard formulas.

Standard formats can be applied not only to the speech as a whole, but to its parts at different levels. For example, in discussing

7. See Wayne Thompson, *Quantitative Research in Public Address and Communication* (New York: Random House, Inc., 1967), 68–70.

the plant and animal life on a mountain, one could arrange the main points in a spatial order, beginning with the foothills and proceeding to the highest peaks. But within the main points (that is, at each altitude level) the flora and fauna could be discussed in chronological order—that is, the speaker could talk about changes in plant and animal life through the four seasons of the year. Or, the main points could be the four seasons, with each season developed in terms of plant and animal life at the various altitudes.

One reason why standard formats are so useful in speech organization is that they reflect very general relationships among ideas of a sort that most of us use almost daily. Consequently, listeners recognize them immediately, and they present no problems of understanding for the average listener. The speaker who uses a standard format can be almost certain that many of his listeners will grasp the overall structure of his ideas without difficulty.

MESSAGE EFFECTS

People respond to communication in a remarkable variety of ways. In fact, it is probably safe to say that any response an individual can make could, under the proper circumstances, be produced by communication. Of course, such responses are never the sole and direct result of any single factor; they always result from the interaction among the speaker, the message, the occasion, and the listener himself. Because we tend to take the characteristics of the speaker, the audience, and the occasion for granted, it is natural for us to assign the results of communication rather directly to the message. We say that the message produced such and such an effect. If we recognize this terminology as a shorthand expression, it can serve as a useful guide to thinking; for it is true that, other things constant, different messages and different versions of the same message produce strikingly different results.

The kinds of message effects that have been most intensively studied are those which have the greatest and most obvious practical significance in the workaday world: *interest-attention, information gain, attitude change,* and *overt behavioral modification.*

Interest-Attention

For centuries men have sought the secret of arousing the interest and directing the attention of their fellow men, and still the problem remains almost as elusive as it was in the beginning. We know that we cannot hope to inform, persuade, or to move to action without first capturing and holding attention. We know also that there are certain characteristics of messages that will usually improve interest and increase attention. We know that change and contrast arouse interest, that well-organized messages hold attention better than poorly organized ones, that, within limits, emotional intensity of any kind commands attention, and that conflict arouses interest. The evidence for these conclusions arises from studies in which messages having these characteristics were compared with messages lacking them.[8] However, such studies tell us little about how to incorporate these interest- and attention-arousing materials into our speeches. It is one thing to say that a beautiful girl will attract more suitors than a plain one; it is quite another matter for a girl to know how to make herself more attractive. To understand the principle is something akin to science, but to apply it effectively is an art. So it is with messages: we can describe some of the properties that make them interesting; but such information is only of indirect use to the speech maker, who still must create the desired properties out of words.

Information Gain

Information gain is a complex matter, and we will deal with it in more detail in a later chapter on communication outcomes. But the most common way of assessing information gained from a speech is to use some sort of "objective" test to measure the number of discrete items of information that the listener "gained." What are the characteristics of messages that improve informativeness in this sense? Surprisingly, information gain seems to vary little with the properties of the message, unless it departs from accepted practice to a very considerable degree. In the sense of imparting isolated bits of knowledge, a well-organized speech accomplishes only a little more than a poorly organized speech, unless the disorganization extends all the way down to the sentence level.[9] Speaking slowly and clearly conveys no more information of this type than speaking rapidly or mumbling, unless these faults are so exaggerated as to impair the intelligibility of individual words. Contrary to popular belief, the use of visual aids contributes little to the learning of isolated bits of information, unless the information is of an inherently graphic na-

8. For summaries of these research studies, see Wayne N. Thompson, *Quantitative Research in Public Address and Communication* (New York: Random House, 1967).
9. See Ernest Thompson, "Does Organization Really Make a Difference?" *Register*, VIII (Spring, 1960): 12–16.

ture (such as visual identification of aircraft, electronic circuit diagrams, etc.). Techniques of verbal emphasis, such as repetition or pointing up by notifying the audience that a certain piece of information is especially important, do have an effect; but it is different from what is usually supposed. Such methods do not increase overall information gain; they do more or less guarantee that most listeners will gain the item of information so emphasized; but this gain is almost always offset by losses elsewhere, so that the net gain of information is fairly constant. The gain of isolated bits of information seems to depend very much more on listeners and circumstances than it does on properties of the speech, except in extreme cases.

Attitude Change

A third effect often attributed to messages is attitude change. Unlike information gain, attitude change appears to be very sensitive to the properties in the speech. To begin with, almost any message will produce some apparent change in audience attitude. We will see later that this appearance may be deceiving, but there is no doubt that people express different attitudes after hearing a persuasive speech than they expressed before it. Interesting speeches change attitude more often than dull speeches. Both positive (reward) and negative (threat) emotional appeals tend to increase the effectiveness of a persuasive speech. Improving the organization of a speech seems to have little effect on immediate attitude change, but the incorporation of "evidence" for assertions does improve the power of the speech to produce attitude change. The interpretation that should be placed on these particular message effects will be discussed in greater detail in the next chapter.

Overt Behavioral Modification

Finally, messages may affect the overt behavior of listeners. Sometimes, of course, the real factor influencing behavior is not the message but some other aspect of the situation, an aspect to which the message merely calls attention. One example is a shout of "fire," which will either cause people to flock around out of curiosity, or disperse to avoid harm. In this case the "persuasive" attributes of the message are trivial, behavior being controlled in fact by a single compelling attribute of the listener's situation. The same is true of a request from some individual or group who has a strong claim on one's loyalty. If my friend asks me to drive him home after work, I will probably comply not because of the persuasiveness of his request, but because of my friendship for him.

In the final analysis, of course, *all* behavior change following communication may be attributed to some factor or factors external to the message. Even the most persuasively composed speech will base its appeals on factors in the listeners' environment: you should stop smoking because it is bad for your health (not because this speech asks you to); you should contribute to the United Fund because the poor and unfortunate need your help; you should buy diet cola because it will make you more attractive. But the difference is one of degree. In cases like the shout of "fire" and my friend's request to take him home, the qualities of the message are relatively unimportant, and my response is more or less automatic once I know what is being said. Even in these two simple instances, however, proofs and support are required. Thus, the closer the desired response to an automatic one, the shorter the message required to elicit the desired behavior and the more nearly certain the listener's response. The more remote the desired response from a habitual or automatic one, the more detail the message calls for, and the greater the persuasive art and effort required to assure an appropriate response.

These four kinds of message effect—interest-attention, information gain, attitude change, and behavioral modification—will all be discussed in the next chapter as major types of communication outcome. Our objective in introducing them briefly here has been to call attention to the fact that these are effects that are very frequently traced to the particular characteristics of the message itself. Moreover, a great deal of thought has been given to the best ways to construct messages so as to produce just these effects. We have observed that the assumption that these outcomes can be produced by message variations alone is very dubious. More than any of the other outcomes, interest-attention seems to be a message effect. It appears that substantial persuasive effects can be traced to messages. Information gain is more dubious, since message variations (short of extreme shortcomings) produce only a little difference in the amount of information gained by listeners. Behavioral modification is frequently seen to be the result not of message characteristics, but of salient features in the situation to which the message happens to call attention. These matters will be taken up in fuller detail and in a broader context in the next chapter.

Messages may be considered from three very different points of view: the message sent, the message received, and the message observed by someone not a direct participant in the communication. The "outside observer" is presumably an "objective" analyst, and his viewpoint has produced much useful information about communication. Some of this is taught to communication participants so that they may improve their own communication by occasionally viewing it from an objective viewpoint.

Message "content" is a variable concept, depending on whether the analyst of content is interested in the linguistic, the ideational, or the implicational level of analysis. Content exists at all three levels, but it is analyzed in radically different ways and is useful for very different purposes.

Message organization conveys some of the meaning of the message. It is usually represented by an outline with divisions and subdivisions reflecting the subordination of ideas in the message. Most often when people talk about content, it is this level of content to which they refer.

Generally, nonverbal communication seems most effective in the transmission of emotions, attitudes, and feelings. But it includes gestures, which can be descriptive as well as expressive.

Structure contributes to clarity and effectiveness of messages. Overall structure is concerned with relations among ideas, and involves the problem of sequencing message elements. Standard formats such as time order, space order, and the like, simplify the organizational problem when they are applicable.

The four kinds of message effects most often thought of are interest-attention, information gain, attitude change, and behavioral modification. These have been discussed in this chapter briefly, with special reference to their relationships to message elements; they are to be discussed in the next chapter as general outcomes of communication.

PROBLEMS AND QUESTIONS FOR DISCUSSION

1. From *The Speaker's Resource Book* by Carroll C. Arnold, Douglas Ehninger, and John C. Gerber (Glenview, Ill.: Scott, Foresman and Company, 1966), select a speech on a topic that interests you. Read the speech and answer the following questions:
    a. Prepare for the speech as thorough an outline as you can. Does the speech fit well into outline form?

b. Does the speaker use any transitional devices to signal movement from one topic to another, or to point up relations between ideas?

c. From the speaker's language alone, can you deduce his attitude toward any of the topics he discusses? List the words that in your judgment reflect his attitude most accurately. (Do you think this attitude would have been projected to the average listener hearing the speech?)

d. What are the principal relations between ideas in the speech? (Does the speaker use a standard format for the whole speech or for any of the points?) Are these relations unique to the subject matter, or are they "general" relations that might be applied to other topics?

2. Watch two people talking together in the cafeteria or some other public place. (Observe physical behavior only, from out of earshot.)

a. What feelings toward each other are reflected in their nonverbal behavior?

b. Can you deduce the status relationship between the two? (If so, what cues did you use?)

c. What moods did each participant express? (Again, what cues did you use in making this judgment?)

d. What expressive and descriptive gestures did each use? Could you guess *what* they were talking about?

3. Cite an example of a communication event in which message sent, message received, and message observed were all different.

4. Apply the linguistic, the ideational, and the implicational levels of analysis to some recent messages in one of your classes. Compare your analyses with those of several other students in the class. Was agreement among your classmates greater for some of the levels of analysis than for others?

8.

SOCIAL INTERACTION

In discussing language, speech production, speech reception, and messages, we have often referred to both the communication source and the communication receiver. However, for the most part we have until now considered them as separate entities. We have concentrated first on the problems of the speaker, then on the problems of the listener, but always individually. Now it is time to put the two together.

In this chapter, we will consider speaker and listener as co-participants in the communication process. By this we mean two things: first, we will focus our attention on properties and actions that concern not so much the individual participants as the relationships between participants. Without losing sight of the individual, we will nevertheless try to see him in light of communication patterns involving one or more other people. Second, we will take account of the fact that in almost all normal communication, no one participant is exclusively a sender or a receiver. As a bare minimum, participants in extended communication exchange roles from time to time; and frequently communicants serve simultaneously as both senders and receivers of messages.

The main point of departure for this discussion will be the two-person communication group, because in these *dyads,* as they are called, the basic processes and relations are most clearly evidenced. However, because the principles we see at work in a dyad can often be generalized to larger groups, we will from time to time extend these principles into communication situations involving more than two people.

In this chapter we deal with five levels of social interaction: alternating monologue, stimulus-response interaction, interaction with feedback, interaction with feedback and feedforward, and interaction with empathy. We will also consider interpersonal roles and games.

ALTERNATING MONOLOGUE

The simplest—and in many ways the least productive—form of social interaction is the alternating monologue. In this pattern of communication, each participant is aware of the presence of the other and superficially addresses remarks to him, but cares little or nothing about the other's response and gives at best sporadic attention to the content of the other's remarks. Consider the following sample exchange:

HE: It's a great day, isn't it?

SHE: It certainly is. I passed my French exam and haven't got a bit of homework to do until Monday.

HE: I don't know when I've seen such tremendous weather this time of year.

SHE: You know, it sometimes seems the faculty deliberately waits till Friday to give you a big assignment, just so you'll have plenty to keep you busy over the weekend. But not this week.

HE: Usually it rains this time of year. Especially on the weekends when you'd like to get out and do something.

SHE: Well, I've got a whole weekend that's all mine. Just think of it, not a single assignment! It's the first time that's happened all year.

HE: Yeah. Come to think of it, this is a lot like northern California weather—you know, warm sunshine but cool breezes. If this weather holds out, it's going to be a great weekend.

SHE: It sure is going to be a great weekend.

HE: No doubt about it.

It is clear that these two people are off in different worlds. True, their verbal interchange has many of the properties of social interaction: each waits for the other to finish before initiating his own remarks; for part of the conversation the message content has some superficial common ground, since both refer briefly to the forthcoming weekend; twice during the conversation—at the beginning and again at the end—there is tacit recognition of something the other said; and the conversation ends on a note of superficial agreement. But there the similarity to productive interchange ends. Far from coming to any meeting of the minds, these two people start from different premises, and at the end of the conversation they are still worlds apart. They have talked *at* one another rather than *to* one another. Not only has each failed to respond to the other's remarks, but neither seems to care very much about the responses of the other. It is almost as if each were in a private reverie, speaking his thoughts aloud but insulated from the thoughts of the other. Each has celebrated his own euphoria without influencing or being influenced by the other. Their dialogue represents speech communication in its most severely limited form.

In the foregoing example, the human contact is almost minimal; but an alert listener will find even more extreme examples of alternating monologue in the daily conversations of people around him. The phenomenon occurs whenever each participant in an interaction is too preoccupied with personal concerns to open up to the other. Because we are all preoccupied some of the time, such interchanges would occur much more often than they do, were it not for the fact that we can all recognize the symptoms of preoccupation in others and either fall in with the other's mood or terminate the interaction. But when chance brings two preoccupied people together, the alternating monologue results.

Some people, of course, are so habitually tied up in their own concerns as to be in effect a walking invitation to the alternating monologue. Such persons make very unsatisfactory conversational partners and even poorer committee members. When such a person makes a public talk, the speaking situation becomes a kind of alternating monologue on a large scale. Because he anticipates no response from his audience and is oblivious to its reactions, the speaker drones on while the audience privately retires to its own thoughts.

STIMULUS-RESPONSE INTERACTION

From the alternating monologue, a step up on the interaction ladder brings us to stimulus-response interaction. In this pattern of communication, at least one of the participants is trying to manipulate the behavior (responses) of the other by stimulating him with appropriate messages. The "manipulator" is interested in the behavior of his interaction partner only to the extent that he is able to observe whether his message had its intended effects.

We all rely on such stimulus-response interaction to a marked extent in our daily lives. In the simplest case, we ask someone else to perform some small task for us: to close the door, pass the salt, give us a specific bit of information, or supply some other simple need. In such cases the interaction may be limited to a request, followed by behavior, followed by a "thank you."

Extensions of Stimulus-Response Interaction

A more extended example is the case of the "structured" interview in which the interviewer asks a preformulated list of questions and records the answers as they are given. Each question is a stimulus, and each answer a response. Both participants understand that the interviewer will serve as "stimulator" and the interviewee as "responder." The interviewer in a structured interview will generally pay attention to the responses of the interviewee, but only to the extent of making sure that he has a satisfactory answer to each question before proceeding to the next. His interrogative behavior is very similar from one interview to another; that is, in his own behavior he makes almost no adjustment that depends on the responses of the interviewee.

A still more extended example is the "indoctrination" type of lecture or informative speech in which the lecturer is imparting information to auditors who will be expected to display their retention of the information through some future behavior. They may be expected to pass a written test covering the material, or perform some nonverbal task such as adjusting a carburetor or calculating a square root. The speaker's object is to elicit the desired response through administration of an appropriate stimulus. In the typical indoctrination lecture the speaker is concerned only that the auditor display attention during the lecture, and retention when tested afterwards. No further information regarding the listener's reaction is necessary. Quality control is maintained in an operation of this type by carefully selecting listeners for adequate preparation and motivation, then flunking, "washing out," or transferring those who fail to acquire the desired information or behavior. That is, the effectiveness of the message is assured not by adapting it to individual differences in listeners, but by selecting as listeners those who display the appropriate response to the chosen stimulus. When a large number of people are to be "taught" some basic skill, and when learners can be selected from a very large group of candidates, this stimulus-response approach is an efficient method. It does not work well when all, or virtually all, members of a particular population or group must be taught the same thing. Under those circumstances, the method must be fitted to the learner, not the learner to the method.

Relativity of Stimulus and Response

From the foregoing examples it may seem that in the stimulus-response interaction pattern, one of the participants manipulates the behavior of the other. This is not quite true. In the stimulus-response pattern at least *one* of the participants manipulates the behavior of the other, but in some cases each participant is both manipulating and manipulated, and each message in the interchange is both stimulus and response. Consider the following message exchange:

SUE: Hello, Jack. (*Message #1*)
JACK: Hi, Sue. How are you? (*Message #2*)
SUE: Great. How are you? (*Message #3*)
JACK: Fine, thanks. (*Message #4*)

Now, to first appearances, Message #1 is a stimulus, and it may be so considered. But what if Jack, before anything was said, had just caught Sue's eye and waved to her? Then we would have to consider Sue's first remark a response, wouldn't we—a response to Jack's nonverbal message? The same behavior on Sue's part would thus be considered both stimulus and response: a response if we consider the behavior from Sue's point of view, since it was something she did; but a stimulus from Jack's point of view, since for him it represents an incoming message to which he will respond.

Jack's Message #2 is also stimulus and response—response from Jack's point of view, a stimulus to Sue. Message #3 is also both stimulus and response, and it is only when we come to Message #4 that we have an unambiguous response (though it is possible that even this message might trigger further response in Sue). Now, the variety of forms that interchanges along the above lines can take is quite limited. For the most part, once begun, such a sequence runs off in a predictable way. Both participants are thus more or less locked into a pattern of stimulus and response. The pattern is to wait for the stimulus, emit an appropriate response, wait for another stimulus, and so on until some terminal behavior is reached.

Practical Applications of Stimulus-Response Interaction

Such exchanges are noncreative in the extreme, but they do serve a purpose. In a situation where social contact cannot be avoided, they allow people to interact with one another without spending much energy or becoming really involved. When meeting strangers for the first time we may use the stimulus-response pattern as a way of stalling for time while we make an initial estimate of the other. And even for good friends such patterns provide a period of transition from non-interaction to interaction on any specific occasion, a transitional period during which we can put out our antennae, so to speak, to size up our friend's mood and frame of mind. Because the interaction in one of these standardized stimulus-response patterns does not occur at a very deep level, it is safe; and since little attention need be paid to the content of the message, it buys time for making interpersonal judgments against which the remainder of the interchange (if any) will be conducted.

The stimulus-response pattern is natural wherever the nature of the interaction between people is highly routine; for when we know exactly what we want from another, and where the nature of our relation is such that we can assume some willingness to give it, the stimulus-response pattern is the most efficient form of communication. We do not expect to experience an in-depth relationship with the customs inspector, the clerk who sells us an auto license, or the student assistant who issues us a class card for our freshman English course. Though such interactions can be managed pleasantly— even charmingly—the basis for our interaction in these routine situations is the need to give and obtain very specific information so as to achieve specific and limited goals. In these situations we expect others to know what questions to ask and to have straightforward answers for our questions so as to transact the relevant business with a minimum of wear and tear on all concerned. Such contacts need not be dehumanized, and life would be more pleasant if more of us knew how to manage these situations more humanely, but the person who treats all such contacts as the occasion for creative personal contact will experience—and cause—considerable frustration.

Frustration can arise, too, when one of the participants in an interaction regards it as a routine stimulus-response situation, while the other persists in treating it as an occasion for closer interpersonal contact. At the time of this writing, shopping for an automobile or a house frequently leads to this kind of misunderstanding. The buyer almost always wants to treat his interaction with the auto or real estate salesman as a routine affair. He wants to shop around, get as much information as possible about the available alternatives, and accomplish this information-gathering as quickly and painlessly as possible.

Some salesmen will cooperate, but many insist on making a highly personal affair of it. Some—because they are naturally extremely gregarious, others because they have studied "salesmanship"

—pitch the discussion on a personal level from the beginning. They try to establish a relationship with the client that will make it all but impossible for him to buy from anybody else. The effort takes many forms, including such nonverbal cues as the friendly smile, the warm handclasp, moving in close to an "intimate" distance to talk, the confidential tone, and so on. Then there are the verbal approaches, such as the inquiry about family, job, and hobbies, which may lead to common acquaintances or interests, the sharing of trade secrets or inside information, and the offer of friendly advice. Such tactics are probably successful often enough to reinforce their perpetrators; otherwise they would not be continued; but to the client with three more agencies to visit and time running short, the discrepancy between desired and observed behavior can be irritating. Probably the most successful salesmen are sensitive to the signs of discontent and can switch "styles" when the need arises. This leads us to the concept of feedback, which is the topic we will take up next.

INTERACTION WITH FEEDBACK

Whenever a speaker alters his speaking behavior by adapting in some way to response from his listener, he may be said to be responding to feedback. Neither the foregoing statement nor the process to which it refers is nearly as simple as it seems, but the feedback function is so important in human communication that it is worth taking time to understand it.

The term *feedback* comes from cybernetics, the branch of engineering science dealing with control systems.[1] Such systems control operations by using information about effects. The now-classic example of a simple cybernetic system is the thermostat on a furnace. When the temperature in a room drops below a minimal level, the thermostat closes a switch, sending a signal that turns on the furnace. The thermostat continuously monitors the room temperature; and when it reaches the desired maximum, the thermostat opens the switch, sending a signal that turns the furnace off. Engineers would refer to the signal that turns the furnace off as "negative feedback": it causes the furnace to discontinue what it has been doing. Positive feedback has no place in a thermostat system because furnaces burn at a more or less constant temperature, and the effect of positive feedback would be to cause the furnace to burn hotter and hotter. In both cases, information about the effects of the operation (in this

1. See Norbert Wiener, *Cybernetics* (Cambridge, Mass.: The M.I.T. Press, 1948).

case, the effect upon room temperature of the firing of the furnace) is used to control the operation (turning it off or causing it to burn hotter). Positive feedback says, in effect, "Do even more of the same," while negative feedback says, "Stop what you have been doing."

Positive and Negative Feedback

Because people use information about the effects of their communication in controlling how they communicate, it is natural to extend the concept of feedback into human interaction. If, for example, one's initial greeting to a stranger meets with a pleasant response, one is likely to continue the conversation, often with a more extended message than the first. This is positive feedback at work. However, if the first message meets with indifference or grouchiness, one is likely to terminate the conversation at that point: here we see the operation of negative feedback. Now, because the words "positive" and "negative" have—in addition to their technical meanings in cybernetics—evaluative meanings for people, it is easy to confuse the two when talking about feedback. In the above example it is not the pleasantness of the listener's response that makes it positive feedback nor the aversiveness of his response that makes it negative feedback. It is simply a question of whether his response causes an increase or a decrease in some aspect of the speaker's behavior. In this case, the question is whether it causes the speaker to enlarge the conversation or terminate it.

As a matter of fact, favorable responses from the listener often signify negative feedback, and unfavorable responses may signify positive feedback. If I am explaining something to you and observe nonverbal cues that tell me you don't understand what I am saying, your response may be characterized as negative; but the feedback it gives to me is positive if it causes me to repeat or enlarge my explanation. On the other hand, if you show that you understand, your response can be said to be positive; but its effect on my behavior will be negative feedback if it signals that I should stop explaining.

Variable Influence of Feedback

From this, it should be clear that the term *feedback* refers not to any catalog of listener behavior, but to a *relationship* between the behavior of the speaker, the response of the listener, and the effect of that response on the further behavior of the speaker. Thus, a response of the listener is not feedback if it has no effect on the speaker's subsequent behavior. I may shake my head, frown, even speak out in an effort to generate feedback signals that will influence your communication behavior to me; but if you fail to note my response, or—noting it—refuse to adapt your message in light of it, then my behavior is not feedback. In a sense, then, we may say that feedback, in order to *be* feedback, must be *used as* feedback.

Just as no listener behavior can automatically be classified as feedback if it does not influence the behavior of the speaker, there is no behavior that cannot serve as feedback if it does influence the further behavior of the speaker. In particular, we need to bear in mind that feedback messages need not be transmitted *deliberately* or consciously by the listener. Indeed, most people seeing a film or videotape of their listening behavior in a group discussion or an audience are appalled at the transparency of their reactions. They thought they were sitting in poker-faced inscrutability, but the tape shows many reactions that can be read clearly by an alert observer. They did not intentionally transmit feedback messages to the speaker, but those messages were there to be used as feedback if the speaker was willing and able to perceive and respond to them.

Using Feedback to Enrich Interaction

To introduce possibilities for feedback into human interaction is to enrich the quality of human contact enormously; for now each partner in the interaction can not only influence and be influenced by the other, but the behavior of each will be conditioned by the behavior of the other. In the alternating monologue we see two people talking in one another's presence. In the stimulus-response interaction pattern, at least one of the people is responding to what the other says. In interaction with feedback, the further behavior of the speaker is conditional upon the nature of the listener's response.

We should note that in order to make use of feedback, the speaker must retain some flexibility in his own behavior. At any given moment several options must be open to him; otherwise, the listener's response cannot influence his behavior, and thus cannot serve as feedback. For example, the public speaker who has written out a manuscript and attempts to present it orally is able to make very limited use of feedback from his audience. He can observe their reactions and adjust features of his delivery to comfortable levels by speaking loudly enough and at a rate that is comfortable for them to listen to. He can pause for laughs, applause, or jeers; he can repeat a passage that did not seem to sink in. But beyond these relatively mechanical matters he cannot adjust without scrapping or ignoring the manuscript. Sometimes it is more important to be precise than to be flexible, and then a manuscript is useful. Most people, however, do not learn how to interact with an audience until they give up the practice of reading speeches from prepared texts.

INTERACTION WITH FEEDBACK AND FEEDFORWARD

Feedback, as we have seen, is the process whereby a system modifies its operations so as to adjust to the known consequences of those operations. In the case of human communication, this refers to the process of adjusting one's communication behavior so as to take account of the observed influence of that behavior on the listener. But how does the speaker know what behaviors to use as feedback from his interaction partner, and how does he decide what alternatives to follow in the event of a particular listener response?

Some feedback adjustments amount to automatic social habits, such as adjusting one's loudness level when the listener displays signs of difficulty in hearing, or asking him a question when he seems bored. But other adjustments seem to result not from habit but from forethought. It is as if the speaker had anticipated certain listener behaviors at specific points in the interaction, and had laid out alternative courses of action depending on whether the expected reactions occurred or not. The setting up of such expectancies and contingencies is called *feedforward.*

Like feedback, feedforward is a term that originated in cybernetic theory. In the same sense that the operation of a thermostat is the simplest example of feedback, setting the thermostat is the simplest example of feedforward. By setting the thermostat to a desired temperature range, the operator may be said to "feed forward" the maximum and/or minimum temperature to the point in the heat cycle where these temperature values will be needed. A more interesting and representative example of feedforward would be an attachment to keep track of both the inside and the outside temperature and to pour into a storage tank ahead of time just the amount of fuel needed to bring the temperature back into the desired range. Such a device could be said to "anticipate" fuel needs. Although there are many significant differences between thermostats and human beings, there are also some intriguing analogies which, if not taken too literally, provide insights into the ways in which we as human beings react and interact.

In human interaction, feedforward most often takes one of three forms: (1) *goal-setting,* (2) *establishing expectancies,* and (3) *planning contingencies.*

Goal-Setting

In some ways, setting a specific goal that we hope to achieve with a listener operates much like feedforward: when that goal is reached, our goal-seeking behavior will cease. If the goal is vague or ill-defined, our behavior will be as unreliable as a furnace without a thermostat, and somebody else will have to turn us off. If we are not sensitive to potential feedback signals that tell us the goal has been reached, we will operate like a furnace whose control circuit from the thermostat has been broken.

We should also note that goals are often revised during interaction, and such revision also qualifies as feedforward. Suppose, for example, that you are trying to sell a subscription to the college humor magazine to a student you have just met, and in the process you discover that he seems to know a good deal about magazine writing and publishing. You may now decide that you want more from him than a subscription. If, for example, you now want him to donate some time to the magazine, you will have fed forward a revised goal into the continuing interaction.

Establishing Expectancies

Marshall McLuhan,[2] along with many contemporary psychologists, would argue that except for the simplest reflex behaviors, human beings seldom communicate without some kind of expectancy. This form of feedforward may occur at many levels, from the linguistic to the social. You will recall, for example, that in the chapter on hearing (pages 65–81) we said that one of the most reasonable theories of language decoding (speech recognition) holds that we use a few clues to "synthesize" or "generate" a best guess as to what the speaker is saying, then check that guess against what we can hear of the utterance. The synthesis of the "best guess" is a kind of feedforward. If we are led to synthesize an estimate of what the speaker will say before he says it, then the synthesis represents the kind of feedforward we call *expectancy.*

As we move from the linguistic to the interactional level, we can find still more examples of feedforward. The "canned" sales pitch is

2. Marshall McLuhan, *Understanding Media: The Extensions of Man* (New York: McGraw-Hill Book Company, 1964).

a study in feedforward. Far from being the rigid "speech outlines" that they once were, such interaction plans are now adapted to a variety of listeners, moods, and circumstances. The planner who organizes the pitch will try to anticipate points in the presentation where a listener will ask questions or raise objections, and at each such point will construct appropriate answers. Thus, anticipation of the questions has been fed forward into the interaction plan.

Not all anticipatory feedforward is the result of preplanning. Indeed, much of it arises during the course of interaction with others. For example, suppose that your hobby is shortwave radio. In talking to me you discover very early in the conversation that I know none of the technical terminology. You may very well feed forward the anticipation that I would think it foolish of you to spend so much time and money on the hobby; for unless I know at least some of the terminology, I am not likely to have experienced the satisfactions arising from operating an amateur station, and I certainly will not have dreamed of the amount of money involved. Having encountered such novices in the past, you may predict that I would be amazed to find out how much your hobby costs. Consequently, you will be anticipating this response and will be either marshalling your arguments in defense of such spending or planning ways to dodge the issue.

Whenever anybody says something to us or reacts to something we have said to him in such a way as to increase our awareness of his attitudes or predispositions, we are likely to feed forward new anticipations regarding that person. Since new insights into others happen frequently in interaction, this type of feedforward is a very common occurrence.

Of course, the fact that such feedforward is common is no guarantee of its accuracy or dependability. In the foregoing example, for instance, your prediction about my reaction might be entirely wrong. By avoiding further conversation about a topic you think might become embarrassing, you may deprive both of us of a satisfying encounter. Or, if you were in a more aggressive mood, you might increase the likelihood of an interpersonal crisis between us. By anticipating negative reactions, you might behave in such a way as to increase the likelihood of obtaining one. Thus, you might perversely exaggerate the amount of time and money you spent on your ham station. To such exaggeration I might respond with genuine surprise, which you might interpret as mild disapproval, which might lead you to become defensive, which I might interpret as belligerence, which might lead me to respond coolly, which you might interpret as an escalation of the hostilities, and so on to an interpersonal breakdown—all of which started with your anticipating a negative response. This behavior leads to paranoia, which can be characterized as a condition of distorted feedforward.

Contingency Planning

In an earlier example, we said that the prepared sales talk is a study in feedforward, and illustrated it with examples of anticipating the customer's questions and objections. A still more sophisticated approach to the prepared sales talk involves contingency planning. The person organizing the talk may go further than anticipating questions or objections from the customer; the sales strategist may, in fact, introduce questions into the talk that demand the customer give some response. By anticipating the different possible responses at each of these points in the talk, the sales person may plan a highly flexible program of information and persuasion capable of being adapted to a very great variety of different customers. The essence of such a plan is the feedforward of contingencies to the crucial choice-points in the discussion, and the preparation of appropriate plans for meeting each imagined contingency. Most experienced salesmen have in effect programed themselves to such a contingency plan. Through long experience of success and failure in marketing a particular product, they have come to know the critical choice-points in a sales interaction, and have developed appropriate means of dealing with each.

Just as goals may be revised and expectancies changed during interaction, so may contingency plans arise or be modified during the course of interaction. Perhaps the most primitive, everyday example is the desperate thought: "If he says that again, I'm going to let him have it." This is a simple contingency plan arising during the course of interaction. More constructive examples occur also:

"If she smiles, I'll ask her to the game."

"If he likes the IBM deal, I'll show him the entire portfolio; otherwise, I'll switch to the chemical stocks."

"If he seems friendly, I'll ask him to join today."

"The question of salary is bound to come up sooner or later. If he mentions a specific figure below twelve thousand, we'll agree to it immediately; but if he asks what we're offering, we'll mention ten thousand."

"We escalate our demands until the president can no longer say 'yes.' Then, if he says 'no,' we occupy the administration building; if he refers it to the faculty senate, we move in and take over the senate meeting. Charlie, you start to work on the speeches and signs for the ad-building bash; Annette, you get the stuff ready for the senate."

"By this point, they ought to have a pretty good idea of what I'm talking about. If they seem to understand, I'll drop out the third example."

All of the foregoing are examples of feedforward of the type we call contingency planning. An ability to develop and execute plans of this sort is a necessary skill in effective social interaction, and most people develop at least some of this ability at an early age. It is obvious that the more one knows about people in general, about his listener in particular, and about the topic under discussion, the more effective can be his planning in this regard.

We have seen three kinds of feedforward in social interaction: (1) goal setting, (2) expectancy, and (3) contingency planning. It should have occurred to you that these three levels of feedforward are not in fact strictly separable from each other. Where one leaves off and the other begins is often difficult to determine. But together the three terms describe a continuum of feedforward activities that clearly play a vital role in human communication. Without feedforward, feedback would be a static and sterile affair; and without flexible feedback, interaction could scarcely be human.

INTERACTION WITH EMPATHY

As we have moved from the alternating monologue through stimulus-response interaction, interaction with feedback, and interaction with feedback and feedforward, we have witnessed a gradual increase in both the depth of the relationship between interaction partners and the amount of information about his listener used by the speaker. In the alternating monologue the relationship between interaction partners is all but nonexistent, and the speaker uses almost none of the available information about his listener; in the interaction pattern with feedforward and feedback, the relationship is much closer, and the speaker spends much effort not only in using relevant information about his listener, but also in actively constructing such information. One last step up the interaction ladder brings us to a pattern that differs from the preceding one not so much in kind as in degree. We shall call the pattern "Interaction with Empathy."

What Is Empathy?

The term "empathy" has a long history in both art and psychology, and has been used with many meanings. One thing all of these meanings have in common, however, is the notion of a "feeling for" —a special understanding of—some person or thing. For example, once you have fished with a fly rod you can experience a very special sensation as you watch another fisherman casting and retrieving. In a way, that special feeling involves an enhanced appreciation for what the other is doing; but it goes beyond that. With only a little additional effort, you can almost feel the rod in your own hands and the line running between your own fingers, can see the low-hanging branch as an obstacle just as the fisherman does, and can view a little patch of clear water between two lily pads as the attractive but difficult target for fly or spinner, just as the fisherman sees it. This special feeling that approaches *identification with the acts, sensations, thoughts, and feelings of another is empathy.*

To the scientifically inclined, the foregoing will sound very mystical and superstitious; and indeed the language describes the feeling of the empathizer more than the process of empathy. Yet empathy is so much a part of our everyday lives that most of us recognize the experience as a familiar one. On the football field the runner is hit hard from two directions at once; and the crowd, empathizing with the ball-carrier, groans. We pause to watch children play, and we feel younger and more lighthearted ourselves. Empathy is one of the reasons some people enjoy getting drunk together and others can't tolerate the sight of an intoxicated person. It is also one major reason people who understand us well are most persuasive in their influence on us. This is not solely because we hold them in higher regard, but also because they understand more fully the turns and complexities of our reactions as they talk to us.

At the time of this writing, research methods have not been developed to deal with complex relations of the type outlined above. *Empathy* in research literature, therefore, refers to the ability of one person to predict the responses of another. For example, I might be asked to answer some opinion questions about the use of insecticides, and you might then be asked to answer the same questions as you anticipate or predict that *I* would answer them. The degree of correspondence between my answers and your prediction of my answers would be said to measure your empathy with me on that issue. About the only advantage of this definition of empathy is that it is clear-cut. In fact, what these operations measure is at most the result or outcome of empathy, and not always that. In fact, one might learn to make predictions about another person without ever experiencing any empathy in the sense described above. In any case, the current research definition of the term ignores both the process and the experience involved.

Empathy and Communication

Now, if we apply the concept of empathy to interpersonal inter-action, what do we have? To refer to another analogy to fishing, it is somewhat as though one could be both fisherman and fish at the same time, or—at least, while being fisherman—could see the situa-tion developing from the fish's viewpoint. If I empathize as I am talk-ing with you, I will do something more than anticipate how you will react to what I am about to say, something more than correctly in-terpret your reactions in terms of my purpose and intent. I will go beyond these superficial aspects to see things through *your* eyes, in-terpret them through *your* meanings and values, and vicariously ex-perience *your* reactions. And I will do all of this while encoding my message to you. I will generate feedforward and will interpret feed-back so rapidly and continuously that the qualitative nature of the experience will be entirely different from any other form of inter-action, even though the elementary constituents of the process are not fundamentally different from other interaction patterns.

Love and love making (as opposed to mere sexual experience) involve empathy, which is why we sometimes hear the clever ob-servation that a certain speaker plays upon an audience as though he were making love to it. Clearly it is not the "love" aspect that dominates this analogy, but the empathic process that underlies all really close interaction ranging from love making to charismatic oratory. Of course, in referring to such dramatic examples as these, we risk creating the impression that empathy occurs only in rare moments of high emotion, whereas in fact it occurs fairly often and need not be accompanied by a high state of arousal.

Some Limitations on the Use of Empathy

We also risk leaving the impression that empathy is always to be desired, the impression that once one has experienced it, he will find it so reinforcing that he will seek to establish it in all relation-ships with others. Nothing could be further from the truth. As we pointed out earlier, on page 120, we do not want a deep interpersonal experience with everyone we meet. Not only is empathy a deeply involving experience requiring some effort and the suspension of other thoughts and activities, but it also involves some measure of risk as well. To empathize with another requires that we see things from his point of view; and if the situation is such that we are unable to act in accord with that viewpoint, that insight is almost certain to cause us some discomfort, perhaps even anguish.

That is why the fisherman, even if he could, would prefer not to empathize with the fish. It might make him a more successful fisherman, but every time he landed a big one he would virtually betray himself. Here is the paradox of empathy: in empathic interaction we may manipulate others more effectively because we understand them more fully; but in this understanding we accrue responsibilities toward them that may block our drive to manipulate them. If, in such a case, our need or desire to manipulate should override our scruples, we are likely to experience a personal trauma, and justly so; for to manipulate one with whom we have achieved empathy may be the ultimate immorality. The inability to feel the strain in such a situation may be the ultimate amorality.

Thus, most of the time, we avoid empathy with those whom circumstances require us to manipulate toward predetermined ends, unless we know that those ends are acceptable to the other, or unless we can convince ourselves that the manipulation is all in their best interest. This latter position, of course, leads to some interesting moral dilemmas of its own.

ROLE CONSTRAINTS ON INTERACTION

Thus far in this chapter we have noted several examples in which the nature of the interaction between two people is conditioned to some extent by the positions they hold in some broader social system: boy to girl, student to fellow-student, teacher to student, salesman to customer, and so on. These terms—boy, girl, student, teacher, salesman, customer—define relations between people within some larger social system; that is, they define roles. Insofar as communication is concerned, a *role* may be defined as a position in some social system having certain relationships to other positions in the same system—relationships which affect the communication behavior deemed appropriate to the role. Most of us occupy roles in a variety of social systems: a family, a profession, a school, various clubs and organizations, informal social groups, and the like. In each of these groups we maintain a good deal of personal autonomy, but our roles strongly predispose us to communicate in certain ways within each of them. No discussion of interaction would be complete without noticing the constraints that social roles place upon it. We will not try to treat the topic exhaustively here, for that would require a large book in its own right. Instead, we will touch on a few representative examples illustrating the broader issues involved.

Who Talks to Whom About What

First of all, one's role may require that he interact or prohibit himself from interacting with individuals occupying certain other roles. A teacher, for example, is expected to interact with students who have been admitted to his class; he may not without justification refuse to talk with any duly admitted student. On the other hand, a lawyer may not talk with an individual juror sitting on a case in which the lawyer is involved. Without some very special reason, a waitress may not refuse to talk with a customer in her restaurant when the customer wants to place an order. On the other hand, the customer may not give orders to another waitress except in unusual circumstances. These constraints on who may talk with whom vary from absolute (lawyer and juror) to very relative (customer to a waitress other than the one who is serving him). In each case they exert definite pressure toward or away from interaction. Moreover, they do so without reference to the specific people filling the respective roles. We must repeat that this does not prevent individuals from breaking out of defined role behaviors; but such rugged individualism usually takes effort, leads to unpredictable consequences, and causes anxiety in those involved. It may be desirable, even necessary; but it is definitely not ordinary or usual.

Often role expectations with regard to who talks with whom are limited to certain topics. For example, the teacher is expected to interact with his student, but not necessarily with regard to all topics. Whether the teacher chooses to talk with the student about out-of-class considerations is a matter of preference on the part of both. The role does not prescribe in this regard, and here the preferences of the individuals come into play. We may say that the teacher is free to develop a style of instruction that relies little or much on informal, non-class-oriented interaction with his students; but he is not free to adopt a style of instruction that rules out interaction over class matters. In the same way, the waitress is "required" by her role to talk to the customer about the menu, but not about their mutual tastes in art or about what she is doing after work.

Role and Style

Roles also tend to permeate the way people talk to one another: both their verbal and nonverbal style. In most organizations, the employee does not put his feet on the boss's desk, even though the boss may do so. This goes back to the degrees of relaxation appropriate to status differences discussed in the chapter on messages (page 92–114). Intonation and word choice also reflect the role relationship between speaker and listener. The "official" or "bureaucratic" style of address is one that we are all becoming more familiar with every day. It reflects the perfunctory nature of the relationship between the speaker and the spoken-to, and so it is often used to define and establish that relationship.

Roles and Nonverbal Behavior

As a matter of fact, nonverbal cues such as gesture, posture, position, rate of speaking, and voice inflections are often used to establish role relations between people. The next time you are walking down a crowded hall or sidewalk, notice who moves out of the way for whom. At least a momentary dominance has been achieved by the person who forces the other to turn aside first; on the sidewalks we all play "chicken" every day. With persons we know, we may assert our dominance by giving this little ceremony a reverse twist: "After you, my dear Alphonse." Alphonse is not fooled; in spite of the overt deference—indeed, because of it—he knows that he has been cast momentarily in an inferior role. He knows this because what should have happened unconsciously as a simple matter of natural status differences has been dragged out into the open for everyone to stare at.

Now, if you think Alphonse a little paranoid for having such thoughts, you are experiencing a typical reaction; and that is what makes the establishment of role relations through nonverbal cues such a beautifully simple matter and at the same time such a sadist's delight. Since nothing is actually *said* to indicate the dominance relationship you are bidding for, you can look blank or act surprised when your hapless victim reacts by calling attention to what you are doing. Surely he has misunderstood. Certainly you didn't intend anything of the sort. Has he seen his psychiatrist lately? The latter is not an unusual reaction, since oversensitivity to nonverbal cues is thought to characterize some behavior disorders. Still, it is a mistake to think that our relations with others are controlled mainly by verbal means. In the area of establishing interpersonal dominance and invoking roles, nonverbal behaviors play a highly significant part.

GAMES PEOPLE PLAY

In a delightful little book about interpersonal behavior and personal relationships, Eric Berne points out that for most of us there are patterns of interaction with others that repeat themselves so often as to characterize our personal style.[3] Since these patterns take more than one to play, Berne calls them "games." His interest centers mostly on games that hold a special relevance for the psychological adjustment of the players, but the concept is a convenient one for dealing with a very wide range of communication patterns as well.

One very confusing little game, for example, could be called "Double Bind." A game of Double Bind begins when one player demands that the other choose one of two alternatives, but is prepared to punish him no matter which he chooses. "Why don't you ever say you love me?" is an opening gambit for one version of the game. If the interaction partner fails to say "I love you," then the opening player can extend the discussion along the lines of "See? I told you you didn't love me." On the other hand, if the interaction partner says "I love you," the opening player can reply, "You're only saying that because I asked you." Like Tic-Tac-Toe, the opening player always "wins" this one, since there is no foolproof way to avoid punishment. To be sure, one can delay the inevitable for a little while by some clever ruse, such as "If I told you how much I love you, you'd never believe me." But, given the opening move, nothing can really prevent a determined opponent from winning.

The same can be said for another game that is fairly popular these days. This one might be entitled "You're a Bigot." There's no way to win this one either. A clever opening player knows how to convert almost any social situation into a game of "Bigot." He also has well-developed trap-plays for all of the standard responses to the opening gambit, such as "Why, some of my best friends . . ." or "Now, look, my record on this goes back a long way . . ." or "How about defining your terms?" Anything the responding player says can be converted into further evidence of bigotry, because "That's just what all of them say." This game is very popular on college campuses, so the reader is likely to see it played fairly often. Rarely, if ever, will he see the hapless victim play to a draw.

3. Eric Berne, *The Games People Play: The Psychology of Human Relationships* (New York: Grove Press, Inc., 1964).

Not all games are malicious, of course. One game that Berne takes special note of, for example, is called "Ain't it Awful?" This is a fairly innocuous pastime that consists mostly of reinforcing one another's dolorous view of some person or thing. The game is fairly desultory, and the players mostly take turns reciting dreadful incidents or depressing particulars. It is against the rules to introduce a bright note or to suggest a solution for the problem (if there is a defined problem); and this perverse negativism is probably the only harmful aspect of the game, and then only to the extent that it prevents our moving to resolve the situation causing our distress. We all know people who prefer this game to any other, and unless we are in a foul mood, they make extremely poor conversational partners. In a problem-solving discussion they get in the way by focusing on the problem rather than on potential solutions. As public speakers, they tend toward the "problem exploration" or the sensational exposé, thus sometimes capturing the public spotlight. But they cannot hold attention because of their conspicuous lack of concrete suggestions.

Some games are positively benign, such as "Gee, You're Wonderful," or "Let's Be Friends." Both of these games are played largely by means of nonverbal cues. "Executive," on the other hand, requires both verbal and nonverbal behavior. They are "games" in the sense that they represent interaction patterns that are repeated over and over again by many different people. Once the opening gambit has been made, an interpersonal game usually is played out to its foreseeable conclusion. Usually the opening player is in charge of the action, but he needs reactions from the responding player as grist for his mill.

In this chapter we have dealt with five levels of interaction: *Alternating Monologue, Stimulus-Response Interaction, Interaction with Feedback, Interaction with Feedback and Feedforward,* and *Empathy.* These "levels" should not be regarded as discrete, but as constituting a continuum of interaction possibilities which—during the encounter—range from tenuous contact with another about whom one utilizes very little information to extremely close contact bordering on identification with another about whom one utilizes a great deal of personal information. We also have taken into account certain emotional and ethical problems associated with empathy.

We have identified *roles* as positions in a social system that predispose the individuals who occupy them to communicate in certain ways with persons who occupy related roles in the system. We have said that this predisposition is not necessarily binding, but that it is effort-demanding and sometimes anxiety-provoking to behave contrary to what the role specifies.

We have used the term "games" to refer to interpersonal communication patterns that are repeated often enough to become characteristic of an individual. We have seen that such games, once begun, tend to dominate the nature of the interaction between people. In a way, an interaction game creates a temporary role for each of the players. Games, we have observed, can be played at any level of interaction.

PROBLEMS AND QUESTIONS FOR DISCUSSION

1. During the next few days, observe and—afterward—take notes on conversations between yourself and others, or between other people; then write a brief description of each of the following:
   a. Alternating Monologue. (How did it end? Did the participants ever become aware of what they were doing?)
   b. Stimulus-Response Interaction. (Was only one of the participants the "Stimulator," or did both play the role?)
   c. Interaction with Feedback. (What kinds of signals or messages was the communicator using as feedback? Was the feedback positive or negative? How did it operate to control the behavior of the communicator?)
   d. Interaction with Feedforward and Feedback. (What goals were set? Could you identify specific expectancies? Was there any evidence of contingency planning?)
   e. Empathy. (How could you tell that an empathic condition had been attained? What was the outcome of the interaction?)
2. From the observations you used to answer the foregoing questions, how many *different* kinds of feedback could you identify?
3. During the course of a single weekday, keep a record of the different *roles* you have played. In what ways did each role affect your communication behavior? Bring the list to class for discussion.
4. Try to identify at least one interaction game that is played by any of your acquaintances. Outline the "rules" of the game, and describe how it is usually played. (You will receive extra credit if you can describe a game *you* play!)

9.

EFFECTS OF COMMUNICATION

Most people are interested in communication because of its effects. We know that communication exerts a powerful influence not only on individuals but also on the social milieu in which they live. In the final analysis, the most convincing reason to study communication is that we need to understand those effects much better, and we need to know how they are produced.

In this chapter, we examine the effects themselves—not all possible effects, but those which have emerged as most prevalent and important. We will not concern ourselves much with *how* the effects are produced, and only rarely will we consider how the effects can be manipulated. This is a topic that is still under very intensive research and goes well beyond the limits of our purpose here. Instead, we will try to show that even the simplest communication act may have a variety of effects, some very short-lived and others perhaps more enduring and far-reaching.

The effects of communication are most conveniently studied from the standpoint of their *locus:* that is, where in the communication complex they occur. We will concentrate on the three most important vantage points for viewing those effects: (1) the *audience*, (2) the *communicator*, and (3) the *social system*.

EFFECTS OF COMMUNICATION ON THE AUDIENCE

Communicating is generally viewed as a purposive activity calculated to produce certain effects in an audience. Although in the next chapter we will see that this is not necessarily always true, and that much communication takes place without any such purpose in mind, certainly the most widely noticed and closely observed effects of communication are those which occur in the audience. By "audience," of course, we do not necessarily mean an assembled group listening to a speech, but any individual or group of individuals who may be exposed to a message.

Since audiences are people, and people are capable of an infinite variety of reactions, we could not possibly identify every conceivable type of audience response to communication. Instead, we will focus on only seven kinds of response, seemingly the most important ones:

1. Attention.
2. Arousal. } *PROCESS*
3. Amusement. *EFFECTS*

4. Learning.
5. Attitude Formation, Reinforcement,
   and Change. *PRODUCT*
6. Behavioral Outcomes: Verbal *EFFECTS*
   and Nonverbal.
7. Changes in the Image of the Speaker.

In saying that these seven types of response are important, we mean that they are the ones most often sought by communicators, noted by observers, and significant for the audience itself.

Process Effects Versus Product Effects

Now, these seven kinds of audience response may be manifested in either of two ways: (a) as process effects or (b) as product effects. *Process effects* occur during the message only, and are of relatively short duration. Although they may contribute to more lasting effects, they themselves are replaced by new effects during the message exposure, or fade soon after the message ends. *Product effects,* on the other hand, are of a more permanent nature, and may be seen only after the message has been concluded, sometimes persisting for years or—in very rare cases—for the lifetime of the receiver.

Process effects are characterized by excitement, suspense, laughter, insight, fervor, attention, agreement, and recognition. These psychological manifestations occur during the period of message exposure and are elicited by the elements of the message as they move through the listener's consciousness. Whatever the listener experiences *during a speech* is a process effect.

Outcomes of product effects include attitude change, information gain, behavioral change, alteration of the receiver's opinion of the communicator, and increased interest in a topic. Whenever they occur, they are no doubt traceable to some combination of process effects; but the products themselves are observable only *when the communication is over.* To the extent that it is possible to compare the receiver as he appears *before* the communication with the receiver as he appears *after* the communication, it is possible to determine the product effects of the communication upon him.

In sum, then, the first three of our seven effects of communication—attention, arousal, and amusement—are invariably process effects. The remaining four—learning; attitude formation, reinforcement, and change; changes in the image of the speaker; and overt behavior—may sometimes be observed as process effects, but are more often regarded as product effects.

An understanding of these effects and at least some of the ways in which they may be generated and controlled is essential to the success of the communicator. We will, therefore, examine each of them in some detail.

Attention

The most basic effect any communication can have on an auditor is to capture and/or hold his attention. Subliminal perception aside, no other effects are possible unless the receiver attends to the message.

Sometimes attention is all the communicator desires. For instance, the producer of a TV show usually is interested primarily (sometimes exclusively) in the number of people who are watching his show at a given time. He may care little whether anybody is enjoying himself, agrees with or appreciates the content, learns anything from it, or changes his opinions or behavior afterwards. The producer of the show (as distinguished from the producer of the commercial advertisements) does not care whether the people watching the show buy the sponsor's product. His job is to attract attention—that is, get the largest possible share of the viewing audience —so as to assure that the maximum number of people are watching when the commercials come on the television screen. It is somebody else's job to write persuasive or compelling commercials, which constitute specialized messages in their own right.

Of course, the TV producer is seldom as one-dimensional as the foregoing description would imply. Most people would rather produce worthwhile material than trash, and the TV industry in general does make an effort to produce quality programs. But in the final analysis commercial television stands or falls on the single criterion of audience attention. And even when questions of program quality, social significance, and other important considerations arise, their possible effect on audience attention must be taken into account. Although we do not often recognize it, control of audience attention is often an important end of communication.

Emotional Arousal

Assuming that receivers are paying attention to a message, it may have other effects upon them. One of these is emotional arousal. Sometimes, as in the case of attention, arousal is an end in itself. The message may be so constructed as to produce emotional reactions, and receivers may attend to the message largely in order to experience the emotions.

One of the main differences between attention and arousal as ends in themselves is that in the case of arousal, receivers may actively seek it—that is, it becomes a goal of the receiver rather than the sender. In such instances, communicators merely devise messages that meet their audience's demands. For example, many people seemingly go to the movies largely to experience emotional arousal vicariously through the exciting situations portrayed on the screen. They are in no way being manipulated by the motion picture or producer. Indeed, they come to the theater in deliberate search of such vicarious emotional experiences, and they are likely to be disappointed and critical if they are not presented with scenes that allow them to experience these process responses. This is perhaps clearest in the case of the "skin-flicks"—the low-budget quasipornographic films often shown in "art" theatres. But it is also present in the most advanced art forms. An important point to remember is that in such cases the initial impetus for communication arises *not* with the communicator's intention, but with the audience's desire for stimulation. The communicator merely responds by providing the receiver with what he wants.[1]

1. For an interesting discussion of the changing roles of the persuader and the persuaded, see Thomas M. Scheidel, *Persuasive Speaking*.

Now, of course, the communicator may have a positive desire to arouse his audience emotionally whether or not they come to the situation with a desire for it. He may experience a great sense of power and take considerable satisfaction in getting his audiences "worked up." This observation was frequently offered as a criticism against "old-time revival" preachers, who sometimes seemed interested only in arousing a powerful emotional response in their congregations, without much regard to any long-lasting effects on either their spiritual lives or their moral behavior.

An important concern for the fledgling public speaker is that a powerful and immediate emotional response from an audience is likely to be a strongly reinforcing feedback for him. This immediate availability of reinforcement from feedback is one significant difference between oral communication in the face-to-face setting and other forms of communication that interpose either time or space between the communicator and the receiver. Thus, if something you do or say in a speech elicits an emotional reaction from the audience, you will be reinforced immediately, and you will be impelled strongly to do the same thing again at the next opportunity. Two or three "successful" experiences of this sort may be enough to establish a firm behavioral pattern that will be highly resistant to extinction. If this should happen, you will almost surely display an overt and readily apparent desire to arouse your audiences emotionally. Probably most successful orators display that desire to some degree and are genuinely gratified when their audiences respond emotionally; but, if carried to excess, this motive may so dominate the speaker's behavior as to interfere with other goals that may be more relevant on a given occasion. The speaker who is intoxicated by the heady wine of his audience's emotional response is not likely to think very clearly about more lasting objectives. He is so wrapped up in the process that the product is ignored.

Sometimes, of course, lasting objectives are not exceedingly important. Many ceremonial occasions fit into this category. To be sure, a speaker may use such an occasion to make an important announcement or policy statement. Government officials often do so when dedicating a building or speaking at a commencement, and we all remember Shakespeare's Mark Anthony, who used a funeral oration to start a revolution. But ordinarily the ceremonial speech is not used to accomplish any ulterior end. If, on such an occasion, the speaker can arouse a powerful emotional response, the audience can have a moving and memorable experience, which may well be all that the occasion demands.

Amusement

In many ways, amusement is closely allied to emotional response, and much of what has been said above applies to both. In particular, amusement is a response which is often actively sought by auditors. They often expose themselves to communication in deliberate search of amusement, as witness the enormous popularity of TV entertainment and the stand-up style of nightclub comics. To an even greater degree than with emotional response, communicators often merely provide their auditors with the amusement they seek, seldom trying to elicit this response from an audience that does not come actively seeking it.

As in the case of emotional response, audience expressions of amusement—laughter, applause, and rapt attention—are powerfully reinforcing feedback for speakers. Once you have learned reliably how to elicit amusement from an audience (actually, very few speakers are more than casually successful in this regard), you will be sorely tempted to seek that response at every opportunity. Moreover, if you become fairly good at it, you will attract listeners who come to hear you mainly for the amusement value itself. Thus, you will develop a tendency to establish a sort of self-perpetuating, positive feedback loop: your audiences will come expecting to be amused; if you amuse them, they will be reinforced; and if they are reinforced, they will tend to come again and expect more of the same. For your own part, you will tend to seek the amusement response in your listeners for the reinforcement it provides you; and whenever you are successful, you will tend to repeat the behaviors that generated the desired response. You and your audiences will thus tend to reinforce one another in your respective roles of amuser and amused, and this pattern will repeat itself until something happens to interrupt or change it.

If your goal is to become known as an entertainer, of course the occurrence of this co-stimulation and mutual reinforcement is just what you will be hoping for. But it sometimes happens that a speaker with other goals in mind will use the amusement response as a means to those other ends. In many speaking situations, in serious dramas, in instructional films, and in a variety of other message-types, amusement can be effectively used as either comic relief or as an attention-getting device. So used, it may contribute to other ends; but the communicator who tries to use amusement in this way should remember how easy it is to slip into the self-perpetuating feedback loop mentioned above. If one is exceedingly amusing, his audience eventually may be comprised almost entirely of people who come to be entertained and who respond to the entertaining material without taking anything else away from the speech. If so, the speaker will tend to give them what they want. Or, the speaker may get so much pleasure out of the audience's immediate responses to his humor that he spends more time on these aspects of his message than he should, and ignores more substantive matters.

Once into the pattern, it is very hard to get out, as Tom Corwin, a famous congressman from an earlier generation, testified. Corwin complained that the public would never listen to his serious ideas, and would remember him only as a joker. But he nurtured that image with a constant barrage of wit and humor. Apparently unable to control his appetite for laughter and applause, Corwin seemingly found it almost impossible to make a speech without telling a story or tossing a few choice barbs. His audiences loved him. He could fill a meeting hall with listeners eager to spread his anecdotes and witticisms among friends and acquaintances. But somehow nobody seemed to remember the serious content of his speeches. Tom Corwin's career testifies to the dangers inherent in using amusement as a means to an end. If one is not good at it, the effort will fail; if he is good at it, he may become the victim of his own success.

Learning

One of the responses supposedly enhanced by judicious use of amusing or entertaining content is *learning*. Whereas attention, arousal, and amusement are process responses to communication, learning—as we have previously noted—is a *product* response. We say that someone has learned as a result of communication when afterward he can do something that he could not do before. By "do something," of course, we refer not only to physical acts but also to mental and verbal behaviors as well. If, after viewing a short TV documentary on the season's London and Paris fashions, you can answer some questions about the subject that you could not answer before, then we would conclude that you have learned from the broadcast.

Relevant versus irrelevant information. The assessment of learning is by no means simple, a fact that is readily proved by reading the literature of educational research. For example, there is the difference between *relevant* and *irrelevant* information. Suppose that you are watching an instructional film on the life cycle of a certain Southeastern butterfly, and you see a sequence in which a caterpillar of that species is feeding on the leaves of an azalea. It is possible that you will retain information about the size, shape, color, and texture of azalea leaves that you had not known before. In the general sense, you would have learned something; but from the standpoint of your biology teacher and the producer of the film, this learning is incidental or irrelevant to the main purpose of the sequence.

Of course, the information is not irrelevant to you. You may have just read something elsewhere about azaleas and wished that you knew more about them. In that case, for you the information about azalea leaves might overshadow in importance anything you might learn about caterpillars. Given this conflict in viewpoint, how do we assess your learning in this situation? For purposes of the biology class, we would probably devise some kind of test over the "relevant" content of the film—that is, that content related to its manifest purpose and principal topic. But that test would not by any means reflect everything that you might possibly have learned from the film. Thus, if we want to know what learning has occurred and how much of it can be traced to a particular communication, we must specify whether we are talking about those elements that the communicator intended to convey to his audience (relevant information) or about anything else that the auditor gleaned from the message independently and outside of the communicator's intention (irrelevant information).

Ways to measure learning. A second problem in assessing learning as a product of communication is the vagueness inherent in words such as "knowledge," "information," and similarly broad, but relevant, concepts. Nowadays, the usual method of measuring information or knowledge is through "objective" examinations, which at their best determine what specific facts and isolated bits of knowledge one has at his disposal. If you did rather poorly on such a test in, let us say, a geology course, you might seek some individual help from a tutor or a classmate. Suppose a tutor gave you special instruction for several hours, and then you took the test a second time and scored much higher than you had the first. Everyone would agree that the tutor had communicated information to you— that you had learned as a result of the communicative interaction.

That, however, is not the only kind of learning that might have taken place, for tests of this type evaluate only one kind of knowledge. You might achieve a very high score on such a test, but be unable to write a perceptive essay on the subject. You would have the bits and pieces of information, but you might not have at your disposal the organizing relations that would allow you to put what you know into a meaningful pattern. These organizing relations are not bits and pieces of information, but represent instead ways of *looking at* the fragments so as to put them into perspective with one another. Whether one has such concepts at his command is usually best determined by asking him to write or speak at length about some aspect of the topic, and it is with a view to testing for such broad understandings that "essay questions" are usually asked in examinations.

Sometimes messages are designed not to impart new isolated facts and fragments of information, but rather to communicate broad understanding or meaningful patterns into which information can be put. Even if your geology tutor fails to provide you with any new items of specific information that you do not already have, he may nevertheless inform you—help you to understand the subject better—by giving you certain organizational or relational concepts about it. Subsequently you may do little, if any, better on "objective" tests over the subject, but you may write and speak about it more knowledgeably by virtue of being able to put the pieces together into more meaningful patterns. Surely this outcome can be called "learning."

Recognition versus recall. Still another important problem that we encounter in the assessment of learning has to do with the difference between *recognition* and *recall*. A multiple-choice question can determine whether you can recognize the correct answer to a question when you see it, and can pick it out from among several alternatives. But a multiple-choice question does not determine whether you could have remembered the correct answer without having it put before you. One test of your learning in this sense is a "cloze" test— one in which some incomplete information about the question is given, and you are asked to fill in the missing information.[2] For instance, you may be shown a sentence with certain key words deleted, and asked to fill in the blanks. There is no list of words from which you are to pick the correct one; you must recall it yourself. This calls for a better grasp of the information than the recognition test.

Of course, in the case of the cloze test, you do have the incomplete or partial information to guide your recall. A more rigorous test of recall would be for you to solve a problem, the solution of which demands the information in question. If you can remember the information that is relevant to the solution of this problem, and can

2.　See Milton Dickens and Frederick Williams, "An Experimental Application of 'Cloze' Procedure and Measures to Listening Comprehension," *Speech Monographs*, XXXI (June 1964): 103–108.

recall the information well enough to solve it, then you have "learned" the information in the fullest sense of the word.

From the foregoing problems and examples, it should be obvious that determining how much an audience has "learned" from a speech or other communication is by no means simple and, indeed, that much of the difficulty lies in knowing just what we mean by "learning." We may use the term to refer to *acquiring* isolated bits and pieces of information or to forming patterns for *organizing* them. We may use it to refer to *recognizing* a correct answer when we see one, or to the more difficult task of recalling the correct answer from memory. If we mean the latter, we may be interested in the receiver's ability to recall the information when asked a direct question about it, or we may be interested in his ability to know when he needs the information in connection with problem-solving tasks and to recall it for use on those occasions. We may wish to restrict our attention to those content elements that the communicator intended the listener should learn. On the other hand we may be willing to consider anything at all that the receiver learns (in any of the senses above), including incidental, "irrelevant" information as well as the more readily identified "relevant" information that the communicator intended to impart.

Attitude Formation, Reinforcement, and Change

In addition to learning, a second product effect of communication has to do with *attitude formation, reinforcement, and change.* In all fairness we should begin by noting that nobody knows exactly what an attitude is, but it seems to be a term that we cannot do without when talking about the effects of communication on people. The fact is well established, however, that an attitude is not something that can be seen or otherwise observed directly. It is perhaps best described as a tendency to respond to something in a particular way; it is something that we infer from behavior. This indirect and unobservable characteristic of attitudes has caused a good deal of frustration on the part of social scientists who want to measure the attitudinal effects of messages, but that need not deter us from using the term in an informal way to help explain some of the things that happen when one person talks to another.

The most important attitudes in nearly all situations are those which represent "evaluations": I like you or dislike you; I agree with what the Senator said or I disagree with it; I approve of the guaranteed annual wage or I disapprove of it; I view the compulsory limitation of family size as desirable or undesirable. Attitudes certainly have other dimensions beyond these purely evaluative ones, but for the sake of brevity let us restrict our attention for the moment to this evaluative dimension, which is usually by far the most important one.

It is probably true that we have attitudes toward everything that we know very much about. You will recall that earlier in this chapter we noted that evaluating is one of the commonest human activities, and that it is all but impossible for us to consider any object or event without evaluating it in some way. Our attitudes grow out of those evaluations. Consequently, whenever a communicator refers to something that we already know about, we respond to him against the background of our preexisting attitudes toward that thing. If we have no preformed attitude, then what we hear from the message will usually lead us to form one.

For instance, if I have no previous knowledge of, or attitudes toward containerized transport of consumer goods, and I learn from you in a conversation that Ralph Nader is opposed to containerization, then I will probably form an attitude toward this method of transport that is based on my attitude toward Nader. If I like him and respect his opinion, then I will probably conclude that containerization is bad. If I dislike him and feel that his opinion is worthless, I may conclude that containerization is probably a good thing. Because you linked your idea to an opinion leader about whom I did know something, the contents of your message to me (assuming that I regarded you as a trustworthy source of information on this topic) would lead me to form opinions on a topic that I previously knew nothing about. Your message, then, was instrumental in forming my attitude toward containerization.

Of course, I might have already had a negative attitude toward the topic before our conversation. In that case, if you expressed a negative attitude, and quoted Nader as having a negative attitude, and if I regarded both you and Nader favorably, then your message would probably have the effect of *reinforcing* my attitude. That is, I would be more likely to express that attitude on future occasions; the attitude would become somewhat more resistant to change, and I might even be more likely to act on the basis of the attitude, should the occasion for action arise.

On the other hand, if my attitude toward containerization had been favorable to begin with, your message would have given me a much more complicated problem: you would have confronted me with the need for an *attitude change*. As a result of your message, (1) I could change my attitude toward containerization; (2) I could change my opinion of Nader; (3) I could question the validity of your report of Nader's opinion (I might decide that you had misunderstood, or that you were deliberately lying or quoting out of context); or (4) I could conclude that on this one issue Nader hadn't really done enough research to understand the problem and that his opinion, therefore, was a temporary one that would surely change when he came to see the issues involved. This latter strategy would allow me to keep my opinion of Nader and my opinion of containerization in separate categories—at least for a while; but all of the other possible outcomes represent attitude change toward you, containerization, or Ralph Nader.

Now, if you wanted to change my attitude toward containerization and you knew that I had a favorable attitude toward some public figure such as Nader, and if you found that he had taken a position on the topic that was different from mine, you might try to engineer an attitude change on my part by quoting him as above. But it would pay you to remember that any such encounter has a number of possible outcomes, only one of which gives the desired result. The message will probably change some of my attitudes, but they may not be the ones you had in mind.

Relationships Between Verbal and Nonverbal Behavioral Outcomes

For a long time social scientists and communication analysts reflected the common bias of our everyday way of thinking about communication: namely, that talk is cheap, and that what really counts as a meaningful outcome of communication is some nonverbal act such as voting, donating to charity, joining the Army, picketing the Dean's office, or giving up cigarettes. What you might *say* about these things was thought to represent "soft" data unworthy of serious attention. But practical men of all ages have known that though it may be cheap, talk is nevertheless exceedingly important. If you can change what men say, you will appreciably increase the probabilities of influencing what they do. If you can induce a thousand people to believe what you say and to repeat it to others, your personal influence will be amplified many times over. Clearly, then, an important goal of much communication is to influence people's verbal behavior.

Certainly influence on verbal behavior is often used as an index of whether a given speech was successful. Do people talk about the speech among their acquaintances? Do they recount certain ideas or details in support of their own ideas? When they talk about the speech, do they express agreement or disagreement? Do they seem to have kept the main points fairly well in mind? Was the speech reported in the newspapers? Were excerpts played back over TV? Did Eric Sevareid or David Brinkley feel obliged to analyze it? Did anybody feel called upon to respond to it? All of these questions can be recognized as important indicators of the significance of a speech, and of the effectiveness with which it accomplished its aims. Whenever such questions are relevant, influence on verbal behavior can be said to constitute at least one of the goals of the speech.

Some speeches are designed solely to elicit some verbal behavior—any verbal behavior—from the greatest possible number of people. Most of the communication of the Students for a Democratic Society in the old days was designed with just such verbal behavior in mind. The idea was to start people talking about the movement and its leaders. Even if they talked negatively, they would at least be compelled to pay attention and that would be better than oblivion. By taking extreme positions and issuing "wild" press releases (only Very Important Persons "issue press releases"), they induced people to pay attention—that is, to talk about them. At this writing there still seems to be some question as to whether the movement will be able to change its mode of operation quickly enough to convert the advantage thus gained into lasting benefits; but however that may turn out, SDS has been a significant part of the American scene—not because of the number of buildings burned, college presidents sacked, or students inconvenienced, but because of the vast amount of verbal behavior they have stimulated.

Thus, there is a sort of hierarchy of behavioral outcomes of communication. If my ultimate goal is to get you to quit smoking, I am obviously in the strongest possible position if I can simply tell you to quit and thereby cause you to do so. Barring that, I may hope to change the verbal behavior of all of the people around you so that you will constantly be bombarded with antismoking propaganda from people you meet. If that is not possible, I may try to change your attitude so that you feel guilty whenever you think about smoking. If that is too much to expect, I may try to get across to you one or two simple ideas about the dangers of smoking, to lay the groundwork for future persuasion. If all else fails, I may have to resort to some stratagem that will at least get your attention.

EFFECTS OF COMMUNICATION ON THE SPEAKER

As the analysis of communication has become more sophisticated, it has become increasingly obvious that one of the most significant outcomes of communication is its profound effect upon the communicator. This is particularly true in the case of speakers, and it is on speakers that we shall concentrate here, whether they speak to an audience of thousands or only to themselves.

Factors Affecting the Speaker's Image

One important effect of communication on the speaker is his concern with his own image. Most individuals and groups are very sensitive to their public image, and in their communication behavior they try to avoid actions that will damage that image. Indeed, a surprisingly large amount of communication has as its primary motivation nothing more than improving, promoting, or preserving the image of the individual or group that initiates the message.

Building and maintaining a favorable image are not only important matters, but difficult ones as well. They are important because a speaker's image is like money in the bank: he draws on it for credibility in attitude-change situations like those mentioned above. The stronger his image, the more likely that people who are exposed to his influence will change their attitudes favorably toward the topics he discusses rather than changing them negatively toward him. However, it is difficult for a speaker to build and maintain an image, because everything he does (or fails to do) is likely to have *some* influence on his image, and it is often hard to predict an unfavorable response in advance.

As in the case of other attitude objects, if the speaker is unknown to a particular audience, his first speech to them will certainly form their ideas of him and their attitudes toward him. If he is known to them, the speech may either reinforce his image (favorably or unfavorably), or change it.

It is surprising how often messages are sent with the explicit purpose of enhancing the visibility, reputation, credibility, or other aspects of the image of the message source. In international affairs, "messages of good will" usually have the purpose of enhancing the image of a government with its own people, or with another government (the message recipient or a third power). Thus, when the Soviet government sent a congratulatory letter on the occasion of the U. S. lunar landing, they produced favorable effects (1) on their own people, (2) on the people and government of the U.S., and (3) on still other governments and peoples. Russian citizens could say, "See how generous we are in recognizing the achievements of even the capitalist countries." U. S. citizens could say, "Wasn't it nice of them to recognize our achievement? Perhaps they are not all bad, after all." And citizens of other countries, on hearing of the congratulatory letter, could say, "Those Russians certainly know how to rise above partisan strife on history-making occasions like this. Haven't they matured a lot since the Bolshevik days?"

At a national level, we are all familiar with the "bandwagon effect" in politics, education, business, and other fields of action. Once a controversial person or policy has been endorsed by enough influential powers to assure victory, all but a few die-hard opponents usually jump on the bandwagon—that is, come out with public statements of endorsement. To be seen on the winning side is thought to be very good for one's image, and in most cases it undoubtedly is. To be heard in favor of "good" programs and causes is also beneficial, which is why politicians and other power-seekers are so often heard in praise of whatever it is that everybody wants. The problem is that usually everybody wants something different, so that the poor image-maker who addresses a mass audience is ordinarily reduced to a choice between the broadest generalities or a strategy that will alienate the smallest number of listeners or the least powerful ones. On a recent occasion, the successful candidate for governor of one of our largest states said, "I'm for everything that is good and against everything that is bad. It's as simple as that."

Unfortunately, it isn't at all that simple. Perhaps there was a time when there were at least a few "safe" topics, things one could come out strongly for or against with assurance of getting some applause and arousing the ire of nobody except a handful of fanatics who could be written off as "fringers" and madmen. Alas, the day of the safe topic is gone. On any subject that is sufficiently important to use for enhancing one's image, there are invariably organized "pro" and "con" groups. Whatever brings cheers from one brings boos from the other. Nowadays, even to argue against poverty, for scientific progress, against crime, for due process, against violence, or for democratic decision-making is not a surefire formula for enhancing one's image. Under such restrictive circumstances, the political image-maker is confronted to an unusual degree with the inevitability of alienating some persons and groups with the very messages that he uses to build his credibility with others.

In concentrating on such elevated topics as international diplomacy and national politics, we should not forget that the image-building function of communication operates at all levels. Much more of it goes on at the individual and small-group level than at any other. The salesman "sells himself before he sells his product"; the psychotherapist "establishes rapport with the patient"; the counselor "seeks a basis of common understanding"; and the new foreman "strives to get off on the right foot with the men." All of these behaviors characterize the initial phases of our interaction with other significant behaviors and reflect a desire to establish in the minds of our receivers an image that will prove conducive to favorable outcomes in future communication situations.

Speaker Susceptibility to Process Responses

Without dwelling on it in great detail, we should notice that speakers experience process responses to communication that generally exceed those of listeners. For instance, the physiological indicators of emotional arousal and stress are invariably higher in speakers than they are in listeners, even where the material is of a highly emotional nature. All of the evidence indicates that during most of a speech a speaker is in a state of highly increased awareness and susceptibility to influences of all kinds.

It is therefore perhaps not surprising that speakers often experience considerable change as a result of making a speech. For one thing, if a speaker starts a speech only half believing what he plans to say, by the end of the speech he is very likely to believe it fully. Sometimes it seems that nobody is as convinced by his words as is the speaker himself. In fact, even if he starts the speech quite convinced that what he is about to say is rubbish, he is likely to end the speech wondering if perhaps there is not something to it after all. Experiment after experiment has shown that when communicators make a speech expressing views different from their own, the communicators change attitudes toward their topic even more than their audiences do. Just why this should be so is not entirely clear, and many theories have been offered to account for it; but the point is well worth remembering. You may never become good enough to hypnotize an audience into accepting what you say, but you will find it no trick at all to hypnotize yourself.

This self-hypnotic outcome of speaking becomes almost irresistible when it is accompanied by favorable audience response. We have already noted that audience response may affect a speaker's behavior by causing him to overemphasize emotionality or entertainment. But unless the speaker is unusually clear-headed, these responses are likely to affect his thinking as well. If he should happen to be expounding a theory at the time the favorable responses occur, he is likely to become more convinced that the theory is valid. If expressing an opinion, he is likely to be more convinced that it is right.

Audience Feedback as Speaker Reinforcement

The ability of audiences to alter the behavior of speakers is well known. Almost every year we hear a new version of a very old story regarding the power of audiences over speakers. One version of the story deals with a professor of biology who, while lecturing, frequently directed his gaze out the window, only occasionally stealing a furtive glance at the dozing class before him. A psychology-minded student decided to modify the professor's behavior and enlisted the aid of the class. He arranged that whenever the professor did happen to glance at the class, everyone would make a special point of looking alert, expressing interest, and taking notes. Over a period of several days the professor began to look at his classes more and more. Their positive behavior increased his enthusiasm. By the end of the term he was looking at the class throughout the lecture, his only "speech training" having been the selective reinforcement of eye contact by his students.

The outcome of experiments in this kind of selective reinforcement is quite predictable on the basis of "verbal behavior" studies. By simply looking interested whenever his subject uses a certain kind of word—say a personal pronoun—an interviewer can alter the interviewee's behavior dramatically, producing an abnormally high percentage of personal pronouns in his speech. Moreover, this effect usually occurs without the subject's being aware of it.

On the basis of these experiments, it is easy to see how selective reinforcement can lead to misunderstanding—how, for instance, a psychoanalyst and his patient can fall into a pattern of interaction that would lead both astray. Suppose that you are the psychiatrist and on the basis of your study of psychoanalytic theory and many previous cases, you believe that this patient's problem is traceable to repressed incestuous impulses. During the course of free association or guided interview, whenever your patient touches on either parent-child relationships or sexual matters, you grow a little more alert, attentive, interested, curious. Your patient, of course, senses your interest and is reinforced. Thus, over the course of treatment he will talk more and more about parents/children and sex.

Finally he is bound to put the two together. Then you give him a tremendous reinforcement: you tell him that he has at last penetrated to the core of his problem; he has experienced insight. He may have just been putting words together—words that you had continually reinforced over many previous meetings—and accidentally come up with (from the standpoint of your theory) the "right" combination. But your reinforcement is likely to convince him that he has said something profound. Now he will talk about it more and more, working harder and harder to dig up relevant facts that can be fitted into the pattern. With each successful effort, you provide additional reinforcement. Finally, he is likely to believe that you have helped him achieve a rare and wonderful insight into his own soul, and that you have helped him to build up a network of memories and explanations in support of that "insight."

Of course, his burgeoning "insight" will at every step reinforce your theory and analysis of his case. And he will be grateful for the help you have given him. Thus fortified with success and rewarded with gratitude, you will approach your next patient with even greater confidence and determination. What we have just witnessed is not the typical course of a psychiatric consultation, but it does happen often enough that psychological clinicians of all kinds need special training in how to avoid just such traps as these.

Immediate Versus Delayed Response as Reinforcement

The fact is that just about any response from an auditor is potentially a reinforcement to a speaker. When we deliberately seek a response, whatever we do that elicits such a response from our auditors is reinforced: we are much more likely to do it again in similar circumstances in the future. Of course, the sooner the speaker gets the feedback on his listeners' response, the greater influence their response will have on him. That is why overt process responses are so powerful as reinforcers: they come back to the speaker immediately after he has done whatever elicits such responses from listeners, and immediate reinforcement is much more powerful than delayed reinforcement.

Moreover, process responses may serve an intermediate role in which they mediate the reinforcing power of delayed audience responses that reach the speaker much later. Consider the case of the lecturer trying to impart information. He is hoping that his listeners will get the highest possible scores on subsequent tests over the subject matter of the lecture. Now, if the listeners show interest and enthusiasm during the speech, that response will have an immediate reinforcing effect in its own right; but if the class members later obtain high scores on the test questions based on that lecture, the lecturer may link the process responses and the scores. In that case, all future expressions of interest on the part of his students will be doubly rewarding, both for their own sake and for the promise they hold for improved test scores.

One final point with regard to audience reinforcement of speaker behaviors: reinforcement is not necessarily the same as reward or pleasure. When we say that almost any audience response can give reinforcement, we include some responses that might be thought highly noxious or objectionable. Given a martyr complex, or a sufficiently low opinion of his listeners, a speaker may extract considerable reinforcement from listeners who deride, revile, and persecute him. The classic case was a young English radical who returned utterly dejected from a trip to Hyde Park. "What did I do wrong today?" he moaned. "No matter what I did, I couldn't get a single boo, not even a hiss."

In this section of the chapter, we have tried to show that some of the more significant outcomes of communication have to do with the effects of communication on the *communicator*, especially when he is a speaker. We have seen that some of those effects can be traced to the speaker's greatly increased arousal-level at the time of communication, and that others can be traced to the effects of audience reinforcement of speaker behaviors. We have seen that the same principles operate in person-to-person communication as in the public-speaking situation, and that even apparently negative outcomes may have reinforcing effects.

EFFECTS OF COMMUNICATION ON THE SOCIAL SYSTEM

Thus far, we have devoted much attention to the effects of communication on individuals—that is, the speaker and listener. This is appropriate because in the final analysis whatever takes place as a result of a communication happens because of the way the communication affects individual people. Sometimes, however, it is more to the point to speak of the effects of communication *on groups or masses of people*, or on the relationships between them. We shall refer to such outcomes as effects on the social system. Ultimately, of course, this "social system" can be determined only by looking at the behavior of people, either individually or in the mass; but it is often more direct to talk about the social system as if it were an entity separate from the particular people who participate in it. Certainly some effects of communication can best be described in this way.

Consider, for example, the well-known fact that the percentage of voters who switch sides during the last week of a national election campaign is almost always very small. That percentage is a property of the system as a whole, not of any individual voter within the system. We cannot predict just who will change sides at the last minute, but we can predict with certainty that some will, and that the number who do so will not exceed five percent. A social psychologist looking at these data might throw up his hands in despair, for he would be unable to predict anything at all about individuals; but the sociologist or political scientist would be delighted that he could predict so well how the system as a whole would behave. The difference in viewpoint between the psychologist and the political scientist in this example is the difference between individuals and systems.

Of course, social systems exist on many levels, ranging from those that extend across national boundaries to those that consist of just two individuals. These systems, and the factors which created them, are established, maintained, and altered by communication.

Behaviors in Small-Group Leadership

"Leadership," to consider an example in some detail, consists of a set of behaviors in some particular situation—usually communication behaviors. Depending on the size, complexity, and function of a group, the types of leadership are extremely diverse. Most groups, for instance, require leadership in group maintenance; that is, now and then somebody has to provide humor, emotional catharsis, expressions of mutual approval and solidarity, and similar elements or factors that improve group morale and increase the sense of mutual respect and cooperation. Leadership in this area can be exercised from time to time by different members of the group. If certain members are especially good in group-maintenance leadership and enjoy providing it, in time others in the group will come to look to them for this kind of leadership. This concentration of the leadership function in one or a small number of individuals is not inevitable, but it does occur often.

There are of course many other kinds of leadership as well. For a task-oriented group, like a corporation's board of directors or a city council, somebody needs to perform leadership functions to keep the group on course, to see that all of the issues are raised, and to keep the group moving toward the actions it needs to take. If someone in the group is particularly skillful in these behaviors, he will likely emerge as a *task leader* and (in strongly task-oriented groups) may eventually be elected chairman and take over formal leadership. Most working groups also require leadership in knowledge and expertise relevant to the problems with which they must deal. If one member of the group consistently comes up with the "right" information when it is needed, he will eventually be looked to as an *information leader* in that group. And of course most groups that exist over any appreciable period also develop *opinion leaders,* people whose judgment is trusted on issues that are controversial or on which it is difficult to obtain reliable factual information. Not often do all of these leadership functions come to rest in a single group member, and usually any one type of leadership can be exercised at different times by different members of the group.

Now the important point about all of this is that the behaviors we call "leadership" behaviors are specialized kinds of communication: promoting morale, putting the group back on course, providing information, guiding opinion. Moreover, one establishes himself in the group by means of such communication patterns. By communicating in certain ways—that is, by sending certain kinds of messages —one creates a position for himself in the group, and thereby may alter the structure of the group as a social system. Beyond the image-making that we referred to in the last section, communicators often seek to strengthen or elevate their position in the social structure of some group by means of communication strategies. Or they may seek through communication to form new social structures, or to destroy old ones. Whenever a speaker accomplishes any of these things, it is simpler to speak of the effect as if it occurred within the social system as such rather than within the individuals making up the system.

The Public Dialogue

Another social-system factor that can be changed by communication is what may be called "the public dialogue." At any given time there is before "the public" a range of issues under discussion. Again, remember that "the public" refers not to any one individual or group of individuals, but to a highly variable and shifting arrangement of people who, like the participants in a floating crap game, drift in and out of the discussion of a particular issue. As people talk about an issue over a period of time (sometimes years or even centuries) a sort of public record accumulates—a record consisting of whatever striking or significant has ever been said about the question. This record, and the process that creates it, may be called "the public dialogue." Individuals who enter the discussion do so against this accumulated background.

While individuals contribute to the public dialogue, it supersedes individuals and may be said to exist as a social-system phenomenon. It is "what people are saying about subject X"—not any particular person or group of people, but a shifting constituency that changes over time. Individuals come and go, but the dialogue goes on. On an important issue nobody ever hears all of it, and some people hear only a fragment of it; but actions and decisions are often based on the accumulated arguments, issues, evidence, opinions, and interpretations that make up the dialogue.

Most communicators have very little effect on the dialogue, except to keep the pot boiling by re-transmitting ideas that are already in the record. Of course, a speaker will give increased prominence to any idea that he uses, and will perhaps introduce new ideas for the listeners he is addressing at a given time; but in the broad and long-term development of the issue about which he is speaking, any individual speaker is more likely to serve as a *channel* for ideas already in the dialogue than as a source of new ideas.

By now it should be clear that one important outcome of almost any communication is its effect on the dialogue of which that communication is a part. That effect may take the form of broadening the range of people who have certain ideas available to them; it may give public emphasis to some notions at the expense of others; it may serve only to keep alive public interest in the issue; or it may on rare occasions introduce new arguments, interpretations, or information, and so advance the dialogue a step or two.

PROBLEMS AND QUESTIONS FOR DISCUSSION

1. From the standpoint of understanding how communication affects you and the world in which you live, the preceding chapter contains some of the most applicable information in this book. Therefore, rather than providing the usual summary, the authors suggest that—as an aid to your comprehension and retention of the concepts it sets forth—you prepare your summary of the chapter in not less than 250 nor more than 500 words.
2. As a check on the thoroughness and accuracy of your summary, your instructor may wish to divide the class into groups of four or five students for discussion. Each should read the summary of each of the other students in his group, noting errors and omissions. The group then may be assigned the task of preparing a joint summary incorporating the contributions of all members of the group.
3. Prepare a short paper on "indicators of attention and interest." Discuss how a speaker, or an outside observer, can tell whether listeners are genuinely interested in and attentive to a spoken message.
4. Using the indicators you have devised in the preceding assignment, closely observe audience response in at least one speech in your class. How well did your indicators work?
5. Prepare an informative speech for presentation to your class, specifying

whether you want the audience to learn specific bits of information or acquire some new way of looking at the subject. Devise a test to measure how well your speech accomplished its purpose.
6. Select a speech from *The Speaker's Resource Book*, Revised Edition, by Carroll C. Arnold, Douglas Ehninger, and John C. Gerber (Glenview, Ill.: Scott, Foresman and Company, 1966). Read it, along with the explanatory material about it, and answer the following questions:
    a. Insofar as you are able to determine, what effects did the author of the speech intend?
    b. What effects did the speech have, insofar as you can estimate?
    c. How noticeable would the process effects of this speech probably have been? Would this have had any probable effect on the speaker?

10.

EVALUATING COMMUNICATION

In preceding chapters we noticed how difficult it is to talk without revealing our attitudes, opinions, and feelings. We also learned that this merely reflects a much more general principle, namely, that *evaluation* is one of the most prevalent human activities. We find it all but impossible to contemplate any object or event without placing some value—positive or negative—upon it. It should, therefore, be no great surprise to learn that a great deal of our concern with communication grows out of a desire to evaluate it more accurately.

In a sense, everything you read or hear about communication constitutes a preparation to evaluate it, since in your evaluations of a specific communication act you bring to bear whatever relevant information you have. In this chapter, however, we explore certain issues that arise very often in evaluating communication; and we consider questions that we can ignore only at the risk of making wrong or irrelevant evaluations.

THREE DISTINCTIONS UNDERLYING EVALUATION

First, before we outline the basic issues in evaluating communication, we should examine three important distinctions that underlie the evaluative process: (1) *consummatory versus instrumental communication,* (2) *effects versus effectiveness,* and (3) *the difference between evaluating process and product.*

Consummatory Versus Instrumental Communication

In considering the distinctions undergirding the evaluation of any communicative act, the first and most basic distinction is between *consummatory* and *instrumental* communication. Much literature in communication—and all of it in certain branches of the subject—assumes that communicating is purposive activity. For instance, we think that people do not speak up in a group discussion or a public meeting unless they intend to produce some effect on their listeners. We further assume that all aspects of the speaker's utterance are in some way related to his purpose or purposes, and that the purpose or purposes will be reflected in what the speaker says and how he says it.

Oftentimes this assumption of purposiveness is valid and provides a reasonable basis for evaluating the speaker and/or the speech. But what of the situation where the speaker is talking merely to be heard, or merely to "get something off his chest"? We all know that such things do occur often enough to constitute an important class of communication events. Communication that springs from an intent to produce some change in one's auditors is called *instrumental:* the communication is an instrument for producing change in the speaker's (or writer's) social environment. On the other hand, communication that springs from a need to "get something off one's chest," or simply from a need to be heard for its own sake, is *consummatory:* the speaker's purpose in speaking is consummated by the very act of utterance, without regard to any effects on the audience. "Pass the salt" is—in the usual case, where one actually wants some salt—a purely instrumental communication. Most expletives —such as "Damn!" when you've just stalled the car on a hill—are purely consummatory communication. Expressions like "Sock it to me, baby!" can be either, depending on whether one intends to communicate a request for something, or simply to express enthusiastic appreciation. The distinction, then, is based not on the content or form of the communication itself, but on *the speaker's intention* at the time of utterance.

Interrelationships between instrumental and consummatory communication. So far we have viewed the difference between instrumental and consummatory communication as if the distinction applied only to entire communication acts—acts as complete entities. This may be true when the communication is of very short duration, as in the examples listed above. In more complex messages, however, we may find instrumental and consummatory elements mixed together. A typical instance is the public speaker who addresses an audience with a particular purpose in mind, but selects some of his ideas or uses certain language because of a personal need or desire to hear himself express these ideas or use these words, rather than with primary regard to their relevance to his purpose. Much speaking by young radicals and old conservatives can be explained on this basis. Even when the primary purpose of the communication is instrumental—for instance, to secure concessions or to quell a riot— such consummatory elements as profanity, irrelevant attacks on "the establishment," moralistic generalizations, etc. are very likely to manifest themselves. Thus, we may say that whenever content appears in a communication without regard to its intended effect on some group of receivers, it represents consummatory communication. Whenever the content is aimed primarily toward producing a certain change in or effect upon a listener or listeners, it represents instrumental communication.

Significance of the instrumental-consummatory distinction for evaluating communication. It should be clear that consummatory communication cannot be evaluated on the same terms as instrumental communication. In fact, it can be argued that consummatory communication is not open to evaluation at all: since the speaker does not intend any effects, perhaps it is irrelevant to inquire into the impact or quality of the communication. In "doing his thing," the communicator has satisfied himself; and from his point of view that is the end of the matter.

Artists, in particular, sometimes may carry this argument to the extreme. They may take the position that their art is nothing more than self-expression, and that, as such, it is not open to comment or criticism from anyone other than the artist himself. From the artist's point of view, this is probably a psychologically useful strategy. It may protect his creativity from excessive or premature self-criticism during the difficult formative stages of an art work. But from the standpoint of anyone trying to understand why some artists "succeed" (i.e., make a living and/or become recognized for their work) while others "fail" (i.e., have to get a job doing something else to support themselves and/or are ignored), it is necessary to look beyond the artist for standards of criticism and evaluation. We must also look beyond him if we want to understand how art functions in a culture. Once the work of art leaves the artist's studio, it is subject to criticism and evaluation, whether the artist intended it to be or not.

What is true of art is equally true of all other forms of communication: consummatory acts of communication or consummatory elements of predominantly instrumental communication are subject to evaluation in spite of the communicator's intent. But the evaluation will be quite different, in that we will not assume that the speaker had purposes or intentions that he did not in fact have; and we will not apply standards of criticism that assume a purpose on the part of the communicator. Therefore, when we evaluate consummatory communication, we must be sure to evaluate it solely on its form and effects. For instance, it may be irrelevant to say that such and such a speech was "not very informative" if the speaker did not intend to convey any information and if the situation did not demand it.

There is, moreover, a second way in which the distinction between consummatory and instrumental communication is important to evaluation. As you may have already concluded, the extent to which a given communication is consummatory may in certain cases in and of itself serve as a basis for evaluation. In therapy situations, such as group counseling, consummatory communication is often encouraged for the self-revelatory insights it provides. The more instrumental an act of communication—the more perfectly it is geared to the achievement of some objective—the less it reveals to us about the communicator. It is through consummatory acts of communication, springing from inward drives and impulses, that we most clearly reveal ourselves; and in clinical, therapeutic situations this is often the chief goal of communication.

On the other hand, many situations call for instrumental communication; and an excess of certain kinds of consummatory communication may waste time or interfere with purposeful objectives. The intrusion of excessive consummatory communication may prevent an otherwise excellent speech or message from achieving any useful purpose. In fact, the presence of certain kinds of consummatory communication may undo any good the speaker may have accomplished with other elements of the message. Moreover, the speaker who fails to recognize a situation demanding instrumental communication for what it is, and who manifests consummatory behavior rather than meeting the challenge of the situation, may properly be called to account. In any of these cases the presence, type, and amount of consummatory communication constitute in themselves a valid ground of criticism and evaluation.

Effects Versus Effectiveness

The second distinction underlying evaluation of communication is the difference between *effects* and *effectiveness*. All communication has effects, though not all is effective. And, paradoxically, the effects of an ineffective speech may be more profound and far-reaching than the effects of an effective one.

How can this be so? The answer lies in what we mean by "effective." We define an effective communication as one that accomplishes what the communicator intended it to accomplish, or that meets certain *a priori* or preestablished criteria of effectiveness. To look for the effects of communication is, in principle, a relatively simple matter, for any change produced by the communication can be identified as an effect. Effects are nothing more than outcomes, such as those discussed in the preceding chapter. But to identify a communication as effective or ineffective requires much more information than simply what happened as a result of it. Effects can be determined by observing or measuring just one thing: *audience response*. But effectiveness can be determined only by measuring the communication and/or its effects against some *external criterion*. Depending upon whether we are talking about effectiveness as defined from the standpoint of speaker purpose, listener satisfaction, or *a priori* standards, this external criterion may be what the speaker wanted to accomplish, what the audience expected to get, or what esthetic, logical, ethical, or social standards can be applied.

Perhaps an example will clarify the point. Suppose that I produce a television documentary on communism in China. No matter what the documentary contains, it is relatively certain to produce some results. Assuming that it is nationally televised, it will surely be watched by at least some TV viewers; and they are certain to see and hear some things that they have not witnessed before. Some of these things they will even remember, and that represents information gain: a measurable *effect* of the show.

But the program may be a real "bomb," so bad that only a few thousand viewers watch it. In these days of highly professional talent and pretested programing, such an eventuality is unlikely, but it has happened; and when it does, the program is evaluated as extremely *ineffective*. The criterion for such evaluation is the percentage of the viewing audience. If a large percent of the national sample watching TV at that hour is watching my documentary, it will be evaluated (by the network and sponsor) as very effective—effective, that is, in attracting viewers, which is a highly relevant criterion in TV programing.

Now suppose that my program is watched by millions, that they are strongly impressed with the contents, and that they carry away a great store of new concepts, information, and images regarding China and communism. In that case, the broadcast is also effective in terms of the criterion of imparting information to my audience. But suppose that the information is partially incorrect and that the show imparts a badly distorted picture. Then the program was ineffective in informing the audience, if by "informing" we mean imparting accurate information and forming valid images.

Whether or not it is effective according to any of these criteria, it may nevertheless have great influence. The information, even if distorted, may so capture the imagination of viewers as to exert profound influence on them. Images and views of my "ineffective" program may be picked up and repeated by other communicators, and all of this may eventually result in a redefinition of our nation's China policy. Thus the broadcast may have great influence or *effect,* even though from one standpoint or another it must be evaluated as highly *ineffective.*

The assessment of effects and the determination of effectiveness are both important aspects of evaluating communication. From the outset, however, it is necessary to understand that effects and effectiveness are not the same, and that confusion of the two can only lead to misevaluation.

Product Evaluation Versus Process Evaluation

The third distinction that must be made in evaluating communication has to do with the types of effects that a message may have on its receiver: *process* effects and *product* effects—a distinction we drew rather fully in Chapter 9 (pages 137–159). We emphasize it again here because, though seldom acknowledged, this distinction between communication as process and communication as product actually underlies much evaluation of communication. For example, one of the distinctions often made between "worthwhile literature" and "trash" is that the former is thought capable of effecting permanent and desirable long-term changes in readers, whereas the latter provides only trivial entertainment and momentary diversion. The product effects of worthwhile literature are in some way supposed to make the reader a better person, while the product effects of trashy literature (in the rare case where any can be found) are thought to promote largely undesirable traits.

In evaluating communication, it is important to distinguish

between these two kinds of effects, for the failure to do so will lead to confusion and error. It can, for example, lead to questions such as "If public speaking is so important in presidential campaigns, why is it that William Jennings Bryan was defeated for that office, even though everyone acknowledged that he was the greatest orator of his day?" The answer, of course, lies in the difference between the process effects and the product effects of public speaking. Bryan was a master of the art of eliciting strongly emotional process effects from a listening audience, but the long-term product effects of his speeches upon listeners were apparently inconsequential. He could make audiences laugh, cry, tingle with excitement, or roar and stamp their feet in righteous indignation—all process effects. Unfortunately for his career, however, he could never induce a sufficiently large number of his hearers to cast a vote for him—a much-desired product effect.

When we distinguish between process and product, the Bryan phenomenon is no great mystery. In general, "oratory" as distinguished from "public speaking" is characterized by speaker efforts to elicit strong process effects. If a speaker is successful in the attempt, he is likely to be called a great orator. If he is successful in producing long-term product effects, he will be characterized as an effective spokesman. Once in a very great while, society will produce a man who excels in both; and given the opportunity, such a man will achieve the status of a charismatic leader: a Lincoln, a Roosevelt, or a Martin Luther King.

Because the speeches characterized both by strong process effects and profound product effects have exerted the greatest influence on the course of human events, they are the ones that most often have been preserved in print—and, more recently, on tape and film—and are most widely read and studied. The analysis of such "great" speeches may understandably lead one to ignore the distinction between process and product because in evaluating these speeches the distinction is not important. But in the overwhelming majority of cases—cases where less distinguished and perhaps more typical speeches are concerned—failure to distinguish between these two very different kinds of effects can lead to misunderstanding and misevaluation.

In order, then, to evaluate communication accurately, we must be able to make these three essential distinctions: consummatory *versus* instrumental communication, effects *versus* effectiveness, and process effects *versus* product effects. We turn now to specific approaches to evaluating communication.

We have noted that determining effectiveness is more complicated than assessing effects, for effectiveness requires the application of criteria to the message, its effects, or to both. Now we are prepared to consider effectiveness from the three standpoints of (1) *speaker purpose,* (2) *listener satisfaction,* and (3) *a priori standards* of evaluation.

Speaker-Purpose Point of View

One way of evaluating effectiveness is to determine whether the speaker accomplished "his purpose." As noted earlier, if my goal is to get millions of people to watch my TV broadcast, then my effectiveness can be measured directly in terms of the number of viewers who do in fact watch it. If my goal is to inform as many people as possible that smoking causes heart disease, then the effectiveness of my series of TV spot announcements can be measured in terms of the number of people who learned that fact from viewing my announcements or talking with people who did. If my goal is to get my face and name known to the greatest possible number of voters in the state, then the effectiveness of my speaking tour can be measured by the increase in the percentage of voters who know about me. If my purpose is merely to enjoy the act of making a speech to the Kiwanis Club, then effectiveness can be measured by asking myself afterwards how much pleasure I took in making the speech. If I want to get a school-bond referendum passed, my effectiveness can be determined by counting the number of votes I swayed to my side. In short, according to this definition, I have been effective to the extent that my speech or other communication has accomplished what I said at the outset I wanted it to accomplish.

This definition of effectiveness is an attractive one, and it does have the advantage of objectivity. However, it leaves out of consideration certain factors that may be important. For instance, the speaker may have certain purposes in mind without being fully aware of them. Most of us, for example, in considering any behavior—including communication—would place maintenance of a good reputation very high on our list of priorities. Although we do not ordinarily verbalize this as a goal, it may nevertheless exert a profound influence on our communication, especially when we must choose between this and some other outcome. I might, for instance, attract much attention to myself and get considerable public visibility by claiming that I had just been visited by emissaries from Venus. But however much I might want publicity, this notoriety would probably detract so much from my general credibility that I would decide against it.

To take a more positive example, I might accept an invitation to speak on behalf of the United Fund in my community partly because of a subconscious desire to become known as a public-spirited citizen. Overtly I might list my speaking goals as increasing public awareness of United Fund and promoting increased contributions. But some of my strategy as a speaker might be designed so as to subtly enhance my reputation for public-spiritedness; and if I found afterwards that my speaking had done little for the United Fund but much for my own image, I might count the effort well spent.

Examples like these, which emphasize what might be called the "personal gain" of the speaker as opposed to the "social gain" (presumably attributable to the more utilitarian ends of the speech), may leave the reader somewhat uneasy. We tend to deprecate self-seeking and, in general, prefer to think that as communicators we concentrate on more laudable motives. Yet it is a fact that communication can be used for purely personal ends; and that being so, some people are certainly going to use it thus. It is well for us to recognize also the possibility of such tendencies in ourselves, for what we are not aware of we cannot control.

The purpose of these examples is not to emphasize self-aggrandizement as an end of communication, but to illustrate the point that we do not always recognize explicitly all of our purposes when we engage in an act of communication. At least some of our intentions are likely to remain implicit and unrecognized. Consequently, a speaker may find out during or after the communication act that it had important consequences he had not anticipated. Now that the returns are in, so to speak, he finds that he has been successful or unsuccessful in ways that he had not consciously anticipated. If we are to get a complete picture of the effectiveness of a speech from the speaker-purpose point of view, we have to consider not only what the speaker *said* he was trying to do, but also what he *intended* implicitly, as well as how he *feels* about unanticipated outcomes. From his point of view, the effectiveness of the speech is the sum total of all of these considerations, each weighted according to its relative importance in his personal system of priorities.

Listener-Satisfaction Point of View

Recently it has come to be recognized that listeners usually expose themselves voluntarily to communication, and that they almost always come with some objective in mind. The extent to which the listener carries away from the encounter what he expected to get is one measure of the effectiveness of communication.

From the listener's point of view, much communication has as its primary goal the derivation of simple amusement. If listeners come to your motion picture theater to be entertained, one measure of the effectiveness of the film you exhibit today is how many of the listeners show signs of having been entertained. If the listener comes to your lecture on gardening to get information that he can use in making his own garden, one measure of the effectiveness of your lecture is how many listeners gain how much useful information. If parishioners come to hear your sermon expecting to have their faith renewed, one measure of your effectiveness is how many members of the congregation feel that the sermon accomplishes this to any appreciable extent. If listeners come anticipating a display of brilliance and wit, one measure of your effectiveness is how many of them go away feeling that they have seen such a display. If the audience comes to your "happening" expecting to exercise their sense of cultural superiority by applauding events that would be incomprehensible to others, they may properly judge your effectiveness according to the weirdness and novelty of your display. In short, one standard of effectiveness is *the extent to which listeners get from the message whatever it is that they want from it,* whether the speaker intended they should get it or not.

As in the case of the speaker-purpose standard, the audience-satisfaction standard is attractively objective. You can ask the auditor what he expects to get from a speech, then afterward assess the extent to which his wants were satisfied. Of course, as in the case of speaker purpose, audience satisfaction is complicated as a standard of effectiveness by the fact that listeners are often not really aware of everything that they want.

For example, I may come to see your play expecting to be exposed to dramatic scenes that will allow me to vicariously experience suspense, dread, anger, relief, and other forms of emotional arousal. In this, I may be disappointed; but the play may have such a significant social message that I feel it was worth attending after all, and I may subsequently recommend the play to a friend on just that ground. Of course, the play may provide both arousal and social significance for me, in which case I have not only received what I came for, but I have also reaped a bonus in unanticipated rewards.

Now, if I see enough plays that vicariously provide me with both emotional arousal and a significant message of some kind, I may without realizing it come to expect both. I may tell myself (and everyone else) that I go to the theater for its entertainment value—that is, to experience the arousal; but I may criticize a play because it "has nothing to say." Or, I may tell myself that I go to the theater for the social and psychological insights it provides—for the "message"; but then I may criticize a certain play because "nothing happens in it," or because "it is completely lacking in dramatic impact." In each of these cases I am asking explicitly for one outcome, but actually expecting two. In assessing my satisfaction, it would be necessary to take both into account.

In seeking to assess communication effectiveness either from the vantage point of speaker purpose or the view of audience satisfaction, we have seen that both *expected* and *unexpected* outcomes play a part. We have said that a speaker's effectiveness may be evaluated *from the standpoint of speaker purpose* by considering three criteria:

1. The sum total of outcomes both favorable and unfavorable *to him,*
2. The sum total of outcomes both expected and unexpected *by him,*
3. The weighting of each outcome according to its relative importance in the *speaker's* personal priority system.

By the same token, *from the standpoint of audience satisfaction* the speaker's effectiveness may be evaluated by considering:

1. The sum total of effects both favorable and unfavorable to him,
2. The sum total of effects both expected and unexpected by him,
3. The weighting of each effect according to its relative importance in the *listener's* personal priority system.

A Priori Standards for Evaluating Communication

An *a priori* standard is one that is established "beforehand." In the sense we are using it here, it is a standard that is established without direct reference to the communication participants. Rather, it is usually a standard that is applied to the message itself. Such standards are employed whenever communication is viewed from the standpoint of some broad system of thought such as *logic, ethics,* or *esthetics.*

Logic. Any communication can be evaluated from the standpoint of applied logic. The evaluation of, let us say, a speech from this point of view would entail no judgments about the speaker or the listener, but would require only a careful examination of the speech itself. To what extent are the premises on which arguments are based expressed or clearly implied in the speech? Do the conclusions flow logically from the premises? Is enough of the argument exposed so that the listener or analyst can evaluate how well the conditions of logical rigor are met? Is evidence offered in support of arguments? If so, is the evidence the best that is available, and does it meet the requirements of adequacy? These are some of the questions raised by logical analysis.

Obviously, some speeches meet the requirements of applied logic much better than others do. Obviously, too, the logical standard is not appropriate in every case. One does not evaluate a comedian's act on the rigor of its logic, but one can reasonably call a political speaker to task for failing to observe logical imperatives in his speaking. Having some feel for the relative importance of logical analysis for evaluating a given communication is clearly an important consideration in using this criterion of evaluation.

Ethics. A second *a priori* standard commonly employed for evaluating communication is ethics. The ethics of public communication has been hotly debated since Plato tried to set down rules of behavior for the ideal speaker. Plato argued, among other things, that the statesman-like orator would never lie, withhold information, advocate a dubious course of action, or use emotional appeals.

Just what is a speaker's responsibility to his audience and to others who, though not present, are nevertheless affected by his speech? How sure must the speaker be regarding the validity of a given piece of evidence before he will use it as support for his argument? How much responsibility does he have to anticipate the possibly negative consequences of actions he recommends, and then how much responsibility does he have to warn his audience about these negative possibilities? What responsibility does he have to disclose his particular interest in the outcome of the issue? Is it proper to use such techniques as "scapegoating," or making jokes at the expense of weak or defenseless third parties? These are only a few of the enormous complex of ethical questions that can be brought to bear in evaluating communication.

It is no doubt true that, despite the concern of communication scholars and teachers over the course of long centuries, in speeches and speech making the ethical criteria are too little applied and too often ignored. Only in very recent years has any serious attempt been made to codify ethical standards for communicators. Although the ethical analysis of communication is still in its infancy, it is already clear that most of the really significant ethical issues have some bearing on communication, and communication may raise important ethical issues that are found nowhere else.

Esthetics. A special kind of *a priori* standard is to be found in the esthetic criteria which may be applied to speaking, writing, and other forms of communication. Quite apart from anything else, messages are sometimes quite appealing purely for the esthetic pleasure they give. A voice may be pleasing or irritating. An idea may be developed awkwardly or elegantly. Movement may be graceful or clumsy. Style may be crude or cultivated. The message may display unity or create a disjointed impression. The treatment may be balanced or lopsided. All of these judgments represent evaluative criteria that have nothing to do with utilitarian, logical, or ethical considerations; they relate only to the beauty of the speech in its own right—the esthetic satisfactions that it provides or fails to provide.

Further, audiences may or may not respond to the artistic elements of a speech, broadcast, or other communication. Sometimes they will refuse to listen to the speaker unless certain artistic criteria are met; and at other times they will regard their presence as intrusive, an irritating emphasis on nonessentials. As in the case of logical standards, the speaker ought to know when the esthetic standards apply with some force, and when such application is entirely beside the point. To make the matter even more difficult, the esthetic response of the immediate audience to a speech or other communication is not necessarily a satisfactory guide to the appropriateness of the standards themselves. If the audience responds inappropriately, the response may represent as much a reflection on its taste as it does on the judgment of the speaker. The point is that although esthetic standards of judgment may always be applied, the amount of weight they should carry in the overall evaluation of the communication will vary from one situation to another.

Additional a priori standards of evaluation. There are of course many other *a priori* standards that may be applied to communication. Consider conformity as an instance. In a communist nation, for example, one standard that is almost universally applied is "Does this message conform in all relevant ways to Marxist doctrine?" Among some right-wing groups in the United States, a criterion seems to be: "Does this message in any way reflect the possible influence of foreign ideologies?" In fact, conformity to *any* doctrine may be used as the basis for evaluation, as witness the enormous variety of "schools" of literary criticism. Thus, the list of *a priori* criteria for communication could be extended endlessly. In some situations one or another of these criteria becomes all important; but the three that we have emphasized here—logic, ethics, and esthetics—are the most universal.

Against the background of these differing standards of effectiveness, we may feel that we have lost the forest in the trees. How, then, is "effectiveness" really to be measured? The answer, we think, is that "effectiveness" is truly and inevitably a *relative* term. We have tried in this chapter to outline the main standards against which judgments of effectiveness are usually made. If you disagree with someone else about whether a given speech, counseling session, play, demonstration, or other communication was "effective," you might take a moment or two to determine whether both of you are using the same standards of evaluation. Very probably, you are not.

In this chapter we have made three important distinctions that underlie all evaluation of communication. The first distinction is between *consummatory communication,* which has no ulterior end beyond satisfying the speaker's need or desire to be heard, and *instrumental communication,* which aims to elicit some particular response from the listener. The second distinction is between *effects,* which are any observable outcomes of the speech, and *effectiveness,* which requires that the speech or its effects or both be measured against some outside standard. The last distinction, noted also in the preceding chapter, is between *process effects,* which occur during the act of communication itself, and *product effects,* which represent changes in the listener after the communication is done.

Three broad standards for evaluating effectiveness have been discussed: speaker purpose, listener satisfaction, and *a priori* standards. We have noted that speakers do not always consciously recognize all of their purposes, so that it may be difficult to apply this standard fully in some cases. We also noted the difficulty in applying the standard of audience satisfaction, since auditors also may be unaware of all of the purposes they bring to a communication. *A priori* standards we discussed primarily in terms of logical soundness, ethical acceptability, and esthetic appeal. We also observed that any philosophical system can be used to set standards for evaluating communication.

PROBLEMS AND QUESTIONS FOR DISCUSSION

1. Read the section entitled "Analyses of Three Speeches" in *The Speaker's Resource Book*, Revised Edition (Glenview, Ill.: Scott, Foresman and Company, 1966), by Carroll C. Arnold, Douglas Ehninger, and John C. Gerber, pages 264–292. Classify the critics' approaches according to what you have learned in this chapter.
2. In addition to the approaches used by the critics in the three "Analyses" indicated in Problem #1 above, were there other approaches that you thought might have been made? Specify the further standards of evaluation that you feel the critics could have found especially relevant to apply.
3. With reference to the above "Analyses," what additional information—if it had been available—might have provided significant grounds for further evaluation of the speeches in question?
4. In the speech entitled "The Method of Scientific Investigation" by Thomas Henry Huxley (pages 264–269), do you feel that process effects or product effects were more important? What responses of each kind do you feel would have been most significant? Would you give process responses and product responses the same order of priority for the speech entitled "Address to Congress" by Douglas MacArthur (pages 277–284)? Explain your judgment.
5. Based on the information provided in the headnote preceding any one of the three speeches referred to in Problem #1 above, how would you describe the probable condition or state of mind of the listeners? Why were they in the audience? What were they apparently expecting? What criteria were they probably prepared to apply to the speech? What did they seemingly hope to get out of it?

II.

SPEECH COMMUNICATION AS A PROCESS

In Chapter 1 several overlapping approaches to the study of communication were explored. The next nine chapters concerned particular aspects of communication: language, meaning, voice, hearing, listening, messages, social interaction, effects, and evaluation. In this chapter we shall return to the question "What is communication?" restricting our attention, however, to speech communication and approaching the question against the background of information provided in the other chapters.

A SYNTHESIS

In the remaining pages, an attempt will be made to fit the facets and elements together in such a way as to build a unified description of the speech communication process as a whole. For the most part we will be using as building blocks the concepts contained in the preceding chapters, adding only a few new ideas that help round out the larger picture. It is this larger picture—the synthesis—that we shall try to grasp in this final chapter. Whereas our attention has heretofore been directed to details, it will now be widened to survey the process in broad outline.

Some theorists would say that what we are now about to do is to "build a model." In this sense, a model is a highly abstract and simplified description that sacrifices detail for the sake of under-standing and generalizability. But if the model is a good one, the details can be put back in without distortion or loss of accuracy. The advantage of a communication model is that it helps us to visu-alize the essentials of the process without getting bogged down in the particulars. Thus it serves as a special aid to understanding—a graphic visualization that helps put a wealth of particulars into a broad perspective.

You now have in hand a sizeable number of particulars about speech communication, and the model about to be built should en-hance your understanding of those particulars by giving you a broader context in which to view them. In one sense, then, this chapter is a kind of synthesis of the book—not all of it, but those parts of it that fit together to form one coherent picture of the speech communication process.

As we shall use the term, *a process is an interconnected series of events which follow one another in a definite temporal order.* Events are interconnected when the occurrence or outcome of one event leads to the occurrence or influences the outcome of one or more other events. Events are interconnected in temporal order when, following the occurrence of some initiating or first event, the other events follow one after another in some predetermined or de-terminable sequence. In this chapter we shall view oral communica-tion as a certain chain or series of events occurring in a particular order, so related to one another that the outcome of each event in-fluences the outcome of one or more of the events which follow it.

THE COMMUNICATION PROCESS VIEWED AS TRANSMISSION

The transmission-reception concept is basic to communication. Re-gardless of what else communication may concern itself with, any approach to the process must recognize the importance of the con-trolled passage of signals or stimuli from one place to another. In Chapter 1 (pages 12–14) we discussed a transmission model that is especially well suited to describe this transmission aspect of com-munication. Now we are looking at transmission in greater detail.

Reproduced in Figure 12 is a diagram model of the major compo-nents of a signal-transmission system. Transmission is accomplished when an information *Source* manipulates the output of a *Trans-mitter* in such a way that a *Signal* is emitted into a *Channel* through which it passes to activate a *Receiver* which, in turn, makes some function of the signal available at a *Destination*. Transmission passes a *Message* consisting of a sequence of *Symbols* from source to destination in some *Code* which is appropriate to the channel employed. The function of the transmitter is to *encode* the message (translate the symbols into code), and the function of the receiver is to *decode* the message (translate symbols out of code). Thus, it is the signal, or coded message, which passes through the channel rather than the message itself. Neither transmitters nor receivers are perfect. Moreover, in addition to the information source, other sources may simultaneously transmit signals into the channel. These extraneous signals can distort, override, or otherwise interfere with the information-bearing signal; and as a result the received signal may differ from the transmitted signal to some extent. All factors which interfere with fidelity of transmission are labeled *Noise,* and any identifiable source of such noise is called a *Noise Source.*

As you recall from Chapter 1 (pages 12–14) this transmission model may be applied to the process of oral communication in the face-to-face situation. Insofar as the audible aspects of speech are concerned, the source may be identified as the mind of the speaker, the transmitter as his vocal tract, the channel as a bandwidth of acoustic energies, the receiver as the ear of the listener, and the destination as the listener's mind. The signal which passes through the channel is a chain of sound waves patterned in the code of some natural language. In the acoustic channel there are many noise sources (such as traffic and competing conversations); and noise

FIGURE 12
Model of Communication as Signal Transmission
(After Shannon)[1]

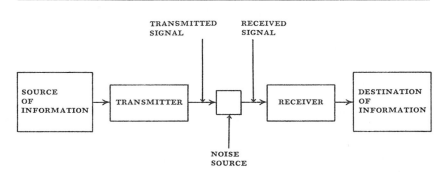

1. C. E. Shannon and W. Weaver, *The Mathematical Theory of Communication* (Urbana, Ill.: University of Illinois Press, 1949).

may also arise in the vocal tract (for example, when the speaker has a cold or a speech defect, or speaks with a mouthful of food) or in the auditory mechanism (when, for instance, the listener has an ear infection or a ruptured eardrum). Redundancy in the language code, as we have previously noted, is insurance against too much information loss due to noise.

Signals Versus Messages

From the standpoint of its human significance, the transmission system of communication is usually viewed as a means of passing meaningful messages from the mind of the speaker to the mind of the listener. However, meaningful messages as such exist only at the source and destination points. The channel carries not a meaningful message but a stream of sound signals which can be regarded at best as no more than an acoustically coded representation of the message. In fact, the acoustic signal represents considerably less than the whole of the message. It is able to carry only that part of the message represented by the phonemes, words, and phrases of the language and by variations in the pitch, loudness, timing, and quality of the voice. Meaning is one aspect of a message which is not adequately represented by these elements.

Ordinarily we think of the meaning of an utterance as being attached to, but somehow transcending the patterned language units that make up the superficial structure of the utterance. Meaning is elicited by the words and phrases, but it is closely related to the experience of the speaker (or listener) and to the total situation in which the utterance is spoken. If the same words may have different meanings for different individuals and in different situations, then it follows that meaning cannot be fully "encoded for" transmission or reliably "decoded from" a received signal. It must be viewed as an aspect of messages as they occur at source and destination—as something which can be created, but cannot be transmitted.

Fidelity in Communication

The significance of this point becomes clearer when we consider a crucial aspect of any transmission system: fidelity of communication. Fidelity concerns the correspondence between a transmitted message or signal and its received counterpart.

Signal versus message fidelity. In oral communication there are several kinds of fidelity to consider. First, there is the problem of *signal fidelity*, the similarity between the sound signal transmitted by the vocal tract of the speaker and the sound signal received by the ear of the listener. Discrepancies here are expressed in terms of physical differences between the two sound signals. Second, there is the quite different problem of *message fidelity*, the similarity between the message intended by the speaker and the message heard by the listener. Under conditions of excellent signal fidelity, certain aspects of message fidelity may be extremely good and other aspects extremely poor. This is because in oral communication the message is a remarkably complex phenomenon displaying several levels of organization—linguistic, ideational, and implicational—and we have to consider a different aspect of message fidelity at each of these levels. In other words, what we mean by "message fidelity" may take a number of different forms depending upon the particular feature of the message we consider.

Intelligibility. The most basic levels of verbal message organization involve phonemes, words, phrases, and sentences. At these purely linguistic levels of organization the question of fidelity is usually called the "intelligibility" problem. A linguistic unit— whether phoneme, word, phrase, or sentence—is intelligible only if the listener can identify or reconstruct it accurately.

In both signal fidelity and message fidelity, intelligibility is determined in the same way: by comparing each symbol of the source message with its counterpart in the destination message so as to determine what proportion of the symbols are identical in the two messages. This comparison is possible and meaningful in the case of linguistic units because if the speaker and the listener use the same language, we can assume some common pool of symbols available to both. Among users of the same language, message fidelity at the level of linguistic units is just about directly proportional to signal fidelity: the better the quality of the signal, the higher the intelligibility of the message. Mutilate the signal or mix noise with it, and intelligibility falls off. In other words, because they can be coded precisely in acoustic form, the symbols of a message can be transmitted.

Meanings, however, present an entirely different problem, for meanings are not "coded" in words in the same way that words are coded in acoustic signals. This stems partly from the fact that, whereas all users of the same language have access to a common store of words, they by no means have access to the same store of ideas. The number and nature of verbal events which can occur at source and destination are strictly limited by a linguistic code common to both. Therefore, with an effective transmission system in operation we can anticipate the symbols occurring at the destination. But the meanings occurring at source and destination are not so strictly limited, and therefore—regardless of the effectiveness of the transmission system—we have no reason to expect that source meanings and destination meanings will correspond perfectly for a particular utterance. Fortunately, the nature of the physical world and the structure of society provide members of the same culture with many common experiences and concepts. Otherwise, verbal communication would not be worth the effort it requires.

Advantages and Disadvantages of the Transmission View

In attempting to assess the usefulness of viewing oral communication as a message-transmission system, we should be aware of its possible benefits and limitations. One major advantage of such a view is its essential clarity: (1) the mind of the speaker and the mind of the listener are connected only by a transmission chain; (2) that chain will transmit reliably only symbols—that is, those parts of a message which can be coded in linguistic units; and (3) meaning cannot be coded fully or reliably in symbols.

There is, however, a considerable inconvenience in discussing oral communication solely from the standpoint of message transmission. This inconvenience arises from the fact that, in the transmission model, source and destination are given different names and are far apart, at opposite ends of the chain. Insofar as transmission is concerned, of course, this nomenclature and placement are quite appropriate. However, oral communicating is done by individuals, and the transmission model divides an individual into two halves: a *source-transmitter* and a *receiver-destination*. In fact, these two halves are contained within a single organism, and therefore we can be reasonably sure that they do not operate independently. For this reason, a model which views communication as organismic behavior better enables us to consider the process of communication from the standpoint of the communicator.

THE COMMUNICATION PROCESS VIEWED AS ORGANISMIC BEHAVIOR

Oral communication is behavior. Whether speaking or listening, an individual is engaged in an ongoing pattern of learned activity through which a degree of learning is always taking place. Some of this activity is overt—that is, visible to an observer. Much of it is covert—hidden under the skin. Some of it is reflexive—automatic, perhaps unconscious response to environmental stimuli. Some of it is intelligent—displaying foresight, planning, and purpose in the adaptation of behavior to circumstances. No view of speech communication is complete unless it takes this variety of behaviors into account.

A model of communication as organismic behavior is presented in Figure 13.

Unlike the transmission process of Figure 12, which has a natural starting point (the source), the behavioral process has no logical starting place. Therefore, rather than following the process through a complete cycle, we will examine certain features of the behavioral system separately.

Receptor Systems

First of all, we should note that the *organism* of Figure 13 is equipped with *receptor systems* which are capable of detecting *stimuli* emanating from *environmental events* outside the organism. By means of these receptors the organism achieves and retains contact with its environment. Certain occurrences in the environment generate energies which impinge upon the receptors, and these respond by setting up electrochemical activity in the nerves leading from the receptors to the central nervous system.

The human receptors are able to detect a wide range of stimuli, making it possible for the human being to become aware of a great variety of environmental events. Of course, not all of them play a part in speech communication. Light radiating or reflecting from the surface of an object becomes a visible stimulus to the eye. Sound produced by collision or vibration of objects becomes audible stimuli to the ear. Molecules detached from the surface of objects or substances waft through the air to produce sensations of smell. If dissolved in the saliva of the mouth, these molecules become tastes. Mechanical forces or changes in pressure on the skin are detectable as tactile sensations. Changes in heat radiation into or out of the body produce sensations of hot and cold. In fact, the organism also has many systems for monitoring internal changes in its own condition and activity. The known human receptor systems for detection of environmental stimuli are the eye (for detecting light), the ear (for detecting sound), the skin (for detecting pressure and temperature), the nose (for detecting airborne molecules), and the tongue (for detecting molecules in solution). Although all of these sensors are important to human existence, the eye and the ear have

FIGURE 13

Model of Communication as Organismic Behavior

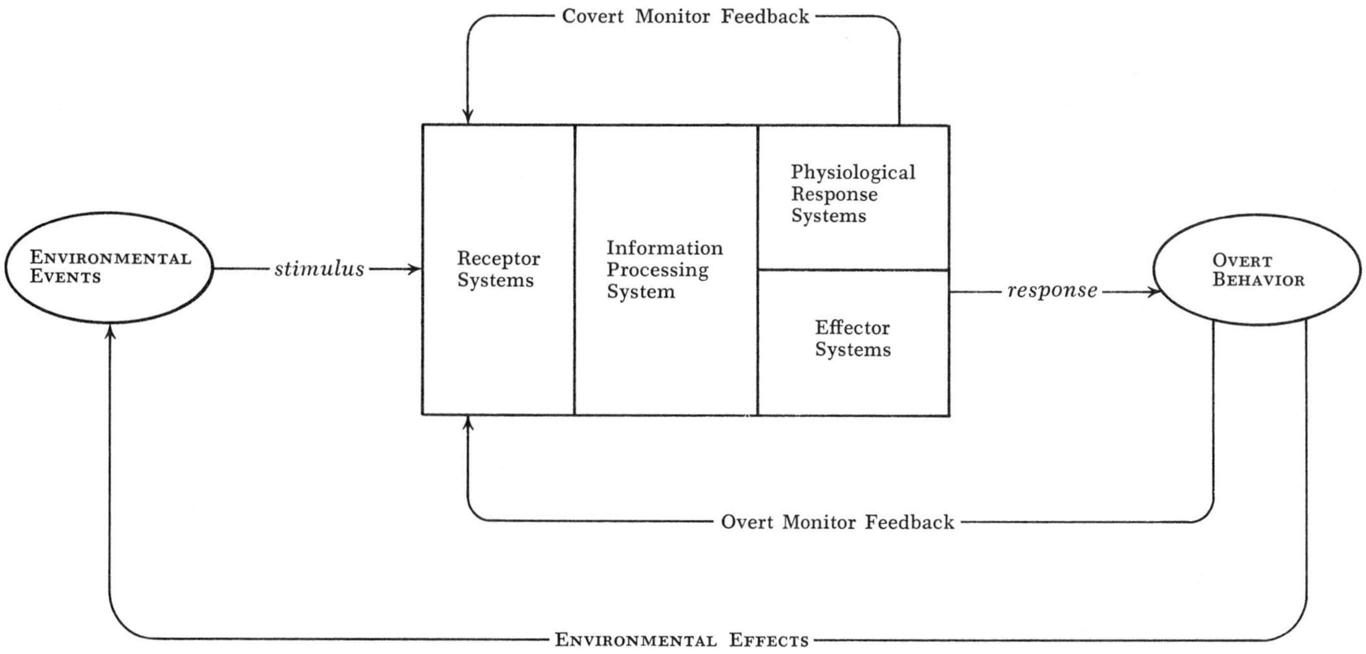

a special significance for man because, in addition to their other functions, they serve him so extensively for communication.

Every environmental event by no means produces stimuli which are detectable by animal receptors. The human senses are inaccessible to many stimuli. In terms of our hearing, for instance—as we learned from our study of the "audible area" in Chapter 4 (pages 59–61)—some are out of range; others are too weak. Still others are not of an energy type which any human receptor is fitted to receive. Otherwise—as we discussed in Chapter 4 (page 59)—we might be able to use super-efficient radio waves for communication. Nevertheless, it is through those energies which are within the range and intensity of the types of stimuli to which the human receptor systems can respond that human beings maintain awareness of the objects and events in their environments—including other human beings. Needless to say, it is through these stimulus modalities also that communication must take place.

Effector Systems

In addition to receptor systems for detecting stimuli coming from the environment, the organism is fitted with *effector systems* capable of generating *responses* which produce phenomena in the organism's environment and which we interpret as the organism's *overt behavior*. This includes, of course, his communication behavior. When we compare the range of stimuli the human organism can receive with the variety of unaided overt bodily responses he can make, the number of the latter seems small indeed. By means of vibrations in the vocal tract, the human being can broadcast acoustic signals, but somewhat fewer than he can hear. He radiates only heat, and that at a constant, uncontrollable rate. He radiates no light at all (as fireflies, glowworms, and certain fishes do); although by muscular contractions he can move the parts of his body into different positions so as to produce variable patterns of reflected light. These same muscles enable him to move around in his environment, to direct some mechanical force against nearby objects, and to manipulate smaller objects. Tiny glands secrete various substances onto the surface of his skin which evaporate slowly into the air. Although this process does vary in activity level from one time to another, it is not controllable; and in any case the molecular concentrations produced by this process are too slight to be detected by other humans even when they are only a short distance away.

Thus the human organism produces controlled outputs to its environment chiefly by means of the vocal tract and the skeletal muscles. These are the primary effector systems. Insofar as human behavior is overt—that is, insofar as it produces detectable environmental signals—such behavior results from muscular action, either in the vocal tract or in the skeletal or facial muscles. It follows that it is exclusively through these forms of activity that communication must take place.

Overt monitor feedback. We have noted that the organism of Figure 13 is equipped with effector systems for generating energies in its environment and with receptor systems for detecting energies in its environment. Ordinarily, whatever energies its effectors generate, its receptors can receive. For example, when you speak, your voice is as audible to you as it is to others. So whatever else may happen as a result of the organism's overt behavior, signals are generated which stimulate its own receptors. This self-stimulation through overt behavior we shall call *overt monitor feedback.* The term feedback refers to any process by which a signal, or a portion or function of a signal is returned to its source. To monitor a process or an event is to observe it, usually with a view to controlling it or controlling some related process or event. Thus, overt monitor feedback is the process by which a portion of the same signal which the organism puts out to its environment returns from the environment through the organism's receptor systems, enabling the organism to observe directly and thus control more effectively its own overt behavior. If you doubt that people use such feedback in speaking, listen to the speech of a deaf person.

Covert response systems. Not all behavior is overt. Numerous events occur more or less under the skin, within the organism, which are not detectable without the aid of special instruments. These events represent the action of the *covert response systems,* and we may speak of them as covert behavior. Human physiological mechanisms are exceedingly varied and interrelated in complex ways; but we shall give as examples here only four systems known to respond to the sorts of stimuli which operate in speech communication: (1) the circulatory system, (2) the respiratory system, (3) the skin, and (4) the skeletal muscles.

The circulatory system includes the heart, veins, arteries, and capillaries. Under varying conditions the heart may increase or decrease its pumping rate, or it may contract more or less strongly—either of which circumstances may cause blood pressure to rise or fall. Blood pressure may also be affected by contraction or dilation of the capillaries in the skin; and this, in turn, may produce an increase or decrease of skin temperature.

The *respiratory system* includes the lungs, diaphragm, and certain muscles of the abdomen and chest. In response to certain conditions these muscles may respond in such a way as to cause the breathing rate to rise or fall, or to cause the breathing to become shallower or deeper.

The *skin*, which is the body's largest organ, contains several physiological systems. We have already noted that contraction or dilation of the skin capillaries may cause the skin's temperature to rise or fall. Earlier we noted the incidence of sweat glands opening onto the skin's surface: those on the palms of the hands and soles of the feet seem to respond primarily to emotional stresses, whereas those distributed over the rest of the body seem to respond primarily to heat and cold. The activity of the palmar sweat glands is also thought to be related to the phenomenon which is sometimes called the galvanic skin response—that is, the tendency of the skin to change its electrical resistance under conditions of exertion or stress.

In the discussion of overt behavior we designated the skeletal muscles as a primary effector system; however, the skeletal muscles may respond covertly without producing an overtly detectable signal. Sensitive electrodes placed on the skin directly over a muscle bundle can record covert tensing or relaxing which is not visible to the unaided eye.

Covert monitor feedback. These four covert response systems are representative of many others, such as the digestive system and the ductless glands—all of which account for a great deal of human behavior, but which produce few overt signals. However, these same covert responses produce many stimuli which are detectable to the person experiencing them. As we noted earlier in this chapter, this is due to the fact that, in addition to receptor systems for detecting stimuli from its external environment, the human organism is also equipped with sensors for detecting changes in its own internal states. Minor changes in blood pressure, skin temperature, heart rate and pumping power, depth and rate of breathing, perspiration, and muscular tension are all sensible to the organism through the operation of *covert monitor feedback.* Among other things, these feedbacks are a significant part of experiencing emotional responses.

Referring again to our model (Figure 13, page 182) and summarizing our discussion of the organismic aspect of the oral communication process up to this point, we have described a person having receptor systems capable of detecting physical stimuli produced by environmental events. He responds in accordance with two systems: (1) effector systems which generate physical responses that are detectable as overt behavior, and (2) covert systems which alter the person's internal condition. He is able to monitor responses produced by either of these systems. He can observe his overt behaviors through the same receptor systems used to detect other environmental events—a process we call overt monitor feedback. He can also observe his covert responses through the use of internal receptor systems—a process we call covert monitor feedback.

Environmental effects. The overt behavior of the human organism leads to certain *effects.* In detecting these effects the person may be said to be observing the consequences of his behavior. This is something quite different from the operation of overt monitor feedback, in which he observes his own overt behavior as he is producing that behavior; for we make a distinction between the behavior and its effects, even though both are detected through the same receptor systems. Overt behavior is composed of the response energies themselves—acoustic, visual, and mechanical; but effects are *environmental events* which occur outside the organism as a consequence of these energies. When a painter dips his brush into paint, and then draws it across a canvas, we refer to his action as behavior. But in behaving, the painter has altered his environment by leaving a mark on the canvas; and we may speak of this alteration as an effect of his behavior. Moreover, the effect in this case is observable to the painter through his own visual receptor system: he can see the consequences of his behavior.

Many environmental effects, like the one we have just described, are essentially physical. However, for the human organism, some of the most significant effects of behavior are those which occur through the intervention of other human organisms. For every human being, all other human beings are parts of his environment. Together they make up what we may call his social environment, and their responses to his behavior are for him among the most important effects of that behavior. In particular, speakers try to manipulate these effects to predetermined ends by constructing messages and otherwise arranging the circumstances of communication to their advantage.

Information Processing and Forms of Behavior

We have now discussed all of the features of the organismic behavior model except one: the central segment of the organism labeled the *Information Processing System.* The importance of this feature is apparent when we consider behavior as response to environmental stimuli. We have observed that the receptors respond to stimuli by sending electrochemical signals along the nerve pathways leading toward the central nervous system, and that effectors are activated by signals traveling over other pathways in the opposite direction. But what links the stimulus signal to the response signal?

In the view we shall take here, stimuli and responses are linked through the operations of an information processing system (hereafter abbreviated IPS) which takes information from the receptor signals, performs certain flexible operations on those inputs, and puts out control impulses to the effectors. Based upon the different patterns of relationship between stimuli and responses, we may distinguish three characteristic modes or levels of operation by the IPS: (1) reflexive, (2) habitual, and (3) intelligent.[2] Externally, these modes manifest themselves as:

Unconditioned reflex
Conditioned reflex
Conditioned operant
Intelligent behavior

Further, as we shall observe, these reflexive, habitual, and intelligent patterns of response—while they all rely upon similar information-handling processes within the organism—differ significantly in the hierarchy of their complexity. To begin, let us examine the outward characteristics of the three different modes, and then see what they have in common.

Unconditioned reflex. The simplest form of behavior is the unconditioned reflex, which is characteristic of the behavior of simpler forms of life, but which is also abundantly present in the higher organisms, including man. When the same stimulus elicits an immediate and invariant response from all normal individuals regardless of differences in experience, the total behavioral pattern is called an unconditioned reflex. Flash a bright light before the eyes, and the pupils contract. Strike the patellar tendon, and the knee jerks. Place food in the mouth, and saliva flows. These behaviors do not have to be learned and are the same for all normal humans. Having specified the stimulus for one of these rudimentary forms of behavior we can predict with great accuracy the response of any biologically normal individual.

Unconditioned reflexes may be important in the infant's ac-

2. In this discussion we are primarily concerned with intelligence as human experience used flexibly to elicit new patterns of behavior, and are defining it as such.

quisition of certain pre-language skills, but they play no very significant role in mature speech behavior. In fact, the unconditioned reflexes account for only a small fraction of all human behavior. Most of it is extremely variable and dependent upon past experiences as well as present stimuli.

Conditioned reflex. Repetitive patterns of behavior that vary according to the previous history of the individual are said to be learned behaviors or habits. The simplest form of learned behavior is the conditioned reflex, exemplified by the conditioned salivary reflex made famous by Pavlov's early experiments. Food placed in the mouth elicits salivation, and this mode of response is an unconditioned reflex. However, if some initially *neutral* stimulus, such as a ringing bell or a flashing light, should occur often just as food is placed in the mouth, this originally neutral stimulus will in time come to elicit the salivary response even when food is not present. At this point a conditioned reflex is said to have been established, and the salivary response is said to have been conditioned to the light or bell. Probably much of our hearing and listening behavior and many of our process responses to communication are traceable to conditioned reflexes.

Conditioned operant. A somewhat more complicated form of learned behavior is the conditioned operant, exemplified by the thirsty rat that learns to thread his way through a maze to find water, or by the hungry cat that learns to operate a lever to activate a food-release mechanism. Such learning is said to occur through a process of reinforcement. Certain stimuli are said to be reinforcing under given conditions because, under those conditions, administration of the reinforcing stimulus increases the likelihood that any behavior which preceded the reinforcing stimulus will recur under similar conditions in the future. That is, if a thirsty rat is given water, then whatever it did immediately prior to drinking will be reinforced. If a hungry cat is fed, whatever it did immediately prior to eating will be more likely to be done again the next time the cat is hungry. A frequently reinforced behavior becomes habitual—that is, its probability of occurrence becomes very high. Most speaking behavior, from sentence construction to the games people play, is based on conditioned operants.

Although reflexive and operant responses may both be learned, the response itself plays quite a different role in the two types of learning. Reflexive behavior is elicited by appropriate stimuli, and its conditioning depends only upon repeated pairings of an unconditioned and a neutral stimulus. The form of the behavior does not change, only the nature of the stimuli which are sufficient to elicit it. Operant behavior, on the other hand, is not, strictly speaking, elicited at all. It must be emitted before it can be reinforced. As operant conditioning proceeds, the behavior itself (rather than just the connection between stimulus and response) may change dramatically. Put still more simply, *through reflex conditioning* the organism cannot be brought to emit any behaviors which it could not emit originally; but *through operant conditioning* the organism may learn entirely new responses. For example, every normal human being—from the time of his birth—can experience fear; through reflex conditioning he merely grows capable of sometimes experiencing it as a response to spoken messages. But nobody is born with the ability to make a speech based on fear appeals. To do that, he must go through a long period of operant conditioning.

Despite this basic difference, certain types of operant behavior bear a superficial resemblance to reflexive behavior in that they occur only following certain stimuli. For instance, a pigeon will learn to peck at a button which activates a feeding machine. However, if the machine is set up so that it delivers food only when the button is lighted up, then the pigeon will learn to peck at the button only when it is lighted. If the hungry pigeon is placed near a dark button, the bird will do nothing; but when the button is lighted up, the pigeon will immediately begin to peck at it. Superficially, it appears that lighting the button has elicited the pecking response. In this situation we say that the lighted button is a *discriminant stimulus*, and that the button-pecking operant behavior has been conditioned to that stimulus. Becoming aware of listener feedback is, in a sense, equivalent to acquiring a set of discriminant stimuli: one learns to recognize in the listener responses that require adaptation.

Intelligent behavior. Undoubtedly a great deal of human behavior, including much communication behavior, is composed of conditioned reflexes and conditioned operants. On the other hand, humans are capable of putting together entirely new patterns of behavior which, although they have never been tried before, are clearly not random combinations of previously learned behaviors and which are successful in coping with novel situations. Under conditions such as these, the person is said to display intelligence. We refer to such behavior as *intelligent behavior*, even though it may not be conscious and even though we might not regard it as wise or good.

Most of us are conscious of performing certain intelligent operations when engaged in planning and decision-making. We are more or less aware of doing things we describe as "analyzing the situation," "defining the problem," "remembering relevant facts and relationships," "thinking out solutions," "inventing alternative courses of action," "considering advantages and disadvantages," "anticipating consequences," and "arriving at a decision." Each of these terms may be thought of as a shorthand expression standing for a complicated sequence of neurological events. Even when one is conscious of the sequence as a whole—that is, when he is monitoring it—he is not conscious of the individual events of which it is composed. I may be aware of "remembering yesterday's lecture" without being aware of the individual neurological events of which that remembering consists. Nor, in fact, is my awareness of remembering the lecture a necessary condition of memory. I may use my memory of yesterday's lecture in answering today's question in class without being aware that I am so using it. Indeed, all of the processes of conscious thought may occur outside of awareness; and, except for the important difference that they are not monitored, they are not essentially different because they occur unconsciously. In other words, a decision arrived at unconsciously is likely to have been reached by processes not essentially different from those involved in conscious decision-making. As we are using the term, then, intelligence is not restricted to conscious thought. It refers to any process by which experience is used in a flexible way to develop novel patterns of behavior. However, if the process can be made conscious, it can also be made public; that is, we can share it with others, even make a speech about it.

There is not a sharp dividing line between habitual behavior and intelligent behavior. The first few times one encounters a recurring problem, he may deal with it through the processes we have described as intelligent; but if the same problem recurs often enough, he will eventually develop some habitual way of dealing with it— that is, some habitual pattern of response to which the total problem-situation is in effect a stimulus. In situations which an individual must confront repeatedly, efficiency requires that as much as possible of his behavior should be habitual. Whenever we talk about something that has become habitual to us, we are likely to rely on many assumptions. If, because of a divergence of experience, our assumptions differ widely from those of our listener, he may find it difficult to follow our train of reasoning.

Mental simulation. Obviously, intelligent behavior calls for even more numerous and more complex kinds of "machinery" for handling and processing information than that required by the un-conditioned reflex, the conditioned reflex, or the conditioned operant. In fact, the variety of processes underlying intelligent behavior is so large that—because of the scope of this book—we will examine only one typical example. The example, which we will consider in some detail, is basic to decision-making in many situations, and we shall term it "simulation."

This process involves a kind of forecasting or predicting of *future* behaviors, and is based on a pre-assessment or pre-programing of alternate sets of *possible* events, outcomes, or responses to organismic stimuli. Stored in the IPS are memory traces of a great many past behaviors, and a great many environmental events. Also stored is additional information making it possible to form estimates of the likelihood that a given behavior will lead to a given event, and of the likelihood that a given event will lead to some other event. That is, information is available for forming *causal estimates*. By processing information on hand, one can say in effect, "If Behavior A is emitted, then Environmental Event J is more likely than Event K; and if J occurs, then Event P is almost certain to follow." Finally, information is available to form an evaluation of any given event with respect to its *desirability*. By processing information concerning possible behaviors, information concerning causal connections between behaviors and events and between events and other events, and information concerning the values of outcome events, one can construct an image of a sequence of events in which the relationship between his own behavior and his own satisfactions is represented. Obviously, the possibility of simulating behaviors and their effects before emitting them is extremely useful, for it enables the organism which has this capacity to avoid costly errors and false starts. Add the ability to communicate, and one can share the results of this thinking—this mental simulation—with others.

Moreover, where the simulation process is a conscious one, it can be tested for *validity*. One may have insufficient or faulty information upon which to base predictions of the outcome of a contemplated response. As a result, the simulated image of the sequence as it occurs in the IPS will correspond very poorly to the sequence of events which does in fact occur in the environment if and when the proposed action is taken. But if one has other information available which enables him to check the inputs to the simulation for sufficiency and quality, this information can help him to evaluate the likelihood that the simulated image is an accurate projection of the environmental state of affairs. This evaluation of the simulation process is a truly remarkable phenomenon. Not only does it make possible an estimate of the predictive value of the simulation, but it also illustrates a complexity of information processing which may be characteristic of human thought processes alone. In evaluating a simulation, the organism is processing information about the processing of information; it is thinking about its own thinking. Of course, if one shares his thoughts with others—communicates them —then others can also check his reasoning by applying the techniques of critical listening.

The hierarchic complexity of response patterns. To review, then, in the preceding paragraphs we have spoken of reflexive, habitual, and intelligent patterns of response as three different kinds of behavior; and, as we have seen, they do represent apparently different patterns of relationship between stimuli and responses. However, they all rely upon basically similar information-handling processes within the organism, even though they differ largely in the number and complexity of basic processes involved.

In the case of the *unconditioned reflex* we need to imagine only the simplest kind of information-processing system: a sort of inherited switchboard that processes the incoming stimulus signal by invariably routing it to a command switch for the appropriate response signal. This basic switching operation is the simplest form of information processing, and is basic to all behavior.

A neurological switchboard arrangement, however, is insufficient to account for even the simplest kinds of learned behavior. To explain the *conditioned reflex,* we also need a storage or memory device for accumulating the experience of numerous paired stimuli. Though not essential to *unconditioned* reflexes, storage is basic to all other forms of behavior.

In addition to a built-in neurological switchboard and a storage or memory device, the formation and maintenance of an *operant* requires some device for making comparisons. Comparison is basic to recognition; and in the execution of an operant, the organism must be able to recognize a discriminant stimulus, issue commands to the effectors, monitor feedback from the effectors as they perform the operant, compare this feedback with internal standards of performance, recognize the reinforcing stimulus, and compare it with internal standards of value.

Finally, we have emphasized that *intelligent behavior*—involving as it does such concerns as conscious and subconscious selectivity, judgmental choice of predictive alternatives, and discriminate response—calls for still more complex information-handling systems than those noted above. Since the variety of intelligent processes is large, and because we wanted to consider in detail one which is basic to much decision-making, we chose a typical example, namely *simulation*.

THE COMMUNICATION PROCESS VIEWED AS BEHAVIORAL INTERACTION

A strictly behavioral point of view requires that every response the organism emits be viewed as the effect of some stimulus or stimuli, however numerous or remote. When one appears to initiate behavior without any apparent stimulation, it may be possible theoretically to account for the behavior as delayed response to prior stimuli. In many cases, however, the stimuli seem so remotely connected with behavior that it is unprofitable to try to identify them. It seems more fruitful to speak of such behavior as if it had been initiated by the person himself—that is, in the Information Processing System. If we allow this viewpoint, then the behavioral process has two possible beginning points: (1) it may begin with an environmental or external event, in which case the organism is responding to stimulation; (2) or it may begin with an event in the IPS, in which case the organism is responding internally, on its own initiative, in accordance with its "intelligence." Another way of saying this is that interaction between a person and his environment may be initiated either by the environment or by the person himself.

When we compare the Transmission Model of Communication (Figure 12, page 177) with the Organismic-Behavior Model (Figure 13, page 182), we find that many features of the former correspond in function to certain features of the latter. Therefore, if we now put the transmission and the organismic aspects together, we can build a more adequate model of the communication process as a whole.

The channel of the transmission model corresponds to part of the physical environment of the behavioral model. The transmitter, which generates a signal in the channel, is identical in function to the effectors, which generate energies in the environment. The receiver, which decodes signals from the channel, performs the same function as the receptors, which detect energies in the environment. The signals themselves correspond to stimuli and responses: considered as a product of effector action (that is, as a transmitted signal), the signal is a response; considered as an activator of receptor action (that is, as a received signal), the signal is a stimulus. Considered as a signal, the response may differ from the stimulus due to the intervention of noise emanating from the environmental stimulus sources which, considered from this point of view, relate to the noise sources of the transmission model. Messages exist in the IPS, which serves the behavioral model as both source and destination: considered from the standpoint of its influence upon the transmission of response, the IPS is a source; but considered from the standpoint of the influence upon it of received stimuli, it is a destination. Viewed diagrammatically, in

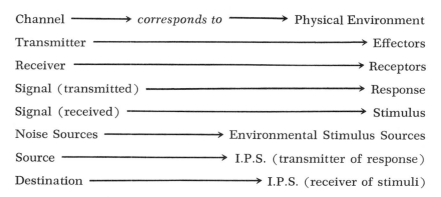

The Transmission Model   as compared with   *The Behavioral Model*

Channel ⟶ *corresponds to* ⟶ Physical Environment

Transmitter ⟶ Effectors

Receiver ⟶ Receptors

Signal (transmitted) ⟶ Response

Signal (received) ⟶ Stimulus

Noise Sources ⟶ Environmental Stimulus Sources

Source ⟶ I.P.S. (transmitter of response)

Destination ⟶ I.P.S. (receiver of stimuli)

It appears, then, that the transmission model and the behavioral model deal with a number of processes in common, each using slightly different terminology and approaching the subject from different points of view. An integration of these two viewpoints is presented in Figure 14, which shows two organisms, L and R, interacting in a common environment through communication.

Each of the organisms, L and R, consists of a receptor system, an effector system, a physiological response system, and an IPS. The overt behaviors of each organism take place in the common environment which serves as a channel between L and R. Viewed from the standpoint of L, his behavior is response; but viewed from the standpoint of R, L's behavior is stimulus.

The behavior of each organism consists of physical signals, transmitted by the effectors of one organism and received through the receptors of the other (and also through the receptors of the transmitting organism as overt monitor feedback). These signals may be mixed with signals emanating from environmental stimulus sources. Considered from this point of view, these extraneous stimuli are noise.

FIGURE 14
Two Organisms Communicating in an Environment

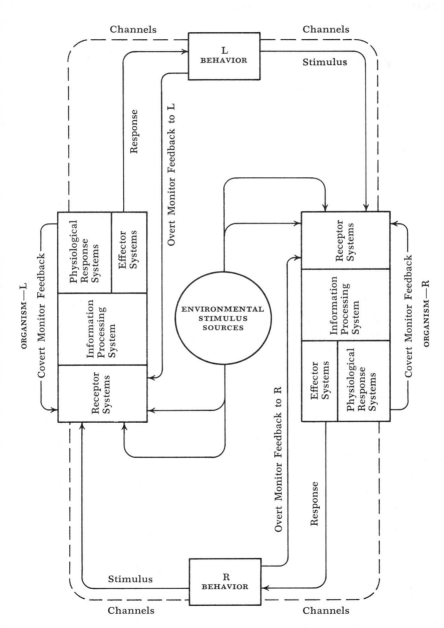

A given cycle of the process depicted in Figure 13 may begin either through the action of some environmental stimulus source or through the action of the IPS of either Organism L or Organism R. The process cannot begin at any other point in the cycle. Once begun, the process may terminate before even one cycle is completed; or it may continue for an indefinite number of cycles.

Some of the effects of the process occur during interaction; thus they represent process responses on the part of either L or R. Other effects are represented by permanent changes in the IPS of either L or R. If L is a public speaker, there may be a multitude of R's; but the principle remains the same.

The process may be evaluated in many ways. It may be evaluated from the standpoint of the messages involved, bearing upon either their excellence according to some predetermined standard, or their predicted, probable effects. Or the process may be evaluated from the standpoint of changes produced in the IPS of either L or R. Invariably, such evaluation will involve not merely an observation of the events of the process, but also a comparison of those events (messages or effects) to criteria of excellence, quality, or effectiveness. Herein lies one of the most vexing problems in the study of speech: it is one thing to know how the process works; but it is quite another thing altogether to know what work it ought to do.

In a way, then, we may view this chapter not only as a synthesis but also as a summary of the preceding ten. We have seen how the previously discussed components and aspects of the speech communication process can be integrated into a single composite picture.

Looking at it from one angle, we have seen communication as the transmission of signals that represent messages. In the transmission model, we have noted the difference between the signals and the messages they represent; and we have taken account of several different kinds—or levels—of fidelity.

Looking at the picture from another angle, we have seen communication as organisms behaving: taking in through their receptor systems stimuli from environmental events, responding overtly and covertly (and monitoring both kinds of response), and generating effects, to which they respond still further. We have paid special attention to the role of information processing in this behavioral complex, noting a hierarchy of complexity ranging from unconditioned reflexes (which require the least complicated information processing) to intelligent behavior using mental simulation (which requires very sophisticated processing of information).

We have noted that the transmission model of the communication process and the behavioral model show some remarkable similarities, with most of the key terms in each model being readily translated into the key terms of the other. In short, we have noticed that, in a very important sense, both models are, in effect, talking about the same thing, with each emphasizing a different aspect and adding certain special considerations. When both of these aspects are combined, and the special features of each model are added, we have a model of communication as *behavioral interaction* which can encompass the most important aspects of the process, of its effects, and of its evaluation.

This model, like every other, is an abstraction; it does not say everything that can or should be said about human communication. But it may properly be regarded as a set of categories and functions. Within it, we can find a place for most of the interesting questions that can be asked about what happens when people talk to one another—including, perhaps, many questions that no one has yet had the foresight to ask.

RECOMMENDED READINGS

ALEXANDER, H. G., *Language and Thinking* (Princeton, N. J.: D. Van Nostrand Co., Inc., 1967).

———, *Meaning in Language* (Glenview, Ill.: Scott, Foresman and Company, 1969).

BARNLUND, D. C., ed., *Interpersonal Communication* (Boston: Houghton Mifflin Company, 1968).

BERLO, D. K., *The Process of Communication* (New York: Holt, Rinehart & Winston, Inc., 1960).

BROWN, R. W., *Words and Things* (Glencoe, Ill.: Free Press of Glencoe, Ill., 1958).

BURKE, K., *A Rhetoric of Motives* (New York: George Braziller, Inc., 1955).

CAMPBELL, J. H., and HELPER, H. W., *Dimensions in Communication* (Belmont, Calif.: Wadsworth Publishing Co., Inc., 1965).

CARROLL, J. B., *Language and Thought* (Englewood Cliffs, N. J.: Prentice-Hall, Inc., 1964).

CHASE, S., *The Proper Study of Mankind* (New York: Harper & Bros., 1948).

CHERRY, C., *On Human Communication* (Cambridge, Mass.: The M.I.T. Press, 1957).

DANCE, F. E. X., ed., *Human Communication Theory* (New York: Holt, Rinehart & Winston, Inc., 1967).

EISENSON, J., AUER, J., and IRWIN, J., *The Psychology of Communication* (New York: Appleton-Century-Crofts, 1963).

FOTHERINGHAM, W. C., *Perspectives on Persuasion* (Boston: Allyn & Bacon, Inc., 1966).

HALL, E. T., *The Silent Language* (Garden City, N. Y.: Doubleday & Company, Inc., 1959).

HAYAKAWA, S. I., et al., *Language in Thought and Action* (New York: Harcourt, Brace & Company, 1949).

HOLTZMAN, P. D., *The Psychology of Speakers' Audiences* (Glenview, Ill.: Scott, Foresman and Company, 1970).

HOVLAND, C. I., *The Order of Presentation in Persuasion* (New Haven, Conn.: Yale University Press, 1957).

HOVLAND, C. I., JANIS, I., and KELLEY, H. H., *Communication and Persuasion* (New Haven, Conn.: Yale University Press, 1953).

HOVLAND, C. I., LUMSDAINE, A. A., and SHEFFIELD, R. D., *Experiments on Mass Communication* (Princeton, N. J.: Princeton University Press, 1949).

JOHNSON, W., *People in Quandaries* (New York: Harper & Bros., 1946).

———, *Your Most Enchanted Listener* (New York: Harper & Bros., 1956).

LANGER, S. K., *Philosophy in a New Key* (New York: Mentor Books, 1951).

McLUHAN, H. M., *Understanding Media* (New York: McGraw-Hill Book Company, 1964).

MILLER, G. A., *Language and Communication* (New York: McGraw-Hill Book Company, 1951).

MORRIS, C. W., *Signs, Language and Behavior* (New York: George Braziller, Inc., 1955).

OLBRICHT, T. H., *Informative Speaking* (Glenview, Ill.: Scott, Foresman and Company, 1968).

REDDING, W. C., and SANBORN, G. A., *Business and Industrial Communication* (New York: Harper & Row, Publishers, 1964).

RUESCH, J., and BATESON, G., *Communication: The Social Matrix of Psychiatry* (New York: W. W. Norton & Company, Inc., 1951).

SCHEIDEL, T. M., *Persuasive Speaking* (Glenview, Ill.: Scott, Foresman and Company, 1967).

SCHRAMM, W., ed., *The Process and Effects of Mass Communication* (Urbana, Ill.: University of Illinois Press, 1954).

———, ed., *The Science of Human Communications* (New York: Basic Books, Inc., Publishers, 1963).

SMITH, A. G., ed., *Communication and Culture* (New York: Holt, Rinehart & Winston, Inc., 1966).

THAYER, L., *Communication and Communication Systems* (Homewood, Ill.: Richard D. Irwin, Inc., 1968).

THOMPSON, W. N., *Quantitative Research in Public Address and Communication* (New York: Random House, Inc., 1967).

WHORF, B. L., *Language, Thought, and Reality* (Cambridge, Mass.: The M.I.T. Press, 1956).

INDEX

ment, 59
Frequency mutilation, 62
Functional equivalence in phonetypes, 21, 33
Game-playing and social interaction, 134–136
Gestures, 104–105
Goal setting as feedforward, 125
Grammars, 28–31; evaluation of, 28; phrase-structure, 28–30; transformational, 30–31
Grammatical theory, 25–27
Graphic representation and language learning, 84

Habitual behavior, 190 (cf. Intelligent behavior)
Hearing, 65–81; auditory perception, 68–72; transduction phase of, 66–68
Hopi Indians and cultural linguistics, 4
Human relations, communication as, 7

Image, speaker, 150–152
Immediate constituent analysis, 28
Immediate versus delayed response, 154–155
Information gain as message effect, 110–111
Information leader, 156–157
Information processing, 186–193
Information Processing System (I.P.S.), 186–187
Inhibitory neurons, 71–72
Instrumental communication, 161–163 (cf. Consummatory communication)
Intelligent behavior, 189–192 (cf. Habitual behavior)
Intensionality and connotative meaning, 38–40 (cf. Extensionality)
Intensity and acoustic measurement, 59–60
Interaction: behavioral, 193–196; with empathy, 128–131; with feedback, 121–124; with feedforward, 124–126; role constraints on, 131–134; social (see Social interaction)
Interest-attention as message effect, 109–110

Interruption mutilation of speech signal, 63

Kernel sentences, 30

Language: artificial, 25–26; code, 25; communication as, 3–5; design features of, 3; Hopi, 4; learning, 10–11, 82–86; linguistic approach to, 4–5; meaning in, 33–47; redundancy in, 19; structure, 18–32; translation, 4; vocabulary of, 2
Leadership: information leader, 156–157; opinion leader, 157; small-group, 156–157; task leader, 156
Learning: as effect of communication, 143–146; language, 10–11, 82–86; measurement of, 144–145; recognition versus recall, 145–146; relevant versus irrelevant, 143–144
Learning new word techniques: contrast, 84–85; division, 83–84; graphic representation, 83–84; imitation, 84
Linguistic: analysis, 3; approach to communication, 4–5; context and meaning, 43–44; environment, 22–23; phonetics, 20–22; units, 24
Listening, 82–91; for assumptions, 88; for bias, 89–90; for comprehension, 86–88; and conscious control, 90; critical, 88–90; for fallacies, 89; kinds of, 82; purpose in, 65, 86–87; for recall, 86–88
Logic, 94, 170–171
Logical fallacies, 89

Meaning, language and, 34–37; linguistic context and, 43–44; paralinguistic features and, 44–45; social context effects on, 45–46; source effects on, 45
Medium (see Channel)
Mental simulation, 190–191
Messages, 92–114; fidelity, 93, 179; intelligibility, 179–180; observed by third party, 93–95; potency, 99; received, 93–95; receiver, 12; reconstructed, 95;

signal, 176–177; by source, 93
Transmitter, 176, 194 (cf. Effector)

Unconditioned reflex, 187–188
Units, linguistic, 24

Vibratory patterns, 12–13
Viewpoints of communication, 15–17

Vocabulary: and content analysis, 101; and culture, 2
Vocal tone, 52–53
Vocal tract, 12–14, 48–50
Voice, 48–64
Voicing of consonants, 55–57

Weaver, W., 12, 177
Word: content, 34–41; structure, 41–43
Written communication, 4